JOHN LENNON
1980

For Oreo Cookie,

A Friend Indeed

JOHN LENNON

1980

THE LAST DAYS IN THE LIFE

KENNETH WOMACK

OMNIBUS PRESS

London / New York / Paris / Sydney / Copenhagen / Berlin / Madrid / Tokyo

Everything will be okay in the end. If it's not okay, it's not the end.
– attributed to John Lennon

A dream you dream alone is only a dream.
A dream you dream together is reality.
– Yoko Ono

Contents

CHAPTER 1

Kitchen Diplomacy

It was late December 1979, with the Christmas holidays in all of their seasonal glitz and glamour having firmly taken hold of New York City. Experiencing one of its mildest winters on record, the Tri-State area had been treated to unusually warm and sunny conditions all month, at one point reaching a balmy 65 degrees Fahrenheit (18 degrees Celsius). But with Christmas looming on the horizon, snowfall had finally descended upon the city, with nearly four inches of the white stuff blanketing the Upper West Side, where John Lennon, the 39-year-old erstwhile leader of the Beatles, lay in wait. He had been a virtual recluse since an April 1975 television appearance in which an acoustic-guitar playing Lennon performed 'Imagine', his most vaunted peace anthem, and then quietly slipped back into the fortress-like Dakota apartment building. A few months later, his wife Yoko Ono had given birth to the couple's first child, Sean, on John's 35th birthday. And then, as far as the wider world beyond the Dakota was concerned, he had all but disappeared from public life.

In truth, John had been exhausted by his multiyear legal fight to stay in the United States, finally earning his much-coveted green card in 1976. During that same period, he and Yoko, who turned 46 in February 1979, had been reunited after John concluded his debaucherous "Lost Weekend" on the West Coast with hard-drinking Harry Nilsson, former bandmate Ringo Starr, the Who's Keith Moon, and John's girlfriend May Pang. But by the time the winter of 1979 made its belated appearance,

John had been largely absent from the headlines, save for a January 1977 appearance at President Jimmy Carter's inaugural eve gala. At this point, he hadn't released a studio album since 1975's *Rock 'n' Roll* LP, which was chock-full of the old standards that set his heart ablaze, including the likes of Gene Vincent's 'Be-Bop-A-Lula', Ben E. King's 'Stand By Me', and Buddy Holly's 'Peggy Sue'. After *Rock 'n' Roll* hit the record stores, notching a Top 10 showing on the *Billboard* charts, John's solitary output had come in the form of a greatest hits LP. A compilation of John's solo singles releases, *Shaved Fish*, had been released only a few weeks after Sean's birth and the resolution of John's immigration battle. Tellingly, the album's liner notes featured a conspicuous message from Dr Winston O'Boogie, John's comic *nom de musique*: "A conspiracy of silence speaks louder than words." If John had left a clue directing listeners to his coming exile, this was surely it. Even more significantly, *Shaved Fish* completed the ex-Beatle's obligations to his bandmates' EMI contract, which formally expired a few months later in January 1976. Having opted not to sign a new deal with the label that had been his recording home since 1962, John was left – for the first time since the onset of his professional life – without the necessity of prepping a new release for the pop music marketplace.

And John's absence from the music scene would prevail for much of the late 1970s only to be interrupted by, of all things, a newspaper ad. In May 1979, he briefly suspended his self-imposed retirement with a full-page message in *The New York Times*. Signed as "A Love Letter from John and Yoko to People Who Ask Us What, When, and Why", the couple implored the world to understand "our silence" as "a silence of love and not of indifference. Remember, we are writing in the sky instead of on paper – that's our song. Lift your eyes and look up in the sky. There's our message." Pointedly, nearly a decade had passed since the couple's last message to the world. In December 1969, they had launched an elaborate billboard campaign in major cities across the globe, declaring "WAR IS OVER! If You Want It – Happy Christmas from John & Yoko."[1]

But this time, the stakes were dramatically different – and *lower*. Back then, the famous couple had joined the mounting ranks of the counterculture to protest the ongoing atrocities of the Vietnam War. Ten years later, they were clearly dipping a very public toe into the roiling, increasingly crowded waters of late 1970s pop culture. While some readers found the Lennons' message of goodwill to be confusing, even elliptical – were they simply trying to reassert their relevance in a world that had otherwise passed them by? – others felt refreshed by John and Yoko's well-meaning thoughts from their retreat on the Upper West Side. Although the May 1979 missive attributed their absence to the couple's long-term engagement in a "spring-cleaning of our minds", the notion that Lennon had earned his retirement many times over was a matter of little, if any actual debate. He'd spent nearly the entirety of his adulthood on the music business' ceaseless merry-go-round, devoting his late teen years and early twenties to trying to wrestle his way onto the damned thing in the first place.

But even still, John and Yoko had their share of detractors. Chief among the unconvinced was *Rolling Stone*'s brash writer Dave Marsh. The 29-year-old music critic had made a name for himself as arguably the most acerbic and malcontented reviewer in the magazine's vaunted pages. And the reading public loved him for it. Yet when it came to Lennon – a bona fide hero of Marsh's from his formative years in the 1960s – the prickly writer let down his guard and waxed idealistic. In a series of open letters to John, the second of which was published in response to the Lennons' *New York Times* communiqué, Marsh entreated John to suspend his retirement and assist the citizenry of the Western world in making sense of the beguiling post-1960s, post-Watergate, post-Vietnam landscape.

"I felt pretty smart," Marsh later recalled. "We resented him for leaving us" during the late 1970s. "Like most rock fans, I took it for granted that John Lennon existed to pump out entertainment, inspiration, and insight." And that's when John's reaction to Marsh's open letters trickled back to the writer through mutual friends. "I don't fucking owe anybody anything," John bluntly observed. "I've done my part. It's everybody else's turn now." Marsh was understandably devastated. Rather than inspiring his hero to effect a bravura return to the music world, he had succeeded in eliciting Lennon's well-placed ire. "I felt pretty small," Marsh admitted. "It never occurred to me, until then, that my attitude reduced someone I thought I loved and admired to the status of a vending machine."[2]

When it came to John's exile from celebrity and music-making, the Dakota was the perfect place to secret himself away from it all, to wax nostalgic and settle into enjoying the good life for a change. For one thing, the building's ornate roofline was the spitting image of the gabled rooftop of Strawberry Field, the Salvation Army orphanage mere steps away from Mendips, his boyhood home back in Liverpool. But even more important, the Dakota represented unqualified class and distinction – a luxurious reputation that it had held for nearly a century – along with the promise of some much-needed privacy.

One of New York City's most treasured and enigmatic landmarks, the Dakota had been constructed in the early 1880s at the behest of Edward Clark, cofounder with Isaac Singer of the Singer Sewing Machine Company, the firm that had transformed the garment industry since the midcentury. With Singer's death in 1875, Clark became president of the company. In the ensuing years, Clark emerged as a leader among New York City's social hierarchy. Recognising that not everyone could live in a private urban estate like the über-wealthy Vanderbilts and Astors, Clark subscribed to the vision of architect Calvert Vaux, co-designer of Central Park, who believed that city dwellers should live in French-style flats. Fellow architect Richard Morris Hunt followed Vaux's lead and constructed the first American apartment building, the Stuyvesant, in 1869 in the city's Gramercy Park neighbourhood. Not surprisingly, Vaux was one of the Stuyvesant's original tenants. But to Clark's mind, the future of urban living would be in the leafy streetscapes abutting Central Park, where New Yorkers could enjoy a cosmopolitan lifestyle of elegance and refinement far removed from the hubbub and hoi polloi downtown.

When Clark first contemplated the notion of building a luxury apartment house on the barren Upper West Side, the neighbourhood was so ramshackle that Central Park West (née Eighth Avenue) was still a dirt road. In 1877, Clark purchased two acres at the corner of Central Park West and West 72nd Street for the princely sum of $200,000 ($4.8 million in 2018). Clark selected Dutch architect Henry Hardenbergh to bring his vision to life. For his part, Hardenbergh viewed his design for the Dakota as the opportunity to let his creative imagination loose on what, in good time, would surely emerge as one of the burgeoning city's most distinctive addresses. The result was a series of Old World European embellishments – high-pitched roofs and imposing balustrades pocked with chimneys, flagpoles, turrets, and finials. The Dakota's exterior was constructed of carved stone friezes, along with a dry moat that marked the building's perimeter and was decorated with the bearded face of Neptune entwined with a pair of serpents.

As it happened, Clark wouldn't live long enough to see his dream for a luxury apartment house on the Upper West Side come to fruition. The business magnate succumbed to malaria at age 70 in October 1882 while visiting his country home in Cooperstown, New York, leaving an estate valued at some $25 million. When the building opened in October 1884, the Dakota's many critics took to deriding it as "Clark's folly", referring to its location among the squatters and their rickety shacks in the barren northwestern reaches of the city. Legend has it that the building was bequeathed its unusual name because of its remoteness – that it was so distant from the city's hubbub that it might as well have been constructed in the Dakota Territory. In truth, the Dakota's name found its origins in Clark's passion for Native American lore and the nation's Western expansion into the territories during that era.[3]

While the building had its share of detractors, the New York *Daily Graphic* greeted its grand opening with a bravura headline describing the Dakota as "one of the most perfect apartment houses in the world". And New Yorkers responded in kind, with the city's elite ensuring that the building's 65 units were fully leased long before it was ready for occupancy. Nestled at the corner of Central Park West and West 72nd Street, the Dakota was an architectural wonder, standing out from the landscape, its spandrels and balustrades giving it a German Renaissance character, not to mention the fearsome sight of the menacing gargoyles that guarded its perimeter.[4]

And then there was the imposing archway that opened onto West 72nd Street, the nineteenth-century building's main entrance, a *porte-cochère* that had originally been constructed to admit horse-drawn carriages into the Dakota's cavernous central courtyard, elegantly fitted out with a pair of cast-iron fountains. In later years, a copper-plated sentry box would be erected on the western side of the archway. The carved faces of Isaac and Isabella Singer decorated the crest above the entrance. Even higher still, the image of a Dakota Indian trained his watchful eye on the streetscape below. In counterpoint to the dramatic archway, Hardenbergh had adorned the building's less ostentatious northern façade with a smaller, rarely used back door known as the Undertaker's Gate.

The "John Lennons", as they were known among the Dakota's austere tenancy, had purchased their seventh-floor apartment in 1973, a year after the building had been added to the National Register of Historic Places. In 1976, the Dakota would be declared a National Historic Landmark. Since the late 1960s, the building had been lodged in the national consciousness when famed director Roman Polanski had filmed the exterior shots for the supernatural thriller *Rosemary's Baby* and deployed the Dakota's imposing Gothic architecture to spine-tingling effect. Polanski's movie held plenty of shock value for late-1960s filmgoers, including the aftermath of a suicide in which a character leapt from a seventh-floor window. Even more infamously, *Rosemary's Baby* depicted protagonist Mia Farrow's terrifying rape at the hands of Satan. While the building enjoyed a notorious reputation thanks to Polanski's film, reality had been much kinder to the Dakota, where residents more often than not succumbed to natural causes.

Although there had been no reported Satanic incursions at 1 West 72nd Street, the building was rumoured to be haunted by the so-called Crying Lady. The ghostly presence was purportedly the spirit of Elise Vesley, who had served as a staunch protector of the building's reputation during the prewar years, when she managed the Dakota. She had suffered a personal tragedy in the 1930s, when her beloved son had been struck by a truck and killed instantly on the streetscape in front of the building. More recently, longtime resident and Broadway set designer Jo Mielziner had died in front of the Dakota's archway. The designer behind the immaculate renovation of the building's service elevators, which were nestled within the four corners of the courtyard, Mielziner perished just a few days shy of his 75th birthday while sitting in a taxicab, having only just returned from a visit with his physician. Not long after Mielziner's death, rumours about the Dakota's spirit world returned with a vengeance. In one unforgettable instance, tenants looked on aghast as one of Mielziner's elevators began to rise up from the basement on its own volition. As historian Stephen Birmingham later reported, "It took four strong men, wrestling at the cables, to bring it down again."[5]

As it turned out, the spectre of death had been behind John and Yoko's stroke of luck at landing an apartment in the coveted Dakota in the first place. In 1972, actor Robert Ryan's wife Jessica had succumbed to cancer in apartment 72. The star of such Western classics as *Bad Day at Black Rock* (1955) and *The Wild Bunch* (1969), Ryan was distraught over the loss of Jessica after 33 years of marriage. Struggling with her untimely death, Ryan moved to 88 Central Park South, near the Plaza Hotel, where he died of lung cancer in 1973. During this same period, John and Yoko had been anxious to move out of their Bank Street loft in the West Village, hoping that they could find a larger place with better security. They had recently been looking at properties in Greenwich, Connecticut, and Long Island when they learned about the availability of the Ryans' former home. Eager to take up residence in the building, John and Yoko initially sublet the apartment from Ryan, later purchasing it from his estate. Knowing the circumstances that led to the apartment's unexpected availability – and marvelling at the stunning views of Central Park that apartment 72 afforded – the Lennons hired a medium to conduct a séance in order to assess their new home's supernatural well-being.

After the medium reportedly made contact with Jessica, a delighted Yoko telephoned the Ryans' daughter Lisa to inform her that her mother's spiritual welfare was in fine fettle. According to the medium, Mrs Ryan fully intended to remain within the apartment's supernatural realm, while promising not to disturb the new tenants' connubial bliss. In spite of the medium's ostensible good tidings, Lisa greeted Yoko's news with dismay, later remarking that "if my mother's ghost belongs anywhere, it's here with me – not with them."

As if the apartment building's apparitions weren't enough, the Dakota was also rife with its own, highly active rumour mill. In terms of the Lennons, the building's co-op board worried about potential "social problems" with the likes of John and Yoko taking up residence.[6]

As Gordon Greenfield, president of the Dakota's co-op board, remarked at the time, "We wanted conservative types as tenants, we wanted good, solid family types, we didn't want riffraff. We had always had an interesting group of theatrical people in the building – people like Robert Ryan and his wife, who were solid family types. The Lennons bought the Ryan apartment, and you just can't put John Lennon in the same category as Robert Ryan." Worse yet, residents believed that John and Yoko intended to buy up every last scintilla of space in the apartment house – indeed, by the fall months of 1979, they owned 28 rooms for their relatively small family. Yet another rumour held that a prewar tenant had secreted $30,000 beneath the parquet floorboards of John and Yoko's master bedroom, where it remained into the current day, waiting to be discovered.[7]

When it came to buying up available real estate at the Dakota, the Lennons' neighbours were correct in their long-held assumptions and, in later years, their umbrage. In the words of fellow resident Paul Goldberger, *The New Yorker*'s architectural critic and a member of the co-op board, "There was a little bit of resentment built up against Yoko, more because she kept trying to buy more apartments. I think people didn't dare get mad at John Lennon, so she bore the brunt of any resentment." Other members of the Dakoterie came to the couple's defence, including singer Roberta Flack, who opined that "when you're John Lennon and Yoko and you have all of the money in the world, how come he can't buy all that he wants?" In fact, John and Yoko rarely passed up the opportunity to purchase additional square footage at 1 West 72nd Street. In addition to apartment 72, they had sublet the adjacent, full-scale residence from Allen and Etheline Staley in 1977 when the couple left for a year-long vacation abroad. During Staley's absence, the Lennons also added the couple's Spanish maid, Rosaura "Rosa" Lopéz Lorenzo, to their payroll.[8]

John and Yoko broke in apartment 71 on the occasion of their ninth wedding anniversary on March 20, 1978, locking themselves inside to spend an entire unbroken day together. The night before, John was giddy about the sleepover, saying that "it will be like staying at a hotel without going away from home." Although they had originally leased the property to maintain their privacy, John and Yoko couldn't bear to part with apartment 71, which they intended to use for storage. When the Staleys returned from their vacation, Yoko made them an offer they couldn't refuse. They also maintained Rosa's employment in the bargain. The Lennons had also purchased a first-floor suite to serve as office space, as well as apartment 4, a cosy unit above the archway occupied by Norman and Helen Seaman, and apartment 911, a garret storage unit to handle the overflow from their seventh-floor residences.[9]

In those days, John most often passed through the Dakota's majestic archway when he slipped into Central Park for a stroll or to hotfoot it to one of his favourite eateries. The gaunt, bearded Lennon had become a regular at nearby Café La Fortuna, where he would take his afternoon tea at his favourite table near the front entrance, or, if the weather was properly inviting, in the restaurant's secluded rear garden. A popular neighbourhood eatery among the Upper West Siders, the proprietors of Café La Fortuna were known for allowing their clientele to while away the hours in the restaurant nursing their assortment of coffees and teas, or, better yet, sampling one of the café's tuna fish sandwiches or from a wide selection of gourmet desserts, including a delectable Key Lime cake, assorted pastries, and homemade Italian ices. During the warmer months, regulars like John looked forward to the restaurant's special cappuccino, which the owners served with a scoop of chocolate-flavoured Italian ice floating inside.[10]

As with so many other Upper West Siders in those days, John's life was largely contained inside the space of the few city blocks that comprised his neighbourhood. John's local pharmacist, Dr Said Saber, operated the

West Side Pharmacy on Columbus Avenue just around the corner from the Dakota. Whether he was picking up diapers for Sean or a prescription, John inevitably corrected the humble Middle-Easterner, who insisted on calling him "Mr Lennon". Not missing a beat, John would inevitably correct him: "Said, it's John," he'd reply. "It's just John." His optometrist Dr Gary Tracy opened up shop a few blocks north on Columbus Avenue and 74th Street. For the past few years, he had supplied John with his iconic, granny-style glasses, although when it came to sunglasses, the former Beatle had recently shifted his taste to more contemporary eyewear. Every few months, he would check out the latest frames. "He didn't take much time picking stuff out," the optometrist recalled. "I want this, I want that," John would announce as he scanned Dr Tracy's wares. Although he would go for a long time without a haircut – sometimes, as many as 18 months would pass between his visits to the barber – John had recently begun frequenting the hip salon Viz-à-Viz a block away from the Dakota at 111 West 72nd Street.[11]

But for the most part, John kept to himself. As the 1970s wore on, the Dakota had evolved into a kind of gilded hideaway for the former Beatle, who spent most of his time alone in his seventh-floor bedroom. Tucked away near the apartment's foyer, with a curtain of beads acting as a makeshift doorway, his bedroom was perched high above Central Park West. But the view was largely wasted upon him, with the white shutters about his large window invariably closed.

John passed most of his days sitting cross-legged atop a queen-sized bed, with its mattress and box springs situated atop a pair of old church pews. To his mind, "it comforted him to think of how many people have knelt on those pews to pray. They were full of mending, gratitude, and good wishes." With its sound muted, a giant television screen emitted the flickering images of soap operas. The only sound came from a nearby portable radio tuned to a classical music station. He would jokingly refer to his TV as his "electronic fireplace". John's addiction to television was a poorly kept secret among his fellow Dakotans. His neighbour Rex Reed, a popular American film critic, could attest to that. After Reed signed a petition in support of John's immigration fight, the Beatle had thanked him with a subscription to *TV Guide*. "That was his bible," Reed later recalled. "All he did was lie around stoned watching television."[12]

But for John, the gigantic Sony was a mindless diversion, and, for that matter, the radio station might just as well have been broadcasting the banal sounds of Muzak. His one abiding passion was for the printed word. John's bedroom-retreat was littered with the detritus of an insatiable reader. Books and magazines were strewn about the room, along with empty coffee cups and ashtrays overbrimming with Gitanes cigarette butts. Titles of nearly every genre and stripe were in evidence, revealing John's wide-ranging tastes, which ran from the eye-popping pages of *The National Enquirer* and *The Weekly World News* to such high-minded magazines as *Scientific American* and *The Economist*. As for books, John would read virtually anything he could get his hands on, from arcane tomes about the occult and Asian philosophy to Studs Terkel's recent bestseller *Working* or *The Double Helix*, the popular opus about the discovery of DNA. Always a pushover for political nonfiction, John was known to consume the latest titles with a relish, including G. Gordon Liddy's bestselling *Will* and Nancy Friday's *Men in Love*. In other moments, his literary palate would range to old favourites by the likes of Lewis Carroll, Noël Coward, and W. Somerset Maugham. All the while, mounted on the wall above John's head, was his cherished, albeit rarely played candy apple red Fender Stratocaster. The last time John had seen action with an electric guitar of any kind had been on Thanksgiving Day 1974, when the ex-Beatle joined Elton John onstage for a rousing version of 'I Saw Her Standing There'.

In more recent years, John had begun to associate the similarities between his self-contained, private existence and the last days of Howard Hughes, the maverick aviation pioneer and businessman whose eccentric, reclusive lifestyle made international headlines when he died in 1976. That April, Hughes had perished, somewhat fittingly in retrospect, on a private aeroplane en route from Acapulco to Houston, where the billionaire's handlers sought medical treatment for their ailing employer. In short order, the ensuing news stories about Hughes' bizarre final years captivated the public, especially Lennon, who often gravitated towards the more sensational stories of his day. To John's mind, Hughes' withering final years originated with the slow failure of the once innovative and industrious magnate's creative capacity. "He lost his spark," John soberly concluded. His frequent laments about Hughes' slow demise barely masked his own frustrations about his inability to rediscover his muse – the world-breaking inspiration that had led to such feats of musical fancy as 'In My Life' and 'Strawberry Fields Forever' during his Beatles years and, in the early 1970s, solo gems along the lines of 'Instant Karma! (We

All Shine On)', 'Imagine', and perennial holiday favourite 'Happy Xmas (War Is Over)'.[13]

But by the time the winter of 1979 had left its first snowy imprint upon New York City, John had settled into a kind of retirement, proudly crowing to his intimates that for the first time in his life he was blissfully free of the yoke of a recording contract. Not that any such agreement would do him good. He had become so devoid of inspiration that he purposefully avoided listening to the latest radio hits. For the life of him, John couldn't abide the contemporary music scene. While he adored reggae and enjoyed a number of disco songs, new wave sometimes fell beyond his ken, as did the raucous swagger of punk, with its attendant guitar-driven violence and gnashing of lyrical teeth. To his ears, new wave and punk sounded uncannily like the Beatles' early days in the Liverpool's Cavern Club.

Even worse, he would physically cringe at the sound of something really good that might wash over him in his Dakota bedroom. If a new tune that he really admired happened to wind its way into his sonic orbit, he would find himself growing steadily more agitated, having wished that he had the wherewithal to have composed the latest work of musical genius himself. An inevitable depression would follow in which he lamented his inability to regain the mettle that, only a few years earlier, had resulted in such chestnuts as 'Whatever Gets You Thru The Night', his first number-one solo hit, and '#9 Dream'. Sometimes, he would even wax philosophically about his creative malaise, remarking that when the inspiration "stops coming, the trick is to accept that and not try to force it, because the harder you try the more elusive it becomes." For John, creative inspiration hadn't merely become elusive. It was downright non-existent.[14]

And while he found solace in his regular jaunts among the cosy eateries of the Upper West Side, John had become increasingly suspicious, even apprehensive, about the fans who staked out the Dakota's Gothic archway in hopes of catching a glimpse of the reclusive Beatle. Tony Award-winning actress Lauren Bacall had lived in the Dakota for decades in a spacious apartment three floors below John and Yoko. The Hollywood film legend found the fans loitering about the streetscape to be particularly irksome and was lauded by the other tenants for ordering them to get out of her way in the same stentorian voice that she had used in a spate of television commercials for *The New York Times*. In their zeal to see the Lennons in the flesh, fans had taken to learning the makes and models of John and

Yoko's cars, as well as the limousines that would ferry them about the city. On a good day, the Dakota's doormen would succeed in thwarting the throng of camera-toting fans by redirecting John and Yoko to the basement service door nestled on the west side of the building.[15]

As for John, nothing seemed to upset him more than when he took his meals at Mr Chow's or the Stage Deli, sitting at some out-of-the-way table, thinking he was incognito only to watch one of the diners screwing up his courage to stand up and make his way over to the person he was certain – *just had to be* – Beatle John. Lennon's stomach would sink as his worst instincts had been proven correct yet again, and before long he was hastily scrawling his signature on some cocktail napkin, hoping that an autograph would suffice as a small price to let him dine alone in peace.

And if it wasn't the fans, it was rock 'n' roll's glitterati that really got John's goat. As far as the music industry was concerned, New York City was Ground Zero, the weigh station through which everyone who was anyone either resided or passed through, Seventies jetsetters that they were, on their way someplace else. And for many of his contemporaries, the chance to catch up with ex-Beatle John Lennon was too good to pass up. For John, such moments occasionally went well, but sometimes they proved to be an unwanted imposition. A few years earlier, in April 1976 during a hiatus from the McCartneys' triumphant Wings Over America tour, John and Yoko had spent a convivial evening with Paul and Linda, watching television together and catching up on old times. But the very next day, Paul was back on the Lennons' doorstep.

As John later recalled, "That was a period when Paul just kept turning up at our door with a guitar. I would let him in, but finally I said to him, 'Please call before you come over. It's not 1956, and turning up at the door isn't the same anymore. You know, just give me a ring.' That upset him, but I didn't mean it badly. I just meant that I was taking care of a baby all day, and some guy turns up at the door with a guitar." For his part, Paul would look back on the episode thinking it had been his mere presence that had caused John such duress. Little did he know it had actually been his guitar, the symbol of his creative might – McCartney and his band Wings were lording over the charts at the time – that had foisted such stress upon his former songwriting partner. For better or ill, they hadn't seen each other since.[16]

But on that cold winter's night in December 1979, John was treated to a very different guest – one from his Beatles past all right, but someone, unlike Paul, with whom he had unsettled business. With the apartment all but empty save for his beloved cats – Yoko, four-year-old Sean, and the Lennons' personal assistant Fred Seaman having made themselves scarce for the evening – he ushered George Martin into his seventh-floor foyer. Fourteen years John's senior, the Beatles' lanky, grey-haired record producer followed Lennon past the stark-white music room, with its matching white Steinway baby grand piano, and into the furthest reaches of the apartment, where the family's large, eat-in kitchen was perched high above the Dakota's courtyard.

While John had managed to make up for ancient squabbles, both large and small, with his former bandmates, his war of words with the good-natured Martin had been particularly vexing, not to mention almost completely unexpected. The older man was known as an amiable sort, the kind of person who amassed many allies while making scant few, if any, genuine enemies in the record world. Not surprisingly, it was Lennon who first lit the fuse of their disaffection, name-checking the legendary producer with an abrasive comment nearly a decade earlier in the pages of *Rolling Stone*. During an interview with Jann Wenner, John had called out the producer for his alleged role in the Beatles' achievement, remarking that "I'd like to hear George Martin's music, please, just play me some." Martin took the bait, responding in kind shortly afterwards that John's observation was "silly, of course. I guess I feel sorry for him, because he's obviously schizophrenic in that respect. He must have a split mind… either he doesn't mean it, or if he does mean it he can't be in a normal state of mind." Nobody ever got off easy calling out John for the quality of his mental acuity, which Martin knew all too well. "John had a very sweet side to him," the producer once observed. "He was a very tender person at heart. He could also be very brutal and very cruel."[17]

But as the snow settled onto the rooftops of the Upper West Side, John's tender side was in full flower. Before long, the two old friends were "mulling over past glories like a pair of old codgers," Martin later recalled. At one point, "I tackled him about the *Rolling Stone* interview. I said, 'What was all that shit about, John? Why?' He said, 'I was out of my head, wasn't I?' And that was as much of an apology as I got." But for George, it was enough. Lennon was clearly in great spirits. The night's unexpected visit from Martin had afforded him the opportunity to act normal, to pretend, if only for the space of an evening, that he had not become a prisoner of his own fame. After a while, the producer began to ascertain the state of

John's mind, to recognise that something else had started eating at him – it was no longer McCartney or Martin, but something else altogether. As Martin later recalled, "John suddenly looked up at me. 'You know what, George,' he said. 'If I had the chance, I'd record everything we did again.'" Martin was suddenly aghast: "What?" I replied. "Even 'Strawberry Fields Forever?'" As always, John was quick with his retort: "*Especially* 'Strawberry Fields Forever'."[18]

Much later, after the record producer had disappeared into the night, John knew the bitter truth: that his stunning words to Martin had been an empty boast, that his four-year hiatus from the music business hadn't come about because he wanted to stay home and raise his infant son – a story that he had repeated to almost everyone he knew – but rather, because he had lost his muse. For his part, John adored the old Beatles tunes as much as anybody – possibly even more than the band's most ardent fans. When he happened upon the hokey mid-Sixties Beatles cartoons on television, he turned the sound up and revelled in the pure joy of their music. No, John knew full well that he hadn't meant to offend the older man, that he had no intention of diminishing the magnificent sounds they had fashioned together all those years ago.

What John really wanted was to regain his spark. He wasn't done with music – not in the slightest. It turned out that Dave Marsh hadn't been that far off the mark, after all. As his fourth year of confinement was coming rapidly to a close, John hungered for inspiration – to rediscover his lost muse. In his heart of hearts, he longed to pick up his Stratocaster and breathe new life into his art. But for the life of him, biding his time in the Dakota on the precipice of a new year – a new decade, even – he didn't know where to begin. Or even how, at what felt like an especially inauspicious moment in an otherwise storied career, to get back to where he once belonged.

CHAPTER 2

The Dakoterie

During the late 1970s, Clark's century-old dream of cosmopolitan living on the edge of Central Park had been tarnished by New York City's dwindling fortunes and encroaching urban blight. Teetering on the edge of bankruptcy since 1973, that dismal era in the life of the nation's largest city had been notoriously captured in the headlines of the *Daily News* after President Gerald Ford refused to bail out New York with some much-needed federal assistance: "FORD TO CITY: DROP DEAD". By 1979, the Lennons' sixth year in residence at the Dakota, Central Park had come to mirror the city's desolation. As Birmingham observed at the time, "Tall weeds of lethargy and indifference seem to have grown in the Park, a sense of fatalism, and a feeling that nothing can be done… Grassy areas are turned to dirt from the soles of too many sneakers. The great variety of wildflowers that used to bloom there has diminished steadily over the years. Shrubs, plants and flowers are routinely pulled up and carried away. Branches are occasionally snapped from trees for games of stickball, and statues and monuments have been sprayed with graffiti."[19]

By the summer months of 1979, the Dakota's parkside view had become so dilapidated that a band of residents devoted a Saturday afternoon to gathering up the litter and other debris that had accumulated along Central Park West and inside the teardrop-shaped portion of the park most immediately adjacent to the Dakota. Ranging from the bridle path to the lake and bounded by the bronze statue of American statesman

Daniel Webster, the parkland served, for many residents, as the Dakotans' de facto front yard. During a visit to the park in the new year, Yoko remarked that "this is such a sorry spot", suggesting to her husband that "we should donate some grass or something." As for their neighbours' attempt at reclaiming their parkside view, their efforts proved to be all for naught. Within a few scant days, the area had become overrun with litter yet again, their determination to clean up the park all but obscured by the quickly gathering refuse. That autumn, as one of the Lennons' third-floor neighbours watched from his window in horror, a group of Sunday picnickers dismantled a nearby park bench to provide makeshift kindling for their barbecue.[20]

Not surprisingly, the criminal activity back in those days was hardly limited to assault and battery on a public bench. Jeannine Jones, a lifelong Upper West Sider, remembered that in the 1970s "no one in Manhattan lived above 72nd street if they could avoid it. People were afraid to ride the graffiti-streaked, crime-soaked subways, [and] locals knew to be inside their locked apartments by nightfall, and you were safe." In August 1971, shortly before the Lennons moved to New York City, King Curtis was stabbed outside of his West 86th Street apartment. A pair of junkies attacked the legendary sax player as he was attempting to cart an air-conditioning unit into the building. When the men refused to step out of the way to allow Curtis' entrance, an argument ensued, ending with the musician's death at Roosevelt Hospital less than an hour later. In March 1977, TV producers Mark Mannucci and Mary Larsen conducted interviews with passersby on the streets of the neighbourhood. One man remarked that "you have extremes in this neighbourhood. You have the extremely rich and the extremely poor. You'll always have problems when you have two extremes." Another person remarked that "you gotta keep your eyes open at all times. There's always someone trying to steal, rob from you, kill you."[21]

Putting it even more succinctly, *West Side Rag* columnist Carol Tannenhauser described the Upper West Side during that era as both a "community in the best sense of the word and a place to get drugs or mugged." For his part, actor Ben Stiller saw the neighbourhood as the best of both worlds – idyllic and dangerous at the same time. "I grew up in the Upper West Side of Manhattan in the '70s," he later recalled, "and there were block parties and it was multicultural and it was the aftermath of Vietnam and people were sort of into Earth Day and saving the planet –

it was very genuine and real and sort of connected to something, I think." But at the same time, there were "fires and riots and serial killers."[22]

And nestled in the heart of it all was the Dakota. Back in those days, the Dakota was a sorry sight, indeed, having become covered with soot and blackened by the unkempt city. The building's majestic copper turrets had transformed into a motley green, having grown oxidised after years of neglect. The city was only just beginning to wake up to the reality of the blight that had befallen its more than 10,000 buildings. As was so often the case, it took a tragedy to spur the wheels of change forward. In May 1979, 18-year-old Grace Cold, a Columbia University freshman, had perished at 115th Street and Broadway after a piece of masonry had plunged streetward from an eighth-storey window. Responding to the public outcry, Mayor Ed Koch approved New York City's Local Law 10 in February 1980, requiring building owners to conduct regular maintenance programmes. But even still, this was long before the days of Local Law 11, which called for a more stringent periodic assessment of exterior walls and appurtenances of structures above six storeys tall. To avoid mounting fines – even jail time – building owners acquiesced to the legislation, repointing their structures' brick lines, checking for loose masonry, and regularly cleaning their façades in order to win the approval of their local inspector's critical eye.

But neighbourhood upkeep was only a fraction of the city's ongoing malaise back in those days. For decades, the Upper West Side had been beset by its own internal politics and folkways, with Amsterdam Avenue, just two blocks to the west of the Dakota, acting as an unspoken boundary. For Jim Ryan, who grew up in the 1960s and 1970s in the neighbourhood, people lived their lives in relatively close proximity to their apartments. As Ryan recalled, "Back in the day, there was an invisible line down Amsterdam Avenue. Folks on the east stayed in their neighbourhoods, venturing as far as Central Park and Columbus Avenue, while the west-side folks did their business on Broadway and took their leisure in Riverside Park."[23]

As it turned out, the Upper West Side was beset by an even more pervasive rift with its age-old adversary, the Upper East Side. As Beatles historian Susan Ratisher Ryan has observed, it was a rivalry borne of class warfare and social tension. "The Upper West Side was more working class, while the East Side was, more often than not, old money," she recalled. "On the Upper West Side, you had the bohemians, the socialists, and the Red Diaper Babies," the left-leaning progeny of parents who were either members of the nation's homegrown Communist Party or sympathetic to its sociopolitical objectives. Robert Morgan, an artist who lived in the Majestic apartment building directly across the street from the Dakota, put it more bluntly: "The Upper West Side was the alternative for people who didn't want to spend twice as much to live on the East Side. The Upper West Side was chic for artist-types who didn't know the difference and really didn't care about the trendy shops across the park." Back in those days, the socioeconomic differences were not merely cosmetic, but extended to the residents' quality of life – and their ability to sustain it. When it came to health care, the Upper East Side enjoyed access to New York Presbyterian, one of the finest hospitals in the world, while West Siders were left to contend with Roosevelt, an outdated neighbourhood hospital.[24]

Even as a comparatively recent fixture in his Upper West Side neighbourhood, John restricted much of his wanderings to the eastern reaches beyond Amsterdam Avenue. And while his artistic and political affinities clearly leaned leftwards, the longstanding rivalry among the Upper West and Upper East sides meant scarcely little to a transplanted New Yorker like himself. If his movements were circumscribed by the relatively tiny imprint of the area around the Dakota, it had far more to do with the simple matter of proximity, rather than the insularity of inter-neighbourhood politics. For John, the most pressing issue was always the looming presence of Beatles fans, particularly the ones who camped outside the Dakota or – worse yet – attempted to talk their way inside.

On just his third day of working for the Lennons, Fred Seaman encountered the issue first hand as he followed John into the archway after a shopping trip on the Upper West Side. As they made their way inside, a teenaged girl shouted out, "Hi, John. Wanna party?" Clearly flummoxed by the intrusion, Lennon hurried inside the building, later cautioning Fred about the lengths to which fans might go to cosy up to him. "She'll try to sweet-talk you, bribe you, or even fuck you to get to me," he said. "Don't be tempted."[25]

The 27-year-old Seaman had begun working at the Dakota in February 1979. As the nephew of Norman and Helen Seaman, the affable Fred seemed like the perfect choice for serving as the Lennons' personal assistant. After all, the Seamans were longtime friends of John and Yoko, tirelessly working on behalf of John's immigration fight during the mid-Seventies. The Lennons trusted Norman and Helen implicitly. In the

1960s, Norman, a dyed-in-the-wool Upper West Side communist in his own right, had promoted Yoko's performance art, while also toiling on behalf of other niche performers in his stable, including Ono's one-time roommate Charlotte Moorman, who achieved notoriety under Norman's management as the "topless cellist" of the avant-garde set. Helen, Norman's wife of nearly 30 years, worked as Sean's live-in nanny.

As for Fred, John took to the Seamans' nephew almost immediately. A recent graduate of the City College of New York, Fred had written music reviews for the student newspaper. For his part, John was visibly relieved when he learned that Fred's speciality was jazz criticism and that he wasn't just another Beatles fan trying to worm his way into John and Yoko's orbit. Before Fred was hired, Yoko ensured that his charts were studied, given that she based most of her decisions on astrological and numerological findings. Her astrologer concluded that Fred would get along very well with John because his birthdate was the day after the musician's – John's was October 9 and Fred's was October 10. In short order, Seaman was hired at $175 a week. Although his salary may have seemed like a paltry sum, even by late 1970s standards, working for the Lennons virtually changed Fred's life overnight.[26]

Like many people who found themselves in the famous couple's inner sanctum, Fred would be struck by how different they seemed – both in terms of disposition and background. Indeed, in many ways, John and Yoko were a study in opposites. Seven years Yoko's junior, John was born in Liverpool in 1940, into the working-class household of Julia and Freddie Lennon, who worked as a merchant seaman. Before long, the still-married Julia set up housekeeping with John Dykins, a wine steward, during one of Freddie's frequent seafaring jaunts. Disgusted with her sister's behaviour and determined to provide her nephew with a proper upbringing, Mimi and her husband George Smith, a dairy farmer, took custody of John, who was raised at Mendips, the couple's semidetached wood and stucco home on Menlove Avenue near Penny Lane and across from the Allerton Golf Course. After George's untimely death in 1955, Mimi took in boarders to make ends meet as her nephew pursued his studies at Quarry Bank High School. For John, things came to a head with the accidental death of his mother Julia, who had only recently re-entered his life, in July 1958. In spite of his natural intelligence and intellectual curiosity, John fell into a depression, failed his O-level examinations, and still managed to land a place at the Liverpool College of Art, where he met his first wife, Cynthia Powell.

While John was riding the high tide of Beatlemania in the 1960s, producing dozens of chart-topping hit singles and one landmark album after another – from *Rubber Soul* (1965) and *Revolver* (1966) to *Sgt. Pepper's Lonely Hearts Club Band* (1967), *The Beatles* (popularised as *The White Album*; 1968), and *Abbey Road* (1969) – Yoko was attempting to make her mark on the New York City avant-garde art scene, which was a far cry, indeed, from her privileged upbringing in her Japanese homeland. Born in Saitama, Japan, on February 18, 1933, Yoko was the oldest child of Isoko Yasuda, a wealthy heiress, and Eisuke Ono, a banker who, in his younger days, had pursued a career as a classically trained pianist. Yoko, whose name translates as "Ocean Child", attended Tokyo's elite Gakushuin academy. In the years after World War II, Yoko's family emigrated to Scarsdale, New York, where she continued her education at Sarah Lawrence College.

During this period, Yoko fell in with a bohemian crowd of artists and writers, dropping out of college during her junior year. After a failed marriage to composer Toshi Ichiyanagi, she began a lengthy liaison with radical American composer La Monte Young, who introduced her to the New York art world, including composer John Cage and a host of other influential figures. After her parents whisked her back to Japan in 1962, she met American jazz musician and film producer Tony Cox, whom she married that November – but without first having bothered to divorce Toshi. In order to untangle the ensuing legal mess, her lawyers advised her in March 1963 to annul her marriage with Tony. They remarried in June 1963, and their daughter Kyoko was born on August 8 of that year. Tony and Yoko's marriage deteriorated rapidly in the wake of Kyoko's birth. Years later, Tony would steal away with Kyoko during a custody dispute with Ono, whom he claimed to be an unfit mother because of her struggles with heroin addiction. Father and daughter subsequently disappeared from Yoko's life, having joined a cult known as the Church of the Living Word. Yoko hadn't seen her since a furtive visit in Majorca in 1971.

In the mid-1960s, after successfully establishing herself among the Dadaesque group of artists known as Fluxus (from the Latin word "to flow"), Yoko began exhibiting her performance art in such works as *Cut Piece*, in which she reclined onstage, while audience members cut off her clothing with a pair of scissors until she was naked. During the summer of 1966, Yoko left New York in order to attend the *Destruction in Art*

Symposium, an international congress that Fluxus was hosting in London. Before long, she and Tony took to hanging out with the gaggle of other hipsters who frequented the Indica Gallery. It was there that she met Beatle John on November 9, 1966.

As a way of introducing her upcoming exhibition at the Indica, which would be opened to the public the next evening, Yoko handed John a white card embossed with the word BREATHE. "You mean, like this?" John responded, before breaking into a pant. Almost immediately, Lennon found himself enjoying the humour behind her art. Following the diminutive Japanese woman around the gallery, John happened upon a ladder, above which hung Yoko's *Ceiling Painting*. "It looked like a black canvas with a chain with a spyglass hanging on the end of it," John remembered. At the top of the ladder, John peered through the magnifying glass at the canvas, which sported a single word: YES. Years later, John would fondly recall "that's when we connected, really." While they wouldn't become a couple for another 18 months, the die had been cast. "We looked at each other," John recalled, and "something went off."[27]

While the evolution of the couple's highly public relationship in the late 1960s left many observers believing that they were two very similar peas in the same pod, John and Yoko enjoyed starkly different temperaments and divergent interests. This aspect of their union was often surprising to many outsiders, who believed the pair to be joined at the hip, having witnessed their prolific activities as peace advocates, particularly their much-publicised "bed-ins" for peace.

But even still, the Lennons were able to find a kind of unanimity even in their differences. Take, for example, Yoko's highly superstitious nature. As the years wore on, she became ever more dependent upon a standing group of psychics and numerologists to assist her in navigating her family's nearly every move. Visitors to the Dakota and potential business partners would often be quizzed about their "numbers" – their dates and times of birth – before being invited into the couple's inner sanctum. From his perspective, John wasn't quite so certain when it came to the world of the supernatural, having been a lifelong sceptic and well-known contrarian. But at the same time, he believed in Yoko's sense of intuition implicitly. As Rosa later recalled, "Although John didn't really trust occultism, he definitely preferred not to challenge the unknown. He respected and supported any decision Yoko could make based on the predictions or advice from her consultants." And why should John challenge Yoko's method of decision-making anyway, no matter how unconventional it may have seemed to the workaday world? By the late 1970s, she appeared to be on an unbroken winning streak, and John, more often than not, was the central beneficiary of her good fortune.[28]

For the Lennons, their staff, and the Dakota residents alike, the most pressing daily concern involved the Beatles fans who assaulted the building on a daily basis in an effort to talk on the phone to – or better yet, catch a glimpse of – their hero. On a typical day, Winnie Bodkin, the Dakota's grey-haired, bespectacled switchboard operator, fielded several dozen callers desperately trying to speak with the Lennons. Over the years, Winnie had developed a special fondness for John, and she enjoyed helping him outsmart the paparazzi. On one occasion, "there was a truck with cameras parked across the street for days and days, just waiting for him to come out. But he escaped through the basement when I warned him," she recalled. "The phone is a nuisance, though. I get between 15 and 20 calls a day from people trying to get through to him. People try to leave messages, and they try to leave gifts."[29]

Outside of an unremitting press, most of the Dakota's moveable feast of daily bystanders were good-natured, occasionally overzealous fans who ultimately proved to be harmless. Take "Blonde Brenda", as she was known among the Lennons' staff. At age 17, Brenda Spencer had run away from home, hoping to attend the annual Beatlefest (later known as the "Fest for Beatles Fans") and, perhaps more important, meet John in the flesh. "John used to call me the 'Country Girl'," Spencer later recalled, "because as soon as he heard my accent, he asked where I was from and I told him Minnesota." John subsequently took to describing her as "the girl from 'mmmmiles away'", which he would pronounce with an exaggerated stutter. In the late 1970s, Blonde Brenda managed to meet with John on several occasions, sometimes enjoying longer conversations with him and happily posing for pictures. For his part, Fred couldn't help thinking that she was different from the other fans who loitered outside the building, day in and day out. At one point, he later recalled, "I was suddenly seized with an almost overpowering urge to shake her and say, 'Brenda, Brenda, what are you doing here? There must be a million people in New York who would love to sit down and talk to a pretty girl like yourself. John Lennon puts his pants on one leg at a time, just like everybody else. You are wasting your time."[30]

As with Winnie the switchboard operator, 45-year-old doorman José Perdomo went out of his way to assist the Lennons in navigating the daily nuisance of John's celebrity. A Cuban refugee after the emergence of the Castro regime, the kind-hearted Perdomo contended with the succession of visitors attempting to meet with John. And when they weren't stopping by in person, they often left presents for him. At one point, one of the packages contained a mysterious chalky substance. Worried that something unseemly or even dangerous might fall into the wrong hands – namely, four-year-old Sean's – John demanded that all unsolicited packages be tossed into the garbage.

Despite the best efforts of the Dakota's staff, fans sometimes succeeded in making their way into the building. For the Lennons' fellow residents, the very idea of transient visitors stalking the Dakota's maze of hallways was of paramount concern. As Wilbur Ross, an investment banker and, in later years, president of the co-op board, observed, "One thing that worries us is that if someone got into the building, how would we ever find him?" Birmingham seconded Ross' anxieties regarding intruders, observing that "it is true that in some of the building's dark storage spaces and closets and rooftop lofts a person could conceivably hide out for months undetected. But once he was inside, a prowler unfamiliar with the building would also have a hard time finding his way out, since so many of the Dakota's doors and hallways open into cul-de-sacs."[31]

On more than one occasion, fans had slipped into the Dakota, roaming the hallways and ringing doorbells in brazen attempts to find the Lennons. For the most part, they proved to be harmless. In one instance, David Marlowe, a novelist who lived in an eighth-floor apartment across the courtyard from the Lennons, answered his door to a group of young girls who were patrolling the corridors in search of the ex-Beatle. Seizing the moment, Marlowe fooled them. "This is John Lennon's apartment," he lied. "But he's in Europe for the summer."[32]

Yet not all of the Dakota's residents were as genial towards the Lennons as Marlowe, who enjoyed the novelty of living in the same building as an ex-Beatle. During John's years of self-described retirement, Birmingham fell back on Old World conceptions of "new" and "old" money in his characterisation of John and Yoko's place in the Dakoterie's hierarchy. "The John Lennons are not chic," he observed. "The Lennons may think it is chic, or funny, to enter and alight from their limousines in blue jeans, but they can't have it both ways. They merely seem odd. Besides, the

Lennons have not done much of anything in recent years, and the man who helped revolutionise twentieth-century music now seems to have settled into the ways of the *haute bourgeoisie*."[33]

Still others, including famed composer Leonard Bernstein and his family, were particularly enthusiastic about John's presence in the Dakota. In spite of his classical background, Bernstein had been an early adherent of the Beatles, especially of 'A Day In The Life', Lennon's apocalyptic vision that served as the musical climax of *Sgt. Pepper's Lonely Hearts Club Band* (1967). As Bernstein famously remarked, "Three bars of 'A Day In The Life' still sustain me, rejuvenate me, inflame my senses and sensibilities." The Bernstein family moved into the Dakota in 1975 and met John and Yoko that fall at the annual potluck in the building's courtyard. Held each October, the potluck events offered a rare moment for the residents of the austere address to enjoy each other's company. If it rained, they simply moved the event inside the building's vaulted archway. For the potlucks, the Lennons often shared a plate of sushi; one year, they gifted their neighbours with copies of a book on the merits of living an organic culinary lifestyle.[34]

Years later, Bernstein's teenaged daughter Nina would recall her "great brush with John Lennon" at the dessert table, as the former Beatle stared wistfully at the sweets and playfully announced that "I want something mushy and disgusting" in his Liverpool Scouse accent. Nervous at being in John's presence, the 13-year-old Nina "muttered something about the pecan pie looking good". A few years later, Nina earned a shot at redemption after her father challenged his family to sing a round that he had taught them based upon John's surrealistic poem 'The Moldy Moldy Man' from his first book *In His Own Write* (1964). To John's great amusement, Bernstein's family sang the poem to him at the annual potluck, perfectly executing the round to Leonard's immense satisfaction. For his part, Bernstein relished the opportunity to pay tribute, however slight, from one celebrated musician to another.[35]

As the years wore on, the fans kept coming, having never ebbed in their daily assault on the Dakota's entryways and their brazen efforts to find new and innovative ways into the former Beatle's orbit. Sometimes, John himself was the problem. On the one hand, he recognised the nuisance his admirers created for his family and fellow Dakotans. But at the same time, John felt sympathetic to his fans, regardless of the extent of their obsessions and the lengths to which they were willing to go. On one occasion, a large number of fans were swarming the archway as John and his housekeeper Rosa returned from an errand. As they rode the elevator up to the seventh floor, John told her that "those guys had been there for hours. Some even for days. And just to see me. Maybe it doesn't make sense; however, the least I could do is to avoid disappointing them when they get to see me."[36]

In 1979, two preteen boys hit the jackpot when they made it past the doormen and rang the doorbell to apartment 72. John promptly answered the door, thinking that Yoko had forgotten her keys. When one of the boys politely asked if they could have a word with John, the ex-Beatle invited them inside, where Fred served them juice as they peppered John with questions about the meaning of life. As the boys listened intently, John explained that life was like a movie that played continuously, observing that as you get older, its meaning begins to come into greater and greater relief. When the boys asked him about the looming experience of death, John replied that when a person dies the movie of one's life plays in reverse chronological order, with imagery from the most recent reels coming up first. As Fred later recalled, the afternoon came to an abrupt end when the boys inquired if they could come back again someday and spend more time with John. With nary another word, John beat a hasty retreat to his bedroom, leaving his assistant to send the precocious kids on their way.

Over the years, John had encountered nearly every possible permutation of fandom. In 1971, a homeless man had famously wandered onto the sprawling grounds of Tittenhurst Park, the rural Ascot estate that John and Yoko shared at the time, during the production of the *Imagine* LP. The itinerant fan had sought out Lennon in order to make sense of his wayward thoughts, which had been fuelled on a heavy diet of Beatles lyrics and misconceptions about John's personhood. "Don't confuse my songs with your life," John told the man, who clearly viewed him as a kind of lodestar. "I mean, they might have relevance to your own life, you know, but lots of things do. And so we've met, you know? I'm just a guy, man, who writes songs."[37]

In his role as John's personal assistant, Fred quickly learned that the nightmare scenario in the Lennon household actually had very little to do with Beatle fans, but rather, involved the ongoing threat that someone might attempt to kidnap Sean, extort his wealthy parents, and possibly harm him during the process. Back in November 1977, John and Yoko

25

received a letter threatening Sean's life and demanding $100,000 to ensure his safety. In spite of the FBI's intervention, the case went unsolved when there was no further contact by the would-be kidnappers. After beginning his employ with John and Yoko, Fred soon learned that in spite of such understandable fears, their security was remarkably lax. He couldn't help but chuckle after reading a column by Liz Smith, the doyenne of the city's gossip crowd, who wrote, "Hey burglars, forget West 72nd Street. John Lennon is into locks. He had his digs at the Dakota fortified with more than 50 intricate protective devices that guard everything. It's all something like the little old lady in *The Producers* whose door was lined with locks from top to bottom."[38]

Fred knew all too well that the assertions in Smith's column simply didn't pass muster, recognising that if someone bent on harming the Lennons made it past the doormen on the first floor, the only thing that stood between them and the family in apartment 72 was a standard deadbolt lock. But even still, a paucity of security devices on the Lennons' apartment door was probably a low priority, all things considered, when it came to their safety. The family – Sean especially – was a vulnerable target, particularly in sprawling, densely populated New York City, which was home to more than seven million people in 1979. Concerned with preserving their young son's anonymity, John and Yoko had made a point of discouraging the publication of photos of him until the end of his toddler years. To address the glaring hole in the family's security when it came to safeguarding Sean, Yoko brought ex-FBI man Douglas MacDougall into the Lennons' employ. But for his part, John was sceptical about drawing bodyguards into the family's lives. To his mind, the ethics of being a longstanding pacifist and putting a security guard in harm's way didn't add up. "It's my rationale," he once remarked, "that if they're gonna get you, they're gonna get you anyway. First, they kill the bodyguard." Besides, Fred later recalled, John simply didn't think he was at risk."[39]

But it was more than that. In spite of his admittedly innate sense of paranoia, John felt that living in New York City afforded him a sense of freedom that had long since eluded him in his celebrity life. Since the onset of the Beatles' fame in the early 1960s, the press and the public alike had hounded him virtually nonstop. Over the years, he had seen one outlandish invasion of his personal space after another – beginning, perhaps most notoriously, in February 1964, after the Beatles went for a swim in the pool at Miami Beach's Deauville Hotel. Afterwards, the pool water was bottled and hawked as "Beatle Water". Later that year, makeshift entrepreneurs sold pieces of the bandmates' rug from their suite at Seattle's Edgewater Hotel. And then there was the story of the Chicago DJs who rounded up the Beatles' linens from hotel rooms across their first American tour, cut up the fabric, and resold it in one-inch swathes to ecstatic, souvenir-hungry fans.[40]

As far as the other Beatles went, John wasn't alone in his thinking. To George Harrison's mind, understanding the personal and economic calculus of Beatlemania after a lifetime of unremitting celebrity was ineluctably simple: by his reasoning, the fans "gave their money, and they gave their screams. But the Beatles gave their nervous systems, which is a much more difficult thing to give." For John, the essential loss had always come down to privacy, which he had come to prioritise, at times, even over his own safety. He would begrudgingly admit that his disdain for hiring a security team wasn't just a matter of considering the implications of his pacifism – "first, they kill the bodyguard" – but also the inevitable invasion into his personal space that such round-the-clock safeguards require. And besides, John had come to adore the freedom and anonymity that New York City seemed to beckon and which he had lacked for much of his adult life. John was particularly fond of pointing out that "I can go right out of this door now and go in a restaurant. You know how great that is? Or go to the movies? I mean, people come and ask for autographs, but they don't bug you."[41]

CHAPTER 3

A Phantom

Over the years, New Yorkers would reminisce about observing John during his regular jaunts in Central Park, seeing him at the crosswalk on West 72nd Street, or on his way to one of his favourite eateries. Their stories would often take on the same parameters: a smiling Lennon enjoying a stroll in the city, only to be spotted by a particular fan or passerby. John would catch their eye, their glint of recognition at having seen an actual Beatle in the wild. In such tales, John would invariably lift his index finger up to his lips, as if to say, "This is our little secret." In such moments, the storyteller was happy to see John happily go on his way, unmolested in his adopted hometown. According to Robert Thompson, a lifelong Upper West Sider, an unspoken credo exists among native New Yorkers that celebrities, both famous and infamous, are part and parcel of city life, that they deserve their privacy as much as the next guy standing in line at the neighbourhood bodega or trudging along Amsterdam Avenue. "If there's eye contact, we might smile," said Thompson, but "no autographs, no pictures. If there's any spoken word, it might be a brief compliment for a new movie, record, interview, whatever. But it's always sincere."[42]

But even still, sometimes things would get a little out of hand. On occasion, overzealous fans would trail John about the city, inevitably stammering up to him to ask for an autograph or to snap a picture. But it seemed like a small price to pay to be able to make his regular treks to the West Side YMCA on 63th Street, where he was teaching Sean how to swim in the public pool. Or to push Sean's baby buggy as he and Yoko strolled along the parkside meadows just across the street from the Dakota. Sometimes, he simply had to laugh. In one of his favourite anecdotes, he and Yoko had been serenaded by a Spanish violinist, who, having spotted them in a restaurant, began playing 'Yesterday', a McCartney composition. "He couldn't understand that I didn't write the song. But I guess he couldn't have gone from table to table playing 'I Am The Walrus'." Afterwards, he went so far as to ask John to autograph his violin, and the former Beatle dutifully obliged. In recent years, he had taken to enjoying his afternoon tea in the Plaza Hotel's Palm Court. Occasionally, a tourist would stop by his table and ask, "Aren't you John Lennon?" By now, John had fashioned a variety of gentle retorts such as "I get told that a lot" or "I wish I had his money."[43]

Even still, fans would sometimes go to great and potentially more sinister lengths to meet the former Beatle. As Fred later observed, "John was aware that he attracted the lunatic fringe." For John and Yoko, the fear of intrusion was "a daily anxiety". On some occasions, the perilous nature of a threat made itself immediately and abundantly clear. Rosa recalled one instance in which

> a guy evaded the Dakota security system and knocked on the back door. When I opened, he nervously asked for John. I got so scared, so I told him he was not at home, and I closed the door as fast as I could. I waited a few seconds and opened the door again to check if he was still there. There he was. He took a camera out of his pocket and took some pictures of the house. I slammed the door and went to warn John and Yoko, who were actually in the living room. They immediately called the security guards, who handcuffed him.

However brief it may have been, the incident's potential for danger was not lost on John. "After everything got back to normal," said Rosa, John "walked around the kitchen looking up to heaven and saying, 'Thank God, Thank God, Thank God.'"[44]

And yet, on other occasions, the level of risk was far less apparent to John. In February 1979, one particularly intrepid fan – an amateur photographer named Paul Goresh – had made his way past the building's doormen and all the way upstairs to apartment 72, having disguised himself as the Lennons' television repairman. Hailing from nearby North

Arlington, New Jersey, the 20-year-old Goresh worked as a part-time driver for an electronics shop. With his friend Mario in tow, Goresh commandeered the store's van and piloted the vehicle right into the Dakota's archway, where he was met by the building's doorman. But Goresh was ready, having prepared dummy paperwork to steal his way inside. He was also carrying a copy of *In His Own Write*, which he planned to ask the ex-Beatle to autograph.

As Goresh later recalled, the doorman "didn't even blink" and ushered them inside. "I showed him the service order," said Goresh. "I wrote 'J. Lennon' instead of 'John Lennon' so I could seem totally oblivious about it." As luck would have it, the Lennons' VCR was actually on the fritz that very same day, and John was anxious to get it repaired. When he and Mario arrived at apartment 72, Goresh's enthusiasm got the best of him, and he banged rather loudly on the door. Goresh was particularly flummoxed when John answered the door himself. Not missing a beat, the ex-Beatle remarked that "I thought it was the cops!" and invited them inside the rambling apartment, with its thick, white, wall-to-wall shag carpeting. "My chin must have just dropped. I was just staring at him, amazed that he opened the door," Goresh remembered. "But there he stood, gold-rimmed glasses, chewing gum, and smiling." As it turned out, John had been angry that day – but not at the pair of impostors who had bluffed their way into his apartment. No, John was angry at Helen Seaman for not having informed him about what he assumed to be a legitimate repair call. In the ensuing fracas, the assistant suggested that they return at a later date to make the necessary repairs. As far as Goresh was concerned, "I was disgusted at the way it turned out, especially because I didn't get my autograph."[45]

Not missing a beat, Helen rescheduled the phony repairman's visit for later that same week. When he returned to the Dakota, Goresh brought along his copy of *In His Own Write* and his camera, a Minolta XG1, in his toolbox. But unbeknownst to John's assistant, the ex-Beatle had already purchased a new VCR on his own accord. When Goresh returned, Lennon actually made a point of apologising to *him*, explaining that he had been angry at Helen for not clearing the repair call with him in advance, given the sheer number of fans and other hangers-on attempting to snake their way into his orbit by almost any means. Lennon dutifully autographed Goresh's book, although he pointedly refused to have his picture taken. "Arrivederci Roma!" Lennon quipped as he sent the faux repairman on his way. "I felt bad," Goresh remembered, "because I thought that would be the last time I saw him." Besides, John "had been real nice. I'd gotten what I wanted to get."[46]

But Goresh remained undeterred, still hoping to snap a photograph of his idol. And he had no illusions that his repairman scam had been a complete success. "I honestly think he detected that something was funny," Goresh later recalled. A month later, Goresh took several photographs of John as he strolled on the Upper West Side. This time, John was furious, clearly recognising Goresh from his earlier visit to the Dakota. "I signed your book," Lennon exclaimed. "Don't take my photo. Leave me alone." At this point, Goresh decided that his mission to take John's picture would be better served through stealth. "I could get a telephoto lens, stand across the street from him, follow him, take a few pictures of him, and he'll never be any the wiser," Goresh reasoned.[47]

As it happened, Lennon caught onto Goresh's ruse in short order, brusquely removing the film from his camera and marching towards the safety of the Dakota archway. Now, Goresh was truly despondent, having succeeded in sending his hero away in an angry huff. Leaving his Minolta behind, Goresh caught up with Lennon on the streets of the Upper West Side one more time. "I never meant to cause you grief," he told John. "If you want me to leave you alone, then I'll never come back here again." As they stood together on Central Park West, Goresh could sense Lennon beginning to let down his guard. "I remember he looked right in my eyes and said, 'Stop looking at me as a Beatle. You've got to treat me like you'd treat anyone else.' And he said, 'Come on', and we went for a walk." Quite suddenly, Goresh was living out the fantasy of Beatles fans the world over, regularly accompanying John as he ran errands on the Upper West Side, tagging along as he strolled through Central Park.[48]

But unbeknownst to Goresh, things weren't so free and easy as far as his relationship with Lennon was concerned. Something about the pudgy photographer made the ex-Beatle nervous, even afraid. Perhaps it had been the clandestine way in which he had first entered the Lennons' lives? In an effort to make light of the situation, the Dakota's doormen had taken to referring to Goresh as "Fat Dave" behind his back; as far as they could tell, he was harmless. While John's empathy had gotten the better of him as far as Goresh was concerned, his soul-wrenching anxiety over being stalked and recognised had hardly ebbed. Explaining his constant angst to Fred, John observed that his peculiar brand of celebrity had an omnipresent quality, the kind of fame that forces its wearer into a form of unceasing paranoia. But that's okay, John reasoned, because "paranoia is really a heightened sense of awareness." By this point, John's patience with his fans' hit-and-run tactics had taken a heavy toll on his psyche. He had long been of the mind that the Fab Four's overwhelming celebrity had succeeded in obscuring their most significant accomplishments. Around the time that he met Goresh, John ran into Roger Berkeley, a fellow Upper West Sider with whom he had a nodding acquaintance. Stopping to chat, Berkeley told Lennon about the upcoming fifth instalment of Beatlefest. "Tell the fans that 'the music was the thing'," said John, before disappearing into the neighbourhood.[49]

As he spent more time in the company of his new employer, Fred became ever more cognisant about the nature of Lennon's daily existence. "John's eyes would dart this way and that, anxiously scrutinising passersby, trying to anticipate the moment when he would be recognised and approached by strangers." Struggling to clarify his state of perpetual being to his assistant, John likened his predicament to an interminable parlour game in which the ex-Beatle was engaged in an endless struggle to preserve his selfhood. "It's like a bloody chess game, don't you see?" he told Fred. "I'm the king, and every encounter with pawns weakens me. You're my knight, and it's your job to protect me from such encounters by acting as an intermediary. As far as the public is concerned, I'm a phantom. I only exist in people's imagination. The less I'm seen, the more power I have."[50]

John was a phantom all right. And by New Year's Eve, with the dawn of a new decade in the offing, his power had become truly formidable. Like Hughes, he had disappeared into his celebrity and emerged as a figure of legend. Through his exile and its attendant mystique, he had arguably become even more famous than the other former Beatles, who continued to remain professionally active to varying degrees of success. John's old songwriting partner Paul had developed Wings into a veritable juggernaut, with numerous chart-topping albums and singles to the band's name. While the group's latest record *Back To The Egg* (1979) had failed to achieve such lofty heights, McCartney and Wings enjoyed heavy rotation on the airwaves with singles like the disco head fake 'Goodnight Tonight' and, more recently, 'Wonderful Christmastime', which was a radio favourite as John marked the new year in the Dakota. As for Harrison, the Beatles' lead guitarist had enjoyed an impressive return to form with the release of his eponymous LP the previous February, even going so far as to score a Top 20 hit with 'Blow Away'. When he wasn't churning out new material, Harrison had begun compiling his autobiography for a bravura fall 1980 release.

Although drummer Ringo Starr landed a string of hits in the early 1970s, his musical fortunes had been fading markedly in recent years. His June 1978 LP *Bad Boy* had struggled mightily just to crack the Top 100 records among *Billboard*'s album charts. Concerned about his former mate's flagging results, John never stopped rooting for Ringo to turn the tide on his career. In a 1979 postcard, he even went so far as to provide some unsolicited advice, suggesting that Ringo try his hand at mimicking Blondie's recent string of smash hits: "'Heart of Glass' is the type of stuff y'all should do – *great* and simple," John opined. Although his own muse had deserted him, John always seemed to find time for Ringo. Composed by John during his Lost Weekend with May Pang, '(It's All Down To) Goodnight Vienna' registered a foot-stomping hit for Starr in the summer of 1974.[51]

At one point during that period, Ringo had briefly lived with John and May at their rented house in Los Angeles. As with John, the Beatles' drummer was engaged in wholesale alcohol abuse and trying to right his flagging career. As journalist Larry Kane recalled, John "had a paternal instinct when it came to Ringo and George." May confirmed this aspect of Lennon's personality, remarking that "John always worried about George and Ringo. He was constantly on the phone to George, and heartsick about what Ringo was doing with his life. In California, he watched over Ringo. In New York, at the Apple offices, John made sure he had good time to talk to George, who was a bit insecure about going it alone." At the height of the Lost Weekend – and in spite of his own self-destructive behaviour at the time – John always found time to spend with the Quiet Beatle. As former Apple employee Linda Reig recalled, "John could be a bastard, but when it came to George Harrison, nothing was ever enough. George was a sweetheart, a real gentleman. He came to the office all the time. When he came, John would stop whatever he was doing to spend time with George. I think he viewed him as a younger brother."[52]

In later years, John would describe the Lost Weekend as a period of drunken debauchery, of sowing his wild oats in the company of other wayward rock stars. Drawing the phrase from the 1945 Billy Wilder film noir classic of the same name, John admitted that "I was just insane. The Lost Weekend lasted 18 months. I've never drunk so much in my life, and I've been drinking since I was 15. But I really tried to drown myself in the bottle, and it took an awful lot. I don't seem strong physically that much, but it just seems to take an amazing lot to put me down. And I was with the heaviest drinkers in the industry, which is Harry Nilsson and Bobby Keyes and Keith Moon and all of them, and we couldn't pull ourselves out."[53]

The Lost Weekend had commenced in mid-1973 after Yoko kicked John out of the Dakota, later remarking that "I think I really needed some space because I was used to being an artist and free and all that, and when I got together with John, because we're always in the public eye, I lost the freedom. And also, both of us were together all the time." As it happened, Yoko was entering a crucial phase as an artist. During that period, she had been shifting her experimental music towards a more feminist-oriented rock 'n' roll, as revealed in her 1973 albums *Approximately Infinite Universe* and *Feeling The Space*, which had been engineered by Jack Douglas, the sound man who had earlier shared his talents doing post-production work by overdubbing the Flux Fiddlers' string arrangements for *Imagine*. But it was more than just artistic freedom behind Yoko's restlessness. She had been contemplating an affair during that time with ace guitar player David Spinozza, who had lent his skills to Paul and Linda McCartney's *Ram* (1971), John's *Mind Games*, and, more recently, as a session man on Yoko's *Feeling The Space* LP.[54]

The very public devolution of the Lennons' relationship had begun months earlier when John and Yoko attended an election night party in November 1972 in the apartment of anti-war activist Jerry Rubin. That night, John got thoroughly drunk and demeaned his wife when he had sex with one of Jerry's roommates in a nearby room. As the sounds from their ministrations emanated around the apartment, Yoko could only stand there, waiting until her husband had concluded his very public betrayal. When John was finished, he returned to the party, took Yoko by the hand, and left. As Wayne "Tex" Gabriel, the lead guitarist with Elephant's Memory, later recalled, "That was the only time I remember Yoko breaking down and showing any of us what she was feeling. I gave her my sunglasses so she could leave with some self-respect. Everybody in the room knew what was going on, it was extremely humiliating. And we were all just sort of humiliated along with her, having watched Nixon's landslide."[55]

While John's public humiliation of Yoko was clearly devastating, his increasing substance abuse – namely, his seemingly uncontrollable bouts of heavy drinking – was beginning to take its toll. On several occasions,

John had attended Yoko's *Approximately Infinite Universe* sessions, which he was ostensibly co-producing, in full, disruptive inebriation – that is, when he bothered to show up at all. In his role as chief engineer, Douglas recalled John's spiralling behaviour during this period, including the moment in which his budding alcoholism saw him being banished from the Record Plant – and by his wife, no less. "John was in the control room at a Yoko session I was doing," said Douglas. "He cracked up at something he heard [in the studio], and just then Yoko walked in. He was busted. From that moment on, Lennon was not allowed at Yoko sessions." And it would be the drinking that would spell the end for rock's most notorious couple. "Yoko finally kicked him out," photographer Bob Gruen recalled. "It was very abrupt, and had grown into one of those tired clichés, you know: you always say you're sorry, but you always get drunk and screw things up again. Enough! You're out!"[56]

To effect John's dismissal, Yoko turned to her 22-year-old assistant May Pang. Formerly employed in the New York offices of notorious businessman and one-time Beatles manager Allen Klein, the beautiful young Chinese woman had worked as a production supervisor on Yoko's avant-garde films *Up Your Legs Forever* and *Fly* in the early 1970s. In addition to coordinating Ono's *This Is Not Here* retrospective exhibition at Syracuse's Everson Museum, Pang served as the Lennons' production assistant for the *Imagine* documentary at Tittenhurst Park. She was a trusted member of John and Yoko's inner circle – so much so that when the Lennons decided to relocate to the United States in 1971, May was entrusted to ferry John's prized 1958 Rickenbacker 325 Capri – the selfsame guitar that he had played during the Beatles' bravura *Ed Sullivan* appearances in February 1964 – by plane to New York City.

Yoko set things into motion by tasking May with becoming John's lover. To Yoko's mind, a younger woman was perfect for her husband. "May Pang was a very intelligent, attractive woman and extremely efficient," Yoko later reflected. "I thought they'd be okay." Not surprisingly, May was initially aghast at the thought of such an unconventional – even unethical – arrangement with her employers. "It'll be great," Yoko told her. "He'll be happy. It's cool." But as far as May was concerned, the idea of being with another woman's husband was anything but cool. "It was *wrong*," May remembered thinking, "and I wanted no part of it." By this point, John had begun coming on to his assistant, who eventually demurred when she could no longer resist John's increasingly brazen flirtations.[57]

For her part, Yoko gravitated towards Spinozza with John's full blessing. At times, John even seemed to be pushing Yoko towards the other man, saying, "David's so beautiful. I wouldn't mind having sex with him." For some people – Pang included – John and Yoko's unconventional, even blasé approach to their sexuality may have seemed eccentric, if not downright offensive. As John liked to put it, sex was simply a means to an end as far as he was concerned. "That was one of the main reasons you go on stage, because the guy in the band gets the girls," he once remarked. "There's an old joke, but it's true: Sometimes you'd get this girl after the show and you'd be in bed and she'd ask you which one you are. I'd say, 'Which one do you like?' If she said, 'George', I'd say, 'I'm George'."[58]

But the Lennons' emotional connection was something entirely different. Throughout their separation, John and Yoko barraged each other with daily telephone calls – during one memorable day, May totalled their phone activities to nearly two-dozen different calls. To understand Yoko's looming place in John's life, even during their separation, one need only study the cover art for *Mind Games*, from a hand-cut photo collage by John, which depicts the musician standing forlorn in the foreground of a mountainous image of Yoko on the horizon.

Meanwhile, John and May's affair gathered steam as they crisscrossed the United States, carried out production duties for three albums – *Mind Games*, *Rock 'n' Roll*, and *Walls And Bridges* – and fell in love. At the same time, John's bachelor lifestyle occasionally fell into disarray. With Pang in tow, Lennon and Nilsson got into a series of highly publicised scuffles at LA's Troubadour nightclub. At one point, they were ejected after they heckled the Smothers Brothers. On another occasion, John appeared at the Troubadour with a sanitary napkin affixed to his forehead. "Do you know who I am?" he allegedly asked one of the club's waitresses. "Yeah," she quipped, "you're some asshole with a Kotex on his head." And then there was the time in March 1974 when Paul and Linda dropped by Burbank Studios, where Lennon and Nilsson were recording *Pussy Cats*. That night, the two estranged friends conducted an informal jam session, with Pang, Nilsson, Linda McCartney, Stevie Wonder, and Beatles roadie Mal Evans trying their hands at such classic as Little Richard's 'Lucille', Ben E. King's 'Stand By Me', and Sam Cooke's 'Cupid', among others.[59]

By the spring of 1974, John and May returned to New York City, moving into an East Side apartment during the production of John's *Walls And Bridges* album. By day, the couple spent time with their adopted cats

Major and Minor, before whiling away the hours at the Record Plant, where they recorded tracks like 'Whatever Gets You Thru The Night', his duet with Elton John, and 'Surprise, Surprise (Sweet Bird Of Paradox)', in which he memorialised his relationship with Pang as a kind of intense, erotic liberation. With her delectable body – "sweet as the smell of success" – May lovingly enabled him to survive his "godawful loneliness."

For John and May, 1974 came to a close in South Florida, where they relaxed with Julian on Palm Beach island. "I really like it here," John remarked to a reporter from the *Palm Beach Daily News*. "I really don't want to leave Palm Beach. I'd like to own a piece of it." Later, they took Julian to Walt Disney World, where Lennon famously signed the agreement that ended the Beatles' partnership at the resort's Polynesian Village Hotel. With the new year in full swing, the couple made plans for the future, including the purchase of a cottage in Montauk on Long Island and a February visit to New Orleans, where Lennon hoped to join McCartney and Wings in the studio for the band's *Venus And Mars* sessions.[60]

According to May, the day before the couple's planned trip to New Orleans, Yoko intervened, claiming to have discovered an innovative cure for smoking that she wanted to share with her estranged husband, who had long worried that the habit was damaging his singing voice. "I have a bad feeling," May told John. "Please don't go." In Yoko's memory, her reunion with her husband had been simply a matter of John calling her up and asking her out on a date for tea at the Plaza Hotel. Whatever the impetus, John had spent much of the Lost Weekend openly pining for Yoko. Back in November 1974, he had seen her backstage after his Thanksgiving performance with Elton John at Madison Square Garden, later describing their meeting in highly romantic terms. "Yoko and I met backstage. And somebody said, 'Well, there's two people in love'," John recalled. "There was just that moment when we saw each other. It's like in the movies, you know, when time stands still. And there was silence. Everything went silent, you know, and we were just sort of looking at each other."[61]

By March 1975, John was ensconced back at the Dakota, having been reconciled with Yoko, once and for all. "I didn't think I would lose him," Yoko recalled. "The affair was something that was not hurtful to me. I was prepared to lose him, but it was better he came back." For her part, May was left broken-hearted, and, when her salary from Yoko ran out, unemployed within an industry that was suddenly loath to hire her. In

1975, Lennon would wistfully reflect upon his time with Pang to Larry Kane, remarking that "I may have been the happiest I've ever been. I loved this woman, I made some beautiful music, and I got so fucked up with booze and shit and whatever." When Kane asked him why he returned to his wife, John waxed philosophical, replying that "I love Yoko, too. Finding where you belong can be most difficult, if you know what I mean, young fellow."[62]

To memorialise their reconciliation, Lennon took to wearing a heart-shaped diamond necklace around his neck. For John and Yoko, the jewellery held special significance. In July 1971, the couple had a dreadful fight over whether or not they should appear at George Harrison's upcoming Concert for Bangladesh, the legend-making charity event at Madison Square Garden. John was hell-bent on declining George's offer, while Yoko felt that they shouldn't forgo the chance to perform on the biggest stage of the year – possibly even the decade.

In a fit of anger, John abruptly left Yoko in their New York City hotel suite, making his way back to Europe without so much as telling her where he was going. She caught up with her husband at Tittenhurst Park, where John apologised for his behaviour. As Yoko later recalled, "In Paris he had got me a heart-shaped diamond necklace. I thought it was so touching and sweet, because the heart was so small. He knew I didn't like anything too big and ostentatious. And so we got cosy in bed, and that was that." When John returned to the Dakota at the conclusion of his Lost Weekend, Yoko gave the tiny pendant back to him as a symbol of their reconciliation.[63]

After their reunion, John and Yoko didn't see the inside of a recording studio until June 1976, when they joined Ringo for a session at Hollywood's Cherokee Recording Studios. With his soft spot for the Beatles' drummer in full flower, John provided Ringo with yet another new composition – this time, for inclusion on Starr's *Ringo's Rotogravure* album. Entitled 'Cookin' (In The Kitchen Of Love)', the song featured John performing a rambling piano introduction.

Meanwhile, John hoped to send another winning song Ringo's way. That same year, he had been nursing a bouncy composition entitled 'Everybody's Talkin', Nobody's Talkin'' (also known as 'Everybody'). For the original demo – which he later introduced by announcing that "this one's probably for Richard Starkey, late of the Beatles" – John can be heard performing the tune on his piano in the Dakota along with a drum machine accompaniment. By the late 1970s, John had taken to using a Roland CompuRhythm CR-68 drum machine, complete with the option of deploying break and fill variations, which he rarely toggled. With a heavy dose of piano sostenuto complementing his lyrics, John's song wryly referenced Harry Nilsson, his former Lost Weekend drinking buddy and the pop singer who had covered Fred Neil's 'Everybody's Talkin'' on the road to charting a Grammy Award-winning hit song back in 1969. 'Everybody's Talkin', Nobody's Talkin'' also made mention of John's UFO sighting with May Pang in August 1974, along with an allusion to Milton Hayes' 1911 poem 'The Green Eye Of The Little Yellow God', the subject of frequent and merciless parody on the BBC's *The Goon Show* radio programme in the 1950s:

> There's a one-eyed yellow idol to the north of Kathmandu,
> There's a little marble cross below the town;
> There's a broken-hearted woman tends the grave of Mad Carew,
> And the Yellow God forever gazes down.

By December 1978, John had been outfitted with a brand-new piano rig, courtesy of Yoko, who had Christmas-gifted her husband with the new keyboard in an effort to help him refresh his rusty muse. Yoko had purchased a portable Yamaha CP-80 electric-acoustic grand piano, complete with two high-end speakers, from Manny's Music, a Midtown instrument store nestled among West 48th Street's legendary Music Row. Since its inception in 1935, the firm had come to be known as "Manny's Guitars", but in the late 1970s, as disco and new wave roiled the record industry, the store had expanded its inventory to include a wide range of synth-keyboard options.

As it happened, the CP-80 was "portable" in name only, requiring a minimum of three people to lug it from gig to gig. Self-described by the instrumental conglomerate as the "Rolls-Royce" of keyboards and marketed as being "touring friendly", the Yamaha electric piano featured a full-range 88-key piano board complete with real strings. Not surprisingly, Yoko spared no expense, purchasing all the bells and whistles. The fully loaded CP-80 "Soundboarded" model was primed for recording, including tremolo control, an amplifier, a built-in compressor, and augmented stereo width. The virtual soundboard included two mics that could be positioned adjacent to the piano for demonstration or live recording projects.

In January 1979, scarcely a few days into the new year, the Lennons' staff contacted Manny's Music in a panic: John's CP-80, only recently installed in apartment 72, was on the fritz. The next morning, the store's 22-year-old piano tech Charly Roth was dispatched to the Dakota. With his hair spiked, punk-like, and dyed henna purple, Roth waited downstairs in Studio One, Yoko's first-floor office suite, which consisted of two high-ceiling rooms that formerly belonged to Jo Mielziner. Nicknamed Studio One by John and Yoko, the office served as the headquarters of Lenono Music, while doubling as Yoko's inner sanctum. The outer office served as the nerve centre of the Lenono operation, with banks of white filing cabinets – anointed with labels such as "Royalties, BMI" and "Petty Cash" – towering over the room. Stationed nearby was Seaman's desk, along with the workspace assigned to 33-year-old Rich DePalma, the Lennons' inhouse accountant. Studio One's main room was dominated by a massive gold-inlaid desk set, along with an elaborate glass-covered coffee table, with serpents twisted about the legs situated below a *trompe l'oeil* painting on the ceiling of clouds scudding across a brilliant blue sky – in the process, quite literally, bringing Lennon's signature composition 'Imagine' ("above us only sky") to life.[64]

Moments later, Roth was summoned upstairs to apartment 72. After some good-natured small talk, John led the piano tech into the Dakota's music room, where the malfunctioning CP-80 was splayed out beside an antique Wurlitzer jukebox adorned with decorative bubble tubes across its exterior. A gift from Yoko for John's 38th birthday, the jukebox played 78 RPM records by the likes of Elvis Presley, Chuck Berry, Little Richard, Jerry Lee Lewis, and Buddy Holly. In short order, John got down to business: "We can't figure out what's wrong," he said. "You plug one speaker in, it sounds fine. You plug the other speaker in, it sounds fine. But when you plug both in, it sounds like the Rolling Stones rehearsing in somebody's basement!" Not missing a beat, Roth said, "I take it that's not good?" As Roth looked on, John broke into a smile. "No, not at all," he replied.[65]

Watching the younger man as he attempted to resuscitate the CP-80, John asked if Roth played in a band. As a matter of fact, he had just joined a fledgling group called Regina and the Red Hots. And Roth was really into home recording. "I play drums, bass, and keys, then get guitarists and singers to finish it off," he told John. "It's kinda wacky stuff. Very Zappa like." Now he had the Beatle's full attention. "Wait," John asked, "you play most of the instruments yourself? So, like, what do you do first? Do you play a pilot piano track or a high-hat tempo track?" Roth was only too happy to explain his home-recording techniques to the renowned songwriter. "Well, first we lay down a mechanical click track for tempo," he answered, "and since I know the songs already, I'll do the drums, then I'll play piano. Hey!" Roth suddenly interjected. "Aren't you the guy who made *Sgt. Pepper's Lonely Hearts Club Band*?"[66]

Later that morning, as Roth left John and Yoko's apartment, he couldn't resist asking for an autograph. Lennon helpfully obliged, remarking that "I hope this is the last one of these things I have to do this year." Even still, the younger man hated to leave, revelling in his brush with greatness that day. But Roth would see John again. Two weeks later, back at Manny's Music, he was surprised to hear that John was in the back room with the owner, Henry Goldrich, sizing up a new guitar. "Hey, Charly," said John. "How's your tape coming?" In Lennon's hands was a vintage Gibson Hummingbird acoustic guitar, a spruce-top model complete with the instrument's distinctive floral tortoiseshell pickguard.[67]

Not long afterwards, John made a point of requesting that Fred take an inventory of his massive collection of guitars, many of which were stored next door in apartment 71. "Inside were all of John's guitars from 25 years of performing and recording, piled helter-skelter in the closet. John pointed out his favourite, a jet-black Rickenbacker guitar he had used during the Beatles' first tour of America. It still had the song list from the Shea Stadium concert taped to it." For Fred, "The sight of the old instruments stuffed carelessly into a closet filled me with great sadness, for it reminded me of what a prolific musician John had been before he disappeared from the music scene." At this point, John asked his assistant to spread his guitars out on the floor of one of the empty rooms in apartment 71, acknowledging that his method of storing the instruments stacked one on top of the other in the closet was haphazard at best. One of the most significant guitars on display was John's Gibson Epiphone Casino, which he played, with its finish sanded down to the grain, during the Beatles' famous Rooftop Concert in January 1969. Easily the strangest guitar among his collection was the Sardonyx, a futuristic-looking contraption with two stainless-steel outrigger bars dominating its frame. "When I was finished," Fred recalled, "the entire floor was covered with two dozen guitars in various shapes, sizes, and colors, two banjos, and a sitar."[68]

In spite of the exquisite instrumentation at his beck and call – old and new alike – John only chose to compose new songs sporadically – and often, as was his practice during his earlier heyday, they would emerge, organically, often intermittently, in a haphazard series of bits and pieces. In the prime of his Beatles and solo years, John would frequently reassemble the scraps and fragments of his writing sessions into a splendid, outwardly seamless whole that eclipsed the quality of its component parts. In this fashion, the song-fragments had become an essential aspect of his songwriting process. By the autumn months of 1979, it had been a matter of years since John's last sustained bout of creative expression. Sure, he had been able to come up with the occasional germ of a new song; his mind had been brimming and roiling with the things as far back as he could remember.

No, the real problem often emerged when it came time to bring John's ideas to completion, and, ultimately to be properly inspired enough to shift his fleeting attentions from his aerie in the Dakota to one of the city's coterie of top-drawer recording studios. By the late 1970s, New York was home to several top-flight, state-of-the-art facilities, including the venerable Record Plant on West 44th Street, currently owned and operated by engineer Roy Cicala; Greenwich Village's Electric Lady Studios, which had originally been founded by Jimi Hendrix back in 1970; the Hit Factory's high-tech Times Square location; and, more recently, the Power Station at 53rd Street in Hell's Kitchen.

But for John, the city's plethora of studios was of precious little use. While he liked to tell his friends and confidantes that he was liberated by the idea of not being bound by the strictures of a professional recording contract, music-making was never far from his mind. John had even imagined a planned follow-up LP to *Rock 'n' Roll*, which he had begun referring to as *Between The Lines*, and for which he planned to collaborate with Carlos Alomar, the ace session guitarist with whom he and David Bowie had improvised the chart-topping single 'Fame' in January 1975. That March, John recorded an interview for the BBC's *Old Grey Whistle Test*, remarking that "I've got three quarters of the new album on scraps of paper, which is usual. And now I'm going through the bit of going over them and sort of half arranging them before I go in the studio."[69]

But at the same time, John liked the idea that *Rock 'n' Roll* might be his last LP – a kind of farewell of sorts to the music industry. For John, it was as if he had come full circle. Even the album's cover art – with a leather-jacket-clad John posing in a Hamburg doorway during the Beatles' pre-fame days in the early 1960s – contributed to the symmetry. On 'Just Because', the album's final cut, John concocted a spoken-word outro, announcing that "this is Dr Winston O'Boogie saying goodnight from Record Plant East, New York. We hope you had a swell time. Everybody here says hi. Goodbye." As John later recalled, "a little thing in the back of my mind said, 'Are you *really* saying farewell?' I hadn't thought of it then. I was still separated from Yoko and still hadn't had the baby, but somewhere in the back was a voice that was saying, 'Are you saying farewell to the whole game?' It just flashed by like that – like a premonition."[70]

But as usual, John was of two minds about things. Indeed, his endlessly fecund, always vacillating mind may have been his most salient personality trait. Not only was he an inveterate contrarian, but he was also forever in a state of flux regarding virtually anything or anyone – including, perhaps most of all, himself. "I liked him a lot," journalist Ray Connolly fondly remembered about his friend, but there was no doubt about it, "John Lennon was a complex, often contradictory character."[71]

As the 1970s wore on, John would occasionally meet up with May Pang, who had never really stopped loving him in the years since he had returned to Yoko. She had seen him most recently in December 1978, and, to her mind, John had seemed particularly fragile and uncertain. When they managed to see each other since John's return to the bosom of the Dakota, the couple would often wax nostalgic about their Lost Weekend together earlier in the decade. On that December day, they had even taken to referring to 'Reminiscing', the hit tune by the Little River Band, as "their song". Invariably, their conversation turned to music, and May asked if he ever thought about songwriting and making his return to the record studio. "Of course, I do," John replied. "I never stop wanting to make music."[72]

CHAPTER 4

Emotional Wreck

In addition to unfinished songs like 'Everybody's Talkin', Nobody's Talkin'', John's new compositions by the mid-to-late Seventies had largely emerged through a series of brief spurts of creativity. In 1976, he embarked upon perhaps the most ambitious, albeit unrealised project of his post-Beatles years when he began trying his hand at transforming his life story with Yoko into a full-length stage musical. To be called *The Ballad of John and Yoko*, the musical found its origins in John's earlier attempt to capture the couple's exploits in prose.

During his wife's pregnancy in 1975, he had begun composing a long-form piece, also entitled *The Ballad of John and Yoko*, picking it up again in the months after Roth's visit to the Dakota and sporadically into the late 1970s. For his part, John had long been fascinated by celebrity autobiographies. He had been particularly enamoured with British actor David Niven's *Bring on the Empty Horses*, which was published during the final months of Yoko's pregnancy. Bob Gruen recalled John's infatuation with the book, especially the fact that "Niven had been friends with all the wild stars in Hollywood, and had been to all the crazy parties, but he'd come out sane at the end." To John's mind, Niven had succeeded where so many other celebrities of his ilk had failed. According to Gruen, John announced that "'I'm gonna be David Niven. They're all gonna go on getting drunk, but I'm gonna stay home and write the book.' His plan was to live beyond the wild days and be the one to reminisce. He was gonna be the one that survived."[73]

As a work of prose, *The Ballad of John and Yoko* shifted dramatically from the story of the Lennons' highly public life into a series of thought-pieces about the simultaneously seductive and self-destroying nature of fame. Hunting and pecking at the keys of his portable Brother typewriter, he addressed the nature of his self-imposed retirement – and the public criticisms of folks like Dave Marsh – writing that "it's irrelevant to me whether I ever record again. I started with rock 'n' roll and ended with pure rock 'n' roll (my *Rock 'n' Roll* album). If the urge ever comes over me and it is irresistible, then I will do it for fun. But otherwise, I'd just as soon leave well enough alone. I have never subscribed to the view that artists 'owe a debt to the public' any more than youth owes its life to king and country. I made myself what I am today. Good and bad. The responsibility is mine alone."[74]

John was no stranger to prose writing, of course, having published his anthologies of witticisms, *In His Own Write* and, later, *A Spaniard in the Works* (1965). In 1973, he had famously published an empathetic and widely quoted limerick in Len Richmond's *Gay Liberation Book*:

> Why make it sad to be gay?
> Doing your thing is okay.
> Our body's our own, so leave us alone
> And play with yourself today.

But now, as the 1970s were swiftly coming to a close and his creative motivation was at one of its lowest ebbs, John avowed that he would not force his muse to return for mere commercial gain, or, worse yet, to satisfy a nostalgic, ravenous public appetite for the music of its youth. "I will not make the same mistake twice in one lifetime," he wrote in *The Ballad of John and Yoko*. "This time around, inspiration will be called down by the ancient methods laid down for all to see. If I never 'produce' anything for public consumption than 'silence', so be it."[75]

Yet inevitably, John's crisis of the soul didn't merely concern his creative impasse, but the prison-house of the selfsame fame and fortune he had coveted in his youth – the "toppermost of the poppermost", as he described it, pre-stardom and with unbridled ebullience, to the other Beatles. By this juncture, John had become exhausted by the overwhelming nature of his fame. "Our press-clipping service, which is world-wide, is full of the most bizarre stories," he continued in *The Ballad of John and*

Yoko. "Amongst my favourites is the one that I've gone bald and become a recluse 'locked in my penthouse' – a cross between Elvis Presley, Greta Garbo, and Howard Hughes – occasionally making cryptic statements like 'I've made my contribution to society and don't intend to work again!' If bringing up a child isn't work, what is? The reality behind the mystery is simply that we are doing what we want to do. Period." Never mind that he frequently likened himself to Hughes, and, on more than one occasion, crowed about having fulfilled his debt to the record industry and his fawning public many times over.

But as much as he wanted to make his peace with the fact of his celebrity, John implicitly understood the folly of attempting to imagine a different fate for himself. "All roads lead to Rome," he wrote. "I opened a shop; the public bought the goods at fair market value. No big deal. And as for show biz, it was never my life. I often wish, knowing it's futile, that Yoko and I weren't famous and we could have a really private life. But it's spilt milk, or rather blood, and I try not to have regrets and don't intend to waste energy and time in an effort to become anonymous. That's as dumb as becoming famous in the first place." For John, it always came down to the same longstanding problem: his artistic desires and the requirements of show biz, of being famous, seemed inevitably to go hand-in-hand. In his nearly two decades in public life, he had never known the experience of having one without the other.[76]

During the same period in which he toiled at composing *The Ballad of John and Yoko* as a prose work, he made sporadic attempts at refining the songs that would comprise the musical. "I already have the outline worked out," he told Fred. "It'll open with me meeting Yoko at her gallery show in London, then cut to Yoko in Paris and me in India boogying with the Maharishi and working on *The White Album*. Then the Beatle sessions and our marriage in Gibraltar, the bed-ins – oh, it'll be great!"[77]

In his initial effort, *The Ballad of John and Yoko* took flight with the upbeat tonalities of 'She Is A Friend Of Dorothy's', a bouncy, stage-ready tune for which John and Yoko went so far as to imagine how it might be performed in the eventual musical. Dating back to the Second World War, when homosexuality was criminalised in both the United States and the United Kingdom, the phrase "a friend of Dorothy" functioned as a euphemism for covertly referring to a person's sexual orientation – a kind of gay-friendly shibboleth necessary for survival in uncertain, even dangerous times. The phrase explicitly connotes Judy Garland's performance as Dorothy Gale in *The Wizard of Oz* (1939) and the actress' emergence as one of the twentieth-century's most enduring gay icons, especially given her character's gentle nature and her overarching senses of acceptance and understanding.

For the purposes of 'She Is A Friend Of Dorothy's', John updated the character's clandestine homosexual experience to the 1970s-era, with the seedy essence of gay counterculture on full display. For the song's melody, he borrowed heavily from *Mind Games*' 'Aisumasen (I'm Sorry)', accelerating the cadence to create a series of rolling piano chords to drive the projected musical's narrative. In the lyrics for 'She Is A Friend Of Dorothy's', John's female character comes off as a whirling dervish of prurient imagery, an updated, hyper-clinical version of the Beatles' 'Polythene Pam': she's sexy and shameless, an "art deco decadent". As the song vaults ever forward on the strength of John's buoyant piano, she emerges as a disco queen on 42nd Street, wearing French jeans and "nasty boots". But in contrast with 'Polythene Pam', where the perverted sex in a plasticine bag portends a sexual climax, the woman in 'She Is A Friend Of Dorothy's' is "all fun and no game".

During this same period, John returned to 'Sally And Billy', a composition that dated back to November 1970, when he was in the latter stages of production for his *Plastic Ono Band* LP. Performed on the baby grand piano in apartment 72 with drum machine accompaniment, 'Sally And Billy' finds John veering into metaphorical, even autobiographical terrain as he traces the lives of a forlorn couple who somehow lost their way. In their former lives, they were pointedly more self-actualised. John sings of "proud" Sally: confident, beautiful, intellectual and independent. And then there's Billy, who fronts a band. He's a "lucky man" who spends his time playing mind games, taking drugs, and going after women. But as John laments, it's "too late" for Sally and Billy. With their past glories seemingly lost to them, the couple succumbs to tears of dissatisfaction and encroaching middle-age.

During this same period, John also revived a composition entitled 'Tennessee', a paean to American playwright Tennessee Williams that he had begun back in January 1975. Written along with a work of light, potentially commercial fare aptly entitled 'Popcorn', 'Tennessee' marked the last bit of songwriting that John had attempted before making his return to Yoko and the Dakota in February of that same year. The world learned of John and Yoko's reconciliation on March 1 during the live broadcast of the 17th Annual Grammy Awards, which the couple attended at New York City's Uris Theatre. Wearing a peculiar ensemble featuring a beret, a velvet smock with the word ELVIS emblazoned across the front, and a medallion inscribed with the words WINSTON O'BOOGIE, John presented the award for Record of the Year (Olivia Newton-John's 'I Honestly Love You'; Paul McCartney and Wings earned a pair of statuettes for the megaselling *Band On The Run*). The Lennons' grand coming-out party reached its zenith at the after-party, where longtime friend Bob Gruen photographed the gleaming couple. When asked by the *Washington Star-News'* William Jobes about the details of the couple's breakup and reunion, John replied, "Well, it's not a matter of who broke it up. *It* broke up. And why did we end up back together? We ended up together again because it was diplomatically viable. Come on. We got back together because we love each other."[78]

As for 'Tennessee', the song drew its inspiration from John's recent reading of Williams' play *A Streetcar Named Desire*. Beginning with the phrase, "Tennessee, oh Tennessee, what you mean to me", the composition may have been intended, at one point, for inclusion on *Between The Lines*. While the new album never materialised, 'Tennessee' remained lodged in the composer's consciousness, only to be attempted again as John toiled at transforming his musical into reality. Working again on the baby grand with drum machine accompaniment in apartment 72, John drew the full force of his poetry for the purposes of concocting a tribute to Williams, a visionary in his own right with whom John felt an abiding kinship. With the sustain pedal depressed throughout, John wove a sad tale of forgotten genius in 'Tennessee', along with a gentle nostalgia for a windswept past where poets and playwrights existed as living icons of their age. In 'Tennessee', John offers reassurance that, in spite of everything, America's "faded fear and glory will survive" thanks to the enduring beauty of such works as Williams' classic 1947 play *A Streetcar Named Desire*.

For John, the creative renaissance he briefly enjoyed in the months after Sean's birth was rounded out by 'Mucho Mungo', a song-fragment whose chorus saw its first gestation with producer Phil Spector during the *Rock 'n' Roll* sessions, only to be attempted yet again as a potential contender for inclusion on Harry Nilsson's *Pussy Cats*, which Lennon had produced in 1974. In his 1976 Dakota demo recording, John played the song as a gentle guitar homage to his newborn son, the "sweetest little thing I've ever seen", having concocted new verses in Sean's honour. Fittingly, in the demo for 'Mucho Mungo', infant Sean can be heard crying in the background.

During the years that comprised his "retirement", John's demo recordings also featured a wide number of cover versions and sea shanties, which he often played on his Ovation Legend acoustic guitar, with its distinctive rounded back. John habitually tuned his acoustic guitars a half-step down, often placing a capo on the first fret. These "ditties", as he liked to call them, acted as nostalgic diversions for a composer who had seemed to have lost his way. In one of the more elaborate instances, he records a spirited version of Leadbelly's 'Rock Island Line', complete with electric guitar arrayed against the steady beat of a drum machine. For John and an entire generation of young Brits, Lonnie Donegan's up-tempo take on 'Rock Island Line' had exploded skiffle into a national phenomenon. In a similar vein, John performed a skiffle interpretation of 'She'll Be Coming Round The Mountain' before turning his sights on the classic folk song 'John Henry', for which he concocts a mournful piano ballad.

Not surprisingly, a great number of John's ditties find him navigating the seas of comedy and a nostalgia for the music of his youth. For the former, he shifted easily, albeit hilariously through a swathe of old standards, including 'Beyond The Sea' and 'Blue Moon', which he sang with a Gallic tongue, to 'Young Love' with a Cockney accent and, even more bizarrely still, 'Falling In Love Again' in the voice of Marlene Dietrich, which he recorded while simultaneously watching the daytime soap opera *Search for Tomorrow* on television. John's penchant for nonsensical British comedy reaches its apex with ''Twas A Night Like Ethel Merman', an uproariously funny ballad – not unlike his Joycean poems in *In His Own Write* or *A Spaniard in the Works* – in which he sings, in a mock falsetto voice, about "excavating mucus" on the "long way to Tipperillo".

And speaking of music hall favourites, John's demos find him playing a host of old standards ranging from 'My Old Man's A Dustman' and 'I Do Like To Be Beside The Seaside' to George Formby's 'Chinese Laundry Blues' and 'Leanin' On A Lamp Post'. John's nostalgia for the carefree days of his youth is never more evident than these demos, which joyfully recall the hours he whiled away playing music with Paul and his dad Jim Mac – who fronted his own jazz band back in the 1920s – in the McCartneys' front parlour back on Liverpool's Forthlin Road. During this period, John also recorded a demo for 'Maggie Mae', the traditional ditty about a Lime Street prostitute who fleeces a sailor. A favourite among skiffle bands, including Lennon's Quarry Men in the 1950s, the folk tune about "that dirty, no good, robbin' Maggie Mae" graced the Beatles' *Let It Be* (1970) LP and later served as the subject of a stage musical set around the Liverpool Docks.

In equal measure, John devoted several demo recordings to the sounds of rhythm and blues, including a bluesy take on Bo Diddley's 'I'm A Man' and 'Corrine, Corrina' by way of Elmore James. In addition to a standout performance of the old Chess Records classic 'Too Much Monkey Business', John turns in an edgy acoustic take of Chuck Berry's 'Brown Eyed Handsome Man' that morphs in and out of the Beatles' 'Get Back' before transforming into a fiery blend of both songs at double-tempo à la Jerry Lee Lewis in his rockabilly prime. As the demo comes to an end, John adopts the warm tones of a nighttime radio DJ and enjoins his invisible audience to sit tight: "Don't go away now, we'll be back in just a minute."

More than a year would elapse before John commenced his second spurt of creative activity during his self-imposed "retirement". Interestingly, this era marked a rare flurry of public appearances by John and Yoko, including President Jimmy Carter's inaugural reception in January 1977, and, a few weeks later, their attendance, with toddler Sean, for the Ringling Bros. and Barnum & Bailey Circus at Madison Square Garden. Later that year, as he and Yoko prepared to leave Tokyo after an extended visit with his Japanese in-laws, the couple held a press conference in which John remarked that he had taken a break from music-making in order to raise Sean.

John's parental concern for his youngest son was no doubt genuine – in 1979, he had confided to Fred Seaman that he was desperate to be there for Sean after having spent so many years in estrangement from his older son Julian, who had been born to Lennon and his first wife Cynthia in April 1963. With Sean, John dedicated himself to being a better and eminently more available father than the "self-occupied" person he had been when Julian needed him the most. "I hadn't seen my first son grow up and now here's a 17-year-old man on the phone talking about motorbikes," said John. "I was not there for his childhood at all. I was on tour. I don't know how the game works, but there's a price to pay for inattention to children. And if I don't give [Sean] attention from zero to five, then I'm damn well gonna have to give it to him from 16 to 20, because it's owed. It's like the law of the universe." Even in the doldrums that marked the late 1970s, John managed to wrest himself from his ennui to become a doting parent for his youngest son. When he joined the Lennon household, Fred was awestruck by John's zeal when it came to Sean – even down to his fatherly determination to save every last one of his son's childhood drawings, which he dutifully instructed Fred to frame and display around the Lennons' cavernous apartment.[79]

For John and Yoko, Sean was nothing short of a miracle baby – and understandably so, given Yoko's age at the time (42) and the miscarriages that had plagued their early years together. As with so many 1970s-era couples, the Lennons regularly attended Lamaze classes in order to prepare for a natural birth at home on the Upper West Side. But in the end, it didn't matter. During the first week of October 1975, Yoko was admitted to New York Hospital, where her obstetrician ordered her to undergo a caesarean delivery in consideration of her past difficulties. And that's when things took a turn for the worse:

> Somebody had made a transfusion of the wrong blood type into Yoko. I was there when it happened, and she starts to go rigid and then shake from the pain and trauma. I run up to this nurse and say, "Go get the doctor!" I'm holding on tight to Yoko while this guy gets to the hospital room. He walks in, hardly notices that Yoko is going through fucking convulsions, goes straight for me, smiles, shakes my hand, and says, "I've always wanted to meet you, Mr Lennon, I always enjoyed your music." I start screaming: "My wife's dying and you wanna talk about music!"

For John, it was nothing short of a "miracle that everything was okay." An ecstatic John announced to the press that "I feel higher than the Empire State Building!" As for their Dakota neighbours, the Lennons spread word of the good tidings via a sign – "Baby Boy!" – that they hung in one of the windows of apartment 72 overlooking the courtyard.[80]

Shortly before Sean's fifth birthday, John couldn't help reflecting on the overwhelming attachment that he felt for the boy. "The joy is still there when I see Sean," he remarked. "He didn't come out of my belly but, *by God*, I made his bones, because I've attended to every meal, and to how he sleeps, and to the fact that he swims like a fish… I'm so proud of those things," John added. "He is my biggest pride, you see."[81]

Not surprisingly, John would never characterise Sean as a distraction. But on the occasions when he was able to find time for a bout of songwriting, there was little doubt that the fits and starts of his muse were continuing to wreak havoc on his artistic life. And writer's block was hardly a new phenomenon in his life. Back in June 1973, he had admitted as much to a reporter during his attendance with Yoko at the first International Feminist Conference at Harvard University. "I either write songs or I don't," he remarked. "It's getting to be work. It's ruining the music. It's like after you leave school, and you don't want to read a book. Every time I strap the guitar on, it's the same old jazz. I just feel like breathing a bit." During the autumn months of 1977, John had come up for air yet again, with his creative stalemate having briefly ebbed after the Lennons had returned to New York City after their extended sojourn in Japan.[82]

During this period, John concocted several new song-fragments, including a piece entitled 'Free As A Bird', written most likely in reference to the affirmative conclusion of his longstanding immigration flight and the awarding of his long sought-after green card, which afforded him with carte blanche to travel outside of the United States without the fear of being denied re-entry. For the past several years, John's highly public immigration crisis had taken a mighty toll on the ex-Beatle and his family, with his protracted legal fight no doubt contributing, in its own way, to his tentative, uncertain muse. John first came under the watchful, paranoid eye of President Richard M. Nixon's administration for his anti-war activities after he and Yoko decided to relocate to the United States in 1971. That year, they had released a trio of pacifist-oriented singles in 'Power To The People', 'Imagine', and 'Happy Xmas (War Is Over)', elevating John and Yoko as leading voices of the so-called New Left.

Things came to a head in February 1972, when a rumour developed, at the bidding of American social activist Jerry Rubin, that John was planning to participate in a New Left, anti-Nixon concert in San Diego at the same time as the Republican National Convention. Fearing that John's presence might hamper Nixon's re-election effort – and perhaps even serve to disrupt the convention with a level of violence and political rancour reminiscent of the ill-fated 1968 Democratic National Convention in Chicago – Senator Strom Thurmond authored a memo in which he recommended that "if Lennon's visa is terminated it would be a strategic countermeasure." In addition to seeing his name affixed to Nixon's infamous "Enemies List", John fell into a protracted, four-year legal struggle, led by attorney Leon Wildes, to earn his green card, which the US Immigration and Naturalization Service had been attempting to derail over John's 1968 British drug conviction. In a letter of support, Bob Dylan proclaimed, "This country's got plenty of room and space. Let John and Yoko stay!" Using a more direct tack, veteran *New York Post* columnist Pete Hamill flatly suggested that "John Lennon has improved this town just by showing up."[83]

With Wildes in his corner, John even took his immigration fight to broadcast television, going so far as to make an appearance on *Tomorrow*, Tom Snyder's popular interview programme and a personal favourite for John, who watched the show religiously. Back in October 1974, John had done a similar stint on sportscaster Howard Cosell's *Speaking of Everything* programme. When pressed by Snyder about why he would want to live in a country bent on deporting him, John replied, "Because I'd like to live in the land of the free, Tom." John succeeded in overturning the deportation order on October 7, 1975, two days before Sean's birth. In its ruling, the US Court of Appeals proclaimed that "if, in our 200 years of independence, we have in some measure realised our ideals, it is in large part because we have always found a place for those committed to the spirit of liberty and willing to help implement it. Lennon's four-year battle to remain in our country is testimony to his faith in this American dream." In addition to relieving an ongoing source of tension in his life, the end of his legal battle and the issuance of his green card afforded him with a much-needed sense of relief, of exhalation.[84]

In many ways, 'Free As A Bird' found John attempting to capture this emotional range of experience. For the demo recording, John situated a tiny mic atop his piano to capture both his vocals and the instrumentation. Attempted during a trio of piano takes, the demos sound wistful and, at times, monotonic – as if the composer were creating a guide vocal for future reference. With 'Free As A Bird', John evoked a similar chord structure to, say, the doo-wop balladry of 'This Boy' from his Beatle days back in 1963. In the song, John describes himself as a "homing bird", safe and sound, imbued with enough courage and abandon to find his way in a liberated, alien world. For John, 'Free As A Bird' held out great promise, as did 'Real Life', a composition that would flower into several different songs in the coming months and years. After discovering something "nasty in the sky" in the latter tune, John offers words of consolation – as much for himself as any real or imagined listener. There's "no need to be afraid", he sings in the chorus. The traumas of everyday living – the loneliness, the mayhem of the household, not to mention the outside world – are merely the stuff of "real life".

But as usual, the songs remained largely unfinished, fits and scraps of compositional fragments in need of further polishing – and, perhaps most important, sustained inspiration. During this same period, John returned to his musical conception of *The Ballad of John and Yoko*, which now included a more ominous entry in contrast with the bouncy good times of 'She Is A Friend Of Dorothy's'. In 'Mirror, Mirror (On The Wall)', which had been written expressly for the stage show, John can be heard engaging in the same kind of soul-searching he explored in the prose version. He performs a sombre tune for the purposes of his piano demo, asking his reflection in the mirror, "Is nobody there?" Eventually, having realised that the mirror offers nothing but an empty space as its reflection, John's speaker becomes transfixed and keeps on "staring and staring" before concluding, to his own terror, that the empty space might very well be the hollow essence of his selfhood.

John would explore similar thematic pursuits in such songs as 'I Don't Wanna Face It' and 'Whatever Happened To...', compositions related to his personal crisis of identity during this period, not to mention his ongoing and increasingly prickly relationship with fame. In 'I Don't Wanna Face It', John imagines an Edenic place where he revels in blessed anonymity. But even still, while he dreams of becoming lost in a celebrity-free "oblivion", he can't stop clinging to his stardom and his one-way ticket to "the hall of fame". Realising the hypocrisy of his position, he borrows from an age-old adage, admitting that he can dish it out, but can't take it.

With 'Whatever Happened To...', which he would later append to the bridge of 'Free As A Bird', John continues in the same confessional vein – in this case, projecting his insecurities on an unnamed female character. 'Whatever Happened To...' finds John delivering yet another unfinished micro-story about identity-flux. In the song, his female character hides herself away in the dark, her head concealed by a scarf while she dreams her life away in the books that she mysteriously stores in the folds of her shawl. But with peril in the offing – "the river's rising fast" – John's narrator is determined to share her message with the world before it's too late, before she drowns, along with her diminished sense of self, in the maelstrom.

John likely drew the song's ultimate message – "don't burn the boats till last" – from his voracious reading. Attributed to Hernán Cortés, the phrase referred to the Spanish explorer's fateful decision during his arrival in Vera Cruz in 1519 to eliminate any and all means of escape for his troops, who preferred sailing back to Cuba rather than taking on the entire Aztec Empire. With their options for turning back now lost amid the ashes of their ships, Cortés' soldiers had no choice but to accompany their leader on his journey to Tenōchtitlan and ultimately, his conquest, invasion, and conquering of the Aztecs. In addition to his penchant for devouring the nonfiction of the day, John may have also drawn his inspiration for 'Whatever Happened To…' from Neil Young's 1975 song 'Cortez The Killer', with its blistering, evocative guitar solo highlighting the explorer's unchecked barbarism.

For John, the notion of ceding all his options, of figuratively burning his boats and leaving the safety of the inner sanctum he had built with Yoko in the latter half of the 1970s, was simply too daunting to contemplate with any serious intent at this juncture in his life. In 'One Of The Boys', he spins fantastical lyrics about what it might be like to rejoin the rock 'n' roll fray, in spite of everything that has befallen him as he approaches midlife and "he's no longer *le garçon fatal*". As with many of his demo recordings, the song begins with John engaging in playful banter, if only for himself: "Hello, hello, hello, hello, hello, hello," he announces. "Got it wrong, take 2, folks." As both a reference to his former Beatlehood – when he was, in fact, one of the Boys, those four lads from Liverpool – John imagines a chorus of society's magpies crowing about his enduring good looks and omnipresent wealth. For John, 'One Of The Boys' marked his most humorous take on his predicament during this period, a begrudging acceptance of his peculiar, if enviable lot in life – an increasingly insular world where he still looked good in the paparazzi's pictures and could afford virtually any luxury his heart desired.

By contrast, his other demos during this era found him in varying states of melancholy, despair, and, finally, surrender and acceptance. In the same chilling vein as 'Mirror, Mirror (On The Wall)', song-fragments such as 'I Don't Want To Lose You' (also known as 'Now And Then'), 'I'm Ready, Lord', and 'When This Life Is Done (And The Angels Come)' had apparently not been written for the musical, but rather, offered a window into the delirium of John's creative soul and, ultimately, his growing sense of resignation, as 1977 came to a close. 'I Don't Want To Lose You' offered a perfect case in point. With a mournful, funereal piano melody, John concocts a ballad of longing and despair. The song's middle-eight – Lennon and McCartney's songwriterly shorthand, adopted during their pre-Beatle years, for the bridge – hints at a darker turn in the speaker's story. As John sings, he doesn't want to "lose you or abuse you". In the coming years, John would return to similar themes of remorse and a gnawing, spiralling sense of desperation.

When he wasn't chiding himself in his songs for his feelings of being out of control and expressing his abject fear of abandonment, John – ever the confessional artist – couldn't help responding to his very real critics, like Marsh, who publicly questioned his silence as the decade wore on. Not surprisingly, he had begun drafting a new song, which he called 'Emotional Wreck' in its very earliest stages, to address his conflicted state of mind during this period. On the one hand, he clearly felt a deep-seated need to remind the world that at this point in his career he owed an artistic debt to *no one*. But on the other hand – and perhaps known only to himself and Yoko – he fretted about his fleeting muse and his abiding desire to create new music.

In the demo recording for the song, 'Emotional Wreck' finds John engaged in an imaginary conversation with his critical friends and foes, who suggest that he would be "crazy" for stepping away from his celebrity, for giving up "the big time" in favour of life as a homebody. By the second verse, the song takes a gentle turn into the stormier realities of the entirety of John's life – from his schoolboy years and his Beatles heyday through the present, when his critics, friends and foes alike, accuse him of being lazy and "dreaming my life away". In a later reflection on the composition, John cut to the quick, remarking that "they've been saying that all my life. You wanna read my report card? I have them all from school. That's more of John's life story than John and Yoko's. It says, 'He's lazy, he's lazy', but I was never lazy. How can you think if you're doing something all the time? When you're eating, eat. When you're painting, paint. When you're sitting, sit. There's a time for sitting and a time for running. And just because my life is half-lived in public, people comment on it. I'm not lazy. I've done more in my life than most people would do in ten."[85]

In the demo for 'Emotional Wreck', John can be heard wrestling with the same old demons and contradictions – but this time, something was different, with John seeming to embrace the contradictory aspects of himself in the name of happiness and contentment. Even more significant, he appears to be ready, finally, to lodge a resounding retort to his critics, both real and imagined, who wonder how John could possibly be happy, having opted, by his own volition, no less, to "no longer play the game". As with so many of his song-fragments during this period, 'Emotional Wreck' was brimming with promise, yet remained unfinished in its present state.

CHAPTER 5

Mind Movies

For much of 1978, John busied himself with non-musical diversions – that is, when he wasn't whiling away the hours in his bedroom-sanctuary high above the park, by turns reading and watching TV with the traffic ever-flowing seven storeys below on Central Park West. By this juncture, John and Yoko had developed a close friendship with Elliot Mintz, a Los Angeles radio and television personality who first interviewed the Lennons in 1971 for KLOS FM. The following year, Mintz had been fired from the station after airing John and Yoko's *Some Time In New York City* album – complete with its profanity-laced excoriations of the sociopolitical issues of the day, including sexism, racism, and unjust incarceration – in its entirety. In the coming years, he would become one of the couple's most trusted confidantes. During John's Lost Weekend, which reached its drunken nadir in LA in 1973, Mintz kept a watchful eye over his friend. On New Year's Day 1976, with the Lennons safely ensconced together in the family home with baby Sean, Mintz interviewed the couple for Earth News Radio. Still lost in the connubial bliss of their reunion, John and Yoko broke into an a cappella version of 'As Time Goes By' of *Casablanca* fame during the broadcast, with John later throwing in a hasty rendition of the Beatles' 'What's the New Mary Jane', an outtake from *The White Album*.

During the following year, Mintz joined the family on their annual visit to Japan, where he witnessed John's last public performance to date in the Lennons' Tokyo hotel suite not long after Elvis Presley's untimely death at age 42 in August 1977. The "concert", such as it was, transpired when John picked up his guitar during a conversation with Mintz in the Presidential Suite at the Hotel Okura and began strumming *Imagine*'s 'Jealous Guy'. Just then, an older Japanese couple exited the private elevator, having no idea that they had just strolled into John and Yoko's private suite. As the ex-Beatle continued playing, the couple "had a cigarette or two", Mintz recalled, "and I guess, because no waiter arrived, they finally looked at John, exchanged some words, and got up and left, obviously displeased."[86]

In March 1978, with Mintz as his only audience, John began trying his hand at scripting radio playlets. Deploying the wide array of recording equipment that he had amassed in apartment 72, John described the resulting productions as "mind movies", which he assembled by mixing dialogue from radio and TV programmes with characters wrought from his bizarre, inimitable imagination. Chief among these personages was Maurice DuPont, Agent Provocateur du jour, RET, who featured in a three-act mind movie that Lennon narrated (as DuPont) in an over-the-top French accent. As John completed each of the three instalments in DuPont's espionage saga, he would post them to Mintz in LA as a kind of transcontinental serial. The first act begins with John announcing that he is none other than "Maurice DuPont, speaking to you from the hotel foyer on March the 22nd, 1978. I went to my local air-force recruiter, and now I am forced to let my government hear my story."

By the third act – in spite of all of his attendant adventures and hijinks – DuPont finds himself largely unchanged and unscathed, still sitting in the hotel foyer of John's mind movie. He would attempt a second entry in his self-described genre with a mind movie entitled '[Dialogue for a Silent TV]'. Shifting between an overwrought German accent and an Irish tongue, John's second mind movie offers an exercise in nonsensicality to the extreme: "It has been brought to my attention [that] his mind was empty, but his bowels were full, you see. Or, as his mother put it: his mind was empty, but his bladder was full. You see, that's what she used to say, you see. You see, when your bladder's full, it's hard to think of Rimsky-Korsakov, isn't it, love?"

Outside of his mind-movie excursions, John devoted much of his energies during this period to creating the signature line drawings with which he would ornament his postcards and letters to friends and family.

A lifelong sketch artist, John's fascination with creating line drawings flowered during the later 1940s when he attended Dovedale Road primary school. Long before he took up the guitar, he was enamoured with the work of Ronald Searle, the British gag cartoonist and well-known creator of the *St Trinian's School* series. Adopting Searle's style, John would deploy his early fountain-pen drawings as illustrations for his pre-adolescent poems and stories. For a time, he even published his drawings and jokes in *The Daily Howl*, a comical broadsheet that he circulated among his schoolmates. Naturally, his affinity for cartoon sketches didn't end there, with John continuing to perfect his style across his teen years and eventually studying drawing at the Liverpool Art Institute in the late 1950s. His work in this vein had first become known to the public in 1970, when he staged an exhibition of 14 lithographs drawn from John and Yoko's March 1969 wedding and honeymoon. While drawing was John's "first love", he treated the act of art-making rather nonchalantly, frequently scrawling his telltale, bespectacled self-portraits on napkins or loose bits of paper and giving them away.[87]

As 1978 pressed on, John portrayed himself in a range of guises – often as a loner; as a dreamer, with his head in the clouds; or, on occasion, drifting beyond the corporeal spaces of his earthly existence. Occasionally, he would concoct captions for his line drawings, including a portrait of himself with the phrase "every day, in every way, I'm getting better and better". John would adopt the phrase yet again in an April 1979 postcard to his eldest son Julian on the occasion of the younger Lennon's 16th birthday. In his postscript to Julian, John added a spot of fatherly advice: "the mind is a 'muscle'. It needs *exercise* (to strengthen it)."[88]

In yet another one of his line drawings from this period, John depicts himself sitting high above the clouds, looking earthward, with the caption "he tried to face reality". Another cartoon portrayed John and Yoko in each other's arms and engaged in a dialogue, with John saying, "'Tis the devil's own work, Yoko", to which she replies, "You're beating the bush around, John." In one instance, John even addresses his admirers. The caption reads, "But I'm one of your biggest fans", along with the image of an obese woman holding the leash of her defecating miniature poodle as John dutifully reaches to embrace her. In yet another drawing, a cartoon John happily plays his electric Yamaha keyboard as the sounds of music effortlessly pour forth from one of its speakers. "In which the spirit moves", reads the caption. If only it were that easy.[89]

Another self-portrait, drawn on the occasion of his birthday on October 9, 1978, depicts John thinking to himself, "Then suddenly, I was 38." A second drawing in the same series features John staring at a black circle, along with the caption, "The hole of my life flashed before my eyes." Three-year-old Sean chipped in with several of the captions, including "a small pig is a happy pig", which accompanied John's drawing of a field of prostrate pigs, and "a cat purring", which complemented John's depiction of a contented cat dozing in the vicinity of a goldfish bowl.[90]

John and Sean celebrated their shared birthday at Tavern on the Green, the Central Park restaurant owned by the Lennons' neighbour and fellow Dakotan Warner LeRoy. The happy event was briefly upset when fans crowded the entrance to the restaurant. To remedy the situation, John and Yoko's staff dispatched six different limousines to the restaurant, several of which were empty, in an attempt to outsmart the fans. For his part, John was undeterred. As Rosa later recalled, Sean "spent the whole time on his father's lap. I don't think I have ever seen John so happy. I could even see some tears behind his dark glasses."[91]

During this same period, John fell into another bout of musical creativity, which was largely comprised of a series of parodies. But at least one song-fragment held sway from John's earlier attempts at songwriting. With a gently rolling piano cadence reminiscent of his prelude to 'Imagine', John had reworked 'Emotional Wreck' yet again, now referring to the evolving composition as 'People'. During his latest demo recording of the song, John can be heard admiring the piano lick as one of the nascent song's finest features. At one point, he makes a mental note to delay the lick for as long as possible in order to heighten the effect "until we really hit 'em with it!"

John rounded out the year with a selection of satirical pieces aimed squarely at Bob Dylan, with whom Lennon had carried on a lengthy, and, at times, uncertain friendship and admiration since the mid-Sixties. In many ways, the folk legend had contributed a prodigious influence to John's words and music – indeed, to the Beatles' sound circa *Help!* (1965) and *Rubber Soul* (1965). But Lennon had become perplexed with Dylan after his cryptic parody of John's 'Norwegian Wood (This Bird Has Flown)' on his *Blonde On Blonde* album (1966). In '4th Time Around', Dylan explicitly evokes the sound and flavour of John's composition, which itself owed a great debt to Dylan's songwriting and performance style – an aspect that Dylan pointedly references at the conclusion of

'4th Time Around', when he sings that he hasn't "asked for your crutch", so "don't ask for mine".

In the intervening years, John's paranoia about Dylan had undergone a series of highs and lows – perhaps exacerbated, at times, by the folk icon's blossoming friendship and professional affiliation with Harrison during this same period. John's satires in November 1978 find the former Beatle unleashing his sardonic wit on Dylan with a scathing gusto reminiscent of 'How Do You Sleep?', the *Imagine*-era McCartney diatribe in which Lennon sings, "The only thing you done was 'Yesterday'," as he reels off a litany of insults and diatribes. John would later admit that 'How Do You Sleep?' was "not about Paul, it's about me. I'm really attacking myself. The only thing that really matters is how he and I feel about those things. Him and me are okay."[92]

By the time that Dylan came under John's satirical knife, the American songwriter had been enjoying a mid-career upswing with such LPs as *Before The Flood* (1974), *Blood On The Tracks* (1975), and, with the Band, *The Basement Tapes* (1975). In 1976, his profile was elevated even further still when future President Jimmy Carter quoted Dylan's 'It's Alright, Ma (I'm Only Bleeding)' during his acceptance speech at the Democratic National Convention at Madison Square Garden. "I have never had more faith in America than I do today," Carter exclaimed to the ebullient delegates. "We have an America that, in Bob Dylan's phrase, is busy being born, not busy dying."[93]

In his Dylan satires, John pulls no punches, drawing out his nasal-filled vocals with all the snarl that he can muster. In the first satire, John adopts a highly affected version of the singer-songwriter's voice, reimagines Dylan's persona, name-checks one of his most influential compositions ('Knockin' On Heaven's Door'), and saddles him with an Oedipus complex. Continuing in this vein, John stages his second Dylan parody in the form of a news programme reminiscent of his mind movies back in 1978. In one segment, John adopts the Dylan-accented voice of a groovy foreign correspondent, announcing that "former president Richard Nixon, on his second trip outside the United States since his resignation, was a smiling handshaking politician again, greeting crowds outside his hotel and trying a little French. He sure as hell didn't try it on Pat Nixon." But John saves his real zinger for the last portion of the demo, wherein he casts Dylan as a kind of superstar-sellout and social-activist wannabe, which he delivers along with a swipe at Harrison for good measure:

I got 24 children, 14 wives, three mistresses, 59 accountants, 105 lawyers, two million fans, a posting system that never fails to land me in jail, and look through my mail, perhaps have a garage sale, and you know, go save the whale, and eh, you know, get a boat and go for a sail, and, and, oh, oh, oh, how do you get out of this hell? I'm stuck inside of a lexicon with the *Roget's Thesaurus* blues again. Sometimes I wish I was just George Harrison, you know, got all the answers, oh my God, oh my God.

Having dispensed with his satirical Dylan voice – if only temporarily – John closed out the year with a series of New Year's resolutions for 1979 in the guise of "The Great Wok", a character that he concocted after his Asian cooking adventures in apartment 72's massive kitchen. The Great Wok was patterned after macrobiotic chef Michio Kushi, who had authored numerous cookbooks on living an organic lifestyle with his wife Aveline. In his stilted Asian accent, John announces on his Great Wok recording that "this is the end of the year now and our minds turn towards what is laughably called the future." For his New Year's resolution, John proclaims that in 1979 he intends to renounce absolutely everything "but complete luxury and self-indulgence."

As events would demonstrate, John and Yoko fully intended to live up to this dictum. Over the next several months, the Lennons were nearly constantly on the move, travelling widely to far-flung places like Cairo, which included an excursion to see the pyramids in Giza, and later Tokyo, where they spent a month that summer for their annual sojourn with Yoko's relations. John would never forget the Lennons' return flight from Egypt. As their plane circled JFK during a blizzard, the airline screened *Sgt. Pepper's Lonely Hearts Club Band*, the much-derided movie musical starring Peter Frampton and the Bee Gees. John described the experience aboard the plane as "one of those exquisitely surreal moments in life." In addition to their much-ballyhooed "love letter" advertisement in *The New York Times*, the couple made headlines with Yoko's business successes – particularly her investments in prized Holstein cows; in fact, by the following year, her gambit had paid off handsomely with the sale of a dairy cow known as "Spring Farm Fond Rose" for a record-breaking $265,000. Later that year, John and Yoko made the papers yet again after donating $1,000 to the Patrolmen's Benevolent Society to purchase bullet-proof vests for New York City police officers.[94]

All the while, rumours of a Beatles reunion began to reach a boiling point in the popular press. Speculation about the group's potential bravura return to the stage had been rampant for much of the Seventies, and especially after the bandmates had contributed their musical efforts to several tracks on Starr's 1973 album *Ringo*. At times, the rumours of a possible Beatles reunion would reach absurd levels. At one point during the Lost Weekend, John and May Pang held a raucous party that resulted in a visit from LA police, guns drawn, as they investigated a noise complaint. When the police officers laid eyes on John, they lowered their weapons, dumbstruck in their disbelief that they were standing in the midst of a bona fide member of the Fab Four. Finally, one of the cops spoke up, "Do you think the Beatles will ever get together again?" he asked John. "You never know," Lennon replied. "You never know."[95]

Things began to reach a fever pitch in 1976, when promoter Bill Sargent proposed a $50 million payday for a one-off Beatles concert. "There were phenomenal amounts of money being offered," McCartney later recalled. "But it just went round and round. There might be three of us thinking, 'It might not be a bad idea' – but the other one would go, 'Nah, I don't think so', and sort of veto it." During the April 24, 1976 episode of *Saturday Night Live*, producer Lorne Michaels made light of the increasingly astronomical offers. That evening, Michaels took to the airwaves and made a pitch for the band to reunite. "The National Broadcasting Company has authorised me to offer you this cheque to be on our show," he said, holding up a certified cheque for $3,000 – far less than they had received for their appearances on *The Ed Sullivan Show* back in February 1964. "All you have to do is sing three Beatles songs," Michaels continued. "'She Loves You', yeah, yeah, yeah – that's $1,000 right there. You know the words. It'll be easy. Like I said, this is made out to 'The Beatles'. You divide it any way you want. If you want to give Ringo less, that's up to you. I'd rather not get involved." As it turned out, Lennon and McCartney were watching *Saturday Night Live* that evening across town in John's Dakota apartment building. "Paul and I were together watching that show," Lennon later remarked. "He was visiting us at our place in the Dakota. We were watching it and almost went down to the studio, just as a gag. We nearly got into a cab, but we were actually too tired."[96]

In September 1979, veteran promoter Sid Bernstein – the visionary behind the Beatles' Carnegie Hall and Shea Stadium appearances – amped up the stakes considerably. Earlier that same year, he had bested Sargent's offer with an eye-popping $230 million. Incredibly, the stakes became even higher when United Nations Secretary-General Kurt Waldheim attempted to stage a Beatles reunion as a charity effort on behalf of the Vietnamese boat people – the refugees who had taken to the high seas in order to make their escape from the war-torn Southeast Asian peninsula. Promising a $500 million windfall in the name of charity, Bernstein rallied to support Waldheim, taking out a full-page ad in *The New York Times* in which he entreated the Beatles to consider the UN's offer and its humanitarian intent. "The joy that you gave to people everywhere," Bernstein wrote in his *New York Times* treatise, "gives you a unique place in history. It also gives you an importance and a voice to make a difference in the lives of many human beings who need our compassion and immediate help."[97]

By the autumn months of 1979, John had become fed up with the efforts of folks like Bernstein to meddle in his creative life, such as it was at this juncture. Not surprisingly, Bernstein's potential bonanza ignited a spate of stories in the news media that ultimately painted John as the villain who refused to acquiesce to a Beatles reunion; at one point, McCartney even telephoned John at the Dakota, attempting, albeit unsuccessfully, to change his mind. In his public statements, McCartney often evinced a nonchalance about the possibilities of a Beatles reunion. During the Wings Over America tour back in 1976, he had even fashioned a nifty poem to shoo away nostalgic journalists:

> The Beatles broke up in '69
> Since then, everything's been fine
> But if that question doesn't cease
> Ain't nobody gonna get no peace

On New Year's Day in 1979, when Paul signed a blockbuster deal with Columbia Records rumoured to be in excess of $20 million, his attorneys inserted a clause stating that their client retained the right to produce any music outside of his new contract that involved "John Lennon, Richard Starkey, and George Harrison recording together as the Beatles."[98]

As for John, the Yamaha keyboard setup from Manny's Music, purchased nearly a year earlier by Yoko in order to stimulate her husband's artistry, had seen very little action. And John's attempt at composing a long-form version of *The Ballad of John and Yoko* had lost steam. So when

65

John finally returned to his tape recorder, he held little interest in making music. Instead, he set about the business of creating an audio diary. On Wednesday, September 5, John pressed the record button and began his monologue, announcing "take 1 in the ongoing life story of John Winston Ono Lennon."

As with his satirical efforts the previous fall, John was quick to go on the offensive when it came to Dylan, no doubt spurred on by the folk singer's recent turn to gospel music with his hit single 'Gotta Serve Somebody' from his recently released *Slow Train Coming* LP. "Well I was listening to the radio and Dylan's new single or album, whatever the hell it is, came on," said John. Riffing on 'Gotta Serve Somebody', John remarks that Dylan "wants to be a waiter for Christ" and "the singing was really pathetic and the words were just embarrassing. So, here we sit, watching the mighty Dylan and the mighty McCartney and the mighty Jagger slide down the mountain, blood and mud in their nails."

For John, "the difference between now and a couple of years back is that whenever there was a new thing out by any of the aforesaid, I used to feel a sense of panic and competition. And now," John added, "there doesn't seem any point." Besides, "now at least I get pleasure in it instead of panic. The main pleasure being of course that it's all a load of shit." Even in the heat of the moment, John must have recognised the irony inherent in his verbal attacks against one of his chief influences and his old songwriting partner: while Dylan and McCartney were very much engaged and working in the fray, John contented himself with lobbing grenades under cover from the sidelines in his Dakota bedroom. As he admitted in 'I Don't Wanna Face It', he can dish out criticism with unchecked abandon, but he still can't seem to take it.

As usual, John's capacity for sustaining any project – even his bile-filled audio diary – was decidedly limited at this juncture. He would make a second, aborted attempt at continuing his diary on October 10 – the day after his twin birthday with Sean, which they celebrated yet again at Tavern on the Green. John began his diary entry with a cryptic reference to Yoko's 'Looking Over From My Hotel Window' from her *Approximately Infinite Universe* album, a composition in which his wife had commemorated the passing of her own 39th birthday seven years earlier. "Well, well, here we are," said John, "aged 39, looking out of my hotel window, wondering whether to jump out or get back in bed. So, I got back in bed."

At Tavern on the Green, four-year-old Sean had been the life of the party, which featured a magician and a clown who dazzled the youngest Lennon and his bevy of friends. To mark the occasion, Yoko gifted John and Sean with life-sized dolls that had been fashioned in their likeness, as well as tickets to see *Peter Pan* the next evening at Broadway's Lunt-Fontanne Theatre. As always, John was brimming with pride in Sean, who was becoming ever more precocious by the day – the very sort of independent, self-actualised boy whom John hoped he would be. And he was a kind, good-natured kid to boot. Shortly before Sean's fourth birthday, Rosa overheard a conversation between the youngest Lennon and her 14-year-old son Robert. They were in the playroom, studying the contents of the Wurlitzer jukebox. "What kind of music would you like to hear?" Sean asked the older boy. "I don't know," Robert replied, "the Beatles?" Without missing a beat, Sean said "not bad", although he admitted to a preference for Elvis Presley. "I want to look like him when I get older," he confided in Robert.[99]

As it turned out, John's difficulty in getting out of bed on the morning of October 10 had nothing to do with the passage of yet another milestone or the plight of his aging body, but rather, was the direct result of a relapse of the heroin addiction that had plagued him in the late 1960s. Lennon's experimentation with the drug had begun during Yoko's summer 1968 exhibition at the Robert Fraser Gallery. "I never injected," he liked to say. "Just sniffing, you know." But as journalist and Lennon confidant Ray Connolly observed at the time, Lennon "rarely did anything he liked by halves. Before long, heroin would become a problem for him." Connolly's prediction proved to be frighteningly accurate. By the advent of the Beatles' January 1969 *Get Back* sessions, Yoko openly joked about shooting heroin as the couple's form of exercise. Things reached a crisis point for John and Yoko during the final months before the Beatles' disbandment. "The two of them were on heroin," McCartney later recalled, "and this was a fairly big shocker for us because we all thought we were far-out boys, but we kind of understood that we'd never get quite that far out." In September 1969, John would memorialise his heroin-induced trauma with 'Cold Turkey', a song that illustrated the excruciating throes of heroin withdrawal in all of its brutalising detail.[100]

At Tavern on the Green, John had taken a furtive snort of the opioid during the party, waking up the next morning in a full-blown crisis of regret. "My body's full of smack, but not enough of it," he remarked in his audio diary, "and I'm thinking, 'what the hell am I doing this shit for? I thought I would have quit it all by now.'" John resolved himself to undergoing cold turkey yet again in order to banish the highly addictive opioid from his system. "God help us for the next three days," he continued, lamenting the intellectual cost of his relapse in real terms, especially as it related to his capacity for being creative: "I want to write. I want to talk. I want to think. What I know is inexpressible." As if he needed yet another reminder about his personal artistic stalemate, John woke up on October 25 to the latest international headlines about McCartney being fêted the previous evening at London's Les Ambassadeurs Club by the *Guinness Book of World Records* for being the bestselling composer of all time.

While John's songwriting efforts had seemingly stalled for the moment, his relationship with Sean had flowered precipitously. Sean's swimming lessons at the Y had continued unabated, having become a much-anticipated event on their weekly calendar. After a recent lesson, John and Sean had run into Jack Douglas at an East Side health food store. John was thrilled to see his old friend, happily sharing his private Dakota telephone number with him. For his part, Jack enjoyed seeing their father-son dynamic in action. But as John and Sean left the store that day, Jack resolved not to call. "I didn't want to bother the guy because he was raising his family," he later explained.[101]

As it happened, John had often thought about Douglas – and fondly, at that. In the intervening years since engineering Yoko's solo albums, Douglas' career had skyrocketed with a series of bestselling albums by the likes of Aerosmith and Cheap Trick. When he first met Douglas back in 1971, John had been flabbergasted to learn that Jack was the selfsame American whose picture had been plastered across the UK newspapers back in 1965 after he briefly emigrated to Liverpool with a boyhood chum. Hoping to extend his stay in England, he falsely claimed to a reporter from the *Liverpool Echo* that he and his friend had been held captive on a tramp steamer, which resulted in a raft of sensationalised news stories that John, in turn, had read at the height of Beatlemania. "I'll be damned," said John. "You were the crazy Yanks in the papers!"[102]

As the autumn months of 1979 wore on, John and Sean's evolving bond was evidenced by a number of impromptu recordings that Lennon made with his son during October and November. In easily the most charming of the lot, Sean professes his love for the Beatles' 'With A Little Help From My Friends', which he sings with perfect glee, butchering the words in his childlike abandon. "That's my favourite song," he exclaims to his father. When Sean inquires if John sang the tune, his father sheepishly replies, "No, Ringo, but Paul and I were singing with him." In a later recording, John plugs his electric guitar into an amp – perhaps the candy-apple red Strat in his bedroom – and Sean lets it rip, producing a fusillade of grungy sound:

> Sean: Yeah! I like it very loud.
> John: Well, that's how I like it, too.
> Sean: Won't you make it more louder?
> John: I can't, I can't make it any, any louder than, than it is. It's on full, you see… If you wiggle the volume knob, then you get wow-wow-wow-wow, after you've hit it.

Looking back, Sean recalled that his rudimentary guitar-playing "had no melody whatsoever, but [John] would always go, 'Yeah, that's great. Listen, you're musically talented.' And I'd be like, 'Wow!' And he would always make me feel great."[103]

As the autumn months progressed, John finally returned to the Yamaha keyboard, where he recorded a new demo for 'I'm Crazy', his latest title for 'People' née 'Emotional Wreck'. By this point, he had begun to fashion a rudimentary chorus about gazing at the traffic from his bedroom window. During one of the takes, he ad libs an ironic new verse, referencing people telling him he's stupid for giving his money away. In a more serious vein, John turned to 'That's The Way The World Is', a subtle reworking of 'Real Life' in which he had dispensed with the verses in favour of the chorus about a lonely world with nobody to "call us home". Turning to his acoustic guitar, he also recorded a demo for 'Not For Love Nor Money' (also known as 'Illusions'). For John, life is rife with illusory trappings – chief among them, sex, drugs and "fool's goals". In the song, John pledges to dedicate himself to a future of self-actualisation, as opposed to endlessly reliving the "déjà vu" of his past. Not "for love nor money," he sings, will he do anything he doesn't want to.

Still working on the Yamaha, John turned to 'My Life', a composition that he had likely begun back in Japan, given that the original lyrics were written on Hotel Okura stationery. John tried his hands at three takes of the song, which was clearly in its infancy. Indeed, during one of his attempts at singing 'My Life' with piano accompaniment, he absent-mindedly stumbled into the lyrics of the Little River Band's 'Reminiscing'. At one key juncture during take 3 of his piano demo recordings, John begins to ponder the nature of life itself, trying out an assortment of lyrics about the intrinsic nature of living. In some instances, he seems to be riffing on the syrupy-sweet intent of the original lyrics: life is short, sweet and "nothing without you". Yet in another, less polished section of 'My Life', he wanders into more speculative territory as he struggles to mine the essential nature of his subject. "Life is something that happens to you while you're making plans or something like that," he sings, with a soulful quality to his voice. As with so many of his song-fragments in late 1979, 'My Life' remained unfinished, brimming with words and music like so many other numbers among his growing collection of cassettes. By this point, John had taken to storing his rough drafts and reference recordings in the tan leather shoulder bag that he would cart back and forth from the Dakota to Cannon Hill, the Lennon's Long Island estate.

In addition to 'My Life', John had taken a brief pass at another new composition, 'Stranger's Room', the threads of which he would pick up again in the new year. With dark, descending, even funereal piano chords, he sings about being alone with a stranger, chiding himself for being there in the first place, for the recklessness of his behaviours. As the demo progresses, he tries out a series of different phrases to capture the terrible extent of his dejection: "Stop the bleeding now", "losing out", "dripping down", and "silent shout", before breaking into a bebop scat. As the short demo comes to a close, he flawlessly whistles the melody of his new song-fragment in similar fashion to the Beatles' 'Two Of Us', or, even more fittingly, *Imagine*'s 'Jealous Guy'.

As 1979 was coming briskly to a close, John had become obsessed, like so many others, with the unfolding hostage crisis thousands of miles away in Iran. On November 4, more than 50 Americans had been taken hostage after Iranian students overthrew the US Embassy in Tehran. Earlier that year, Shah Mohammad Reza Pahlavi had been overthrown during the Iranian Revolution. To the great chagrin of the country's new Islamic Republic, the Shah was subsequently admitted into the United States to receive medical treatment. The resulting diplomatic standoff left millions of viewers – Lennon included – glued to their television sets, night after night, as the evening news provided the latest updates about the stalemate that had seen John's adopted homeland outmanoeuvred by a disorganised band of university students.

Over the next few months, John and Yoko carried out a variety of legal activities in keeping with their ever-increasing wealth. First up was John's long overdue will, which he signed on November 12. The four-page document, exclusive of the blind trust, had been prepared by David Warmflash, the Lennons' family attorney since the mid-Seventies. In addition to making provisions for John and Yoko's growing fortune – Mrs Lennon had expanded beyond dairy cow investments to include fine art, real estate, and Broadway productions – the will provided for Sean's guardianship in the case of his parents' untimely deaths. In order to mask the famous couple's identities when conducting real-estate business – any hint of John and Yoko's involvement might very well send a property's asking price rocketing skyward – Warmflash assumed the role of president of Pentacles Realty, Inc. during such transactions. Pointedly, the Lennons also dissolved their longstanding production companies, which included John's Bag Productions and Yoko's Joko Films. By this juncture, Lenono Music had come to represent the couple's interests to the wide world beyond the Dakota, and their old companies, largely inactive since the early 1970s, had become irrelevant.

That same week, rumours began to pick up steam about John's alleged creative activities inside the Dakota, even suggesting that he was on the verge of producing a new album of original material. A *Rolling Stone* magazine article (based upon a story originally published in *Record Mirror*) reported that Lennon would be returning to the recording studio for the first time in four years, adding that ace keyboard session player Nicky Hopkins was slated to join him. "I understand John's not going to do anything for a while," Hopkins told the press. "I was told he's waiting until his son is five-years-old." When asked to confirm the story, John and Yoko's publicist offered a terse "no comment".[104]

With the holidays in the offing and season's greetings already arriving at the Dakota on the wings of the US mail, John fired up the TV in his bedroom to watch the December 5 episode of Tom Snyder's *Tomorrow* programme. That evening's guest was none other than Paul. Later that evening, Wings was booked at London's Rainbow Theatre as part of a 19-date UK tour in support of their *Back To The Egg* LP. The band had recently undergone its third major lineup change in six years, and the exhaustion was written all over Paul's face. "You don't know, you know?" said McCartney, when asked about his uncanny instincts as a hitmaker. "You just trust your judgement. You just hope you're lucky. And you just work hard." For Wings, the 1979 UK tour served as a warmup for the group's upcoming January 1980 dates in Japan. But before the year was out, McCartney and Wings would share their talents as part of the star-studded Concerts for the People of Kampuchea at London's Hammersmith Odeon. Organised by McCartney and Waldheim, the bill included the likes of Queen, the Clash, the Pretenders, the Who, and Elvis Costello. The victims of war-torn Cambodia would get their benefit concert after all. Not surprisingly, rumours abounded about a possible Beatles reunion in advance of McCartney's December 29 performance. London's *Daily Mirror* led the speculation with the headline "Can This Be the Beatles' Reunion?" the day before. As Wings prepared to play 'Goodnight Tonight', Paul poked fun at the rumours when he introduced "Robbo" the drum machine, announcing that "this fellow here is not John Lennon, as has been suggested, and they're [Harrison and Starr] not here tonight, as has also been suggested."[105]

Scant days after reminiscing about old times with George Martin in the Dakota's kitchen, John made careful preparations for ringing in the new year in fine style. He was also desperate to buoy Yoko's spirits after a visit from her daughter Kyoko, now 16 years old, failed to materialise, leaving his wife devastated. John's merriment had been forestalled, if only temporarily, by the unexpected news of an earthquake in Edinburgh over the Christmas holidays. The quake's aftershocks were felt across much of the British Isles, leaving John in a state of panic over the fate of his Aunt Mimi, now 73, who had been living in retirement nearly 500 miles away in coastal Dorset. While they had experienced their share of challenges during his teenage years – she had famously cautioned him at age 14 that "the guitar's all very well, John, but you'll never earn a living from it" – his relationship with Mimi marked his most significant association with his familial past. A week scarcely went by when John hadn't placed his regular telephone call to his aging aunt, who had, not surprisingly, escaped the earthquake unscathed in the safety of her seaside home.[106]

John also managed to keep up with Paul, who had telephoned to offer season's greetings. "I phoned him at Christmas," McCartney remarked to *Rolling Stone*'s Paul Gambaccini. "We talked mainly about our lives, our families. People are calling John a recluse because he isn't doing what they expect him to do. In fact, he's getting on with being a family man. He was cooking, having a great time. I happened to ask him about music and he said, no, at the moment he doesn't particularly feel like doing that anymore. Maybe someday, but it doesn't bug him. He's quite happy, which is the main thing." Paul waxed philosophical about their differing outlooks during this period, while noting that John was finally able to benefit from his fame. "Before the Beatles," said Paul, "we would have said that if we were going to be a big success it would be to free us and allow us to make our way in life without having to be at everyone else's command. I would say that's what he's done. He's gotten there and, unlike me – who's gotten there and thinks I'd better keep going – he's decided he can't be bothered." As for their friendship, Paul added, "there's no venom there."[107]

Meanwhile, with Mintz in tow, John hatched a plan for the "Club Dakota", a private nightclub that he had envisioned for the Lennons' New Year's Eve celebration. The idea had come to John after he heard about the Blues Bar, the private nightclub that Dan Aykroyd and John Belushi had recently opened downtown. To bring his concept to fruition, John outfitted one of the apartment's numerous rooms art-deco style, with an antique cigarette machine, along with his cherished bubbletop Wurlitzer jukebox and his Yamaha electric piano. For the occasion, John dressed up in a white T-shirt and tails, which he accented with his Quarry Bank tie. When the clock struck midnight, with 'Auld Lang Syne' playing on the Wurlitzer, John and Yoko ushered in 1980 with a champagne toast as they watched the fireworks exploding over Central Park.

Back in December 1969, with the long shadow of the Beatles already drifting behind them, John and Yoko had symbolically shaved their heads down to crew cuts and proclaimed that 1970 would be "Year One", that it would usher in a new sociopolitical era of hopefulness and meaningful change. Looking back on the decade receding in his rear-view mirror, John could easily enumerate the many ways in which his vision for the 1970s had come up short. But even still, as he stood on the precipice of 1980, John experienced an eerily similar sense of optimism for the future about to unfold before him.

But John knew, in his heart, that the new decade would have to be – *must be* – markedly different from the last one for everyone's sake. "Wasn't the Seventies a drag?" he would pointedly remark in the coming months. He wanted desperately to reclaim his place as the visionary of his generation. As events would later show, John yearned to pick up his guitar and once again sing his songs of joy and introspection for the new decade – not because he had to in order to fulfil a recording contract, but rather, as the fount of genuine inspiration. John longed to sing and perform expressly for folks like him – now in their thirties and forties – who needed his consoling words more than ever. "Here we are," he would say. "We all survived Vietnam, or Watergate, or the tremendous upheaval of the whole world that's changed." And now, to his mind, the 1980s were a blank slate. "We're going into an unknown future, but we're still all here," he later remarked. "While there's life, there's hope."[108]

As John and Yoko had announced back in May, the spring-cleaning of their minds was once and truly over. By every indication, John knew full well that he had to get back to work – *and do it the right way this time*, and for all the right reasons – if he hoped to regain his footing in the new decade.

CHAPTER 6

El Solano

By the dawn of January 1980, the Lennons had enjoyed an unbroken Dakota residence together since travelling abroad for their Japanese sojourn the previous summer. The only exception had been their Thanksgiving visit to Cannon Hill, their Long Island property overlooking Cold Spring Harbor and, just beyond, the stately shores of Connecticut. As John had explained in his audio diary, Cannon Hill was the result of the Lennons' "endless search for Scotland", but "within an hour of New York". In his diary, John joked that "I've given up on Scotland and the ocean, and I'm settling for some grass and a tree." With Cannon Hill, the couple's longstanding quest for owning a bona fide "country retreat" had paid off – at least in terms of having access to a seaside view. The property was named Cannon Hill because of the antique cannon nestled by the swimming pool. The beachside estate even had its own private dock. Purchased by Yoko the previous spring for $400,000, the oak-shingled, three-storey estate was comprised of 14 bedrooms, numerous parlours and social rooms, and living quarters for multiple staff members. At Thanksgiving, the Lennons had experienced an ignominious maiden voyage at Cannon Hill after realising that the estate was overrun with fleas. As Fred Seaman later recalled, it was John who made the discovery: "We have to leave right away!" he announced as he scratched feverishly at his arm. "This place is infested with fleas. I mean, it's fucking *crawling* with them!"[109]

As the new year unfolded, John and Yoko fell into a hardened, even monotonous routine. With an array of staff attending to Sean, their home, and their every need, the couple spent much of their time by themselves. While John pursued a healthy, additive-free diet after his brush with a heroin relapse the previous fall – save for his beloved Gitanes – Yoko tended to the evolving complexities of the Lennons' business empire, which not only included a web of Beatles-related interests, but also a host of new investments. As for her tastes, Yoko preferred Sherman's Cigarettellos to the acrid smell of John's dark tobacco. In the rare times when they were together, the couple busied themselves with unchecked accumulation, buying nearly every possible kind of consumer good. As unrepentant shopaholics, they had devoted apartment 71, as well as space in their storerooms in the Dakota's basement, to allow for the booty they amassed during their otherworldly spending jags. Of late, their consumerism had tended towards rare Egyptian artefacts – for Yoko, who wanted access to their "magic power" – including a massive sarcophagus that dominated their Dakota living room. John's buying sprees tended towards all manner of electronic gadgetry. To Fred's mind, the basement storerooms had come to resemble the

> warehouse of an old movie studio. Strewn about was a mind-boggling collection of objects, some of them junk and some priceless. John's large surreal oil paintings, collages, and drawings, gold Beatles records, posters, props and sound equipment from concerts, bongo drums and other percussion instruments, pianos, old furniture, damaged antiques, filing cabinets, Sean's discarded toys, cardboard boxes and shopping bags full of fan mail, as well as a toilet seat and a bathtub with claw feet.[110]

Invariably, John's daily routine began in apartment 72's oversized eat-in kitchen. For the Lennons, the kitchen served as the epicentre of their lives in the apartment. Designed by architect Paul Segal, himself a resident at the Dakota since 1969, the kitchen stood high above the building's central courtyard. In Segal's conception, the spacious room would become a "superkitchen", not only large in terms of its size, which was considerable, but also in terms of its plurality of functions in the Lennon family's lives. In contrast with the rooms in apartment 72 that overlooked Central Park West, the superkitchen was largely impervious to the street noise outside the Dakota.

Segal's kitchen had come to define the Lennon's workaday lives – John's especially – in more ways than he could have possibly imagined. Outside of his bedroom, the superkitchen acted as John's comfort zone in much the same way that Yoko valued the privacy Studio One afforded her on the first floor. The kitchen was dominated by a long wooden table, as well as glass-doored refrigerators that revealed the appliances' contents, as well as a wall-length mural of John, Yoko, and Sean holding hands and wearing Superman costumes as they soar upward into the great beyond. Racks of white Formica shelving supported an array of cookbooks, including William Duffy's dietary classic *Sugar Blues*, originally published in 1975, which John regularly consulted about the dangers of refined sugar. In addition to a host of electronics and stereophonic gadgetry, the superkitchen was well stocked with magazines sporting titles such as *Eat Well*, *Better Living*, *New Age*, and *Vegetarian Times*; John and Yoko aspired to a meat-free lifestyle, save for their beloved sushi.

A large butcher-block table, fronted by yellow canvas-covered director's chairs, abutted the kitchen's arched window above the courtyard. Most mornings, John sat alone there in the predawn hours, chain-smoking his unfiltered Gitanes and sipping a cup of tea – his favourite was Red Zinger, though he was determined to swear off caffeine – and taking his breakfast, which invariably featured a bowl of shredded wheat and biscuits adorned with orange marmalade. While John had, for the most part, sworn off drugs during his retirement years, he couldn't manage to liberate himself from tea and coffee, which he often consumed at a clip of 20 to 30 cups a day. The kitchen also served as the regular haunt for the Lennons' trio of cats, a pet posse that included white-coated Sasha, black-haired Misha, and brindled Charo, the mutt. John doted on the cats, who, in turn, adored him – especially for the delectable calf's liver meals that they regularly enjoyed. As Yoko remembered, "John used to have a special love for Charo. 'You've got a funny face, Charo!' he would say, and pat her."[111]

When John wasn't luxuriating in the superkitchen or reading the latest nonfiction in his bedroom, he was making lists – reams of the things that he would prepare for Fred's daily errands. At the beginning of Fred's employment with the Lennons, Rich DePalma would replenish a $1,000 expense account for the assistant's regular tours of Manhattan's finest establishments on the Lennons' behalf; Fred's weekly cash withdrawals would eventually reach $3,000, which he would fetch from the nearby

Bank Leumi on Broadway and 66th Street, to cover his household errands, which become increasingly extravagant.

When it came to the calf's liver, for example, John would dispatch his assistant to one of the high-class uptown butchers, where he would purchase the morsels for as much as $8 a pound. For John, compiling his daily lists had become one of his favourite pastimes. He was known to deploy virtually any available scrap of paper in the service of his list-making. In December, for instance, he had purloined Yoko's notepad, which included a hand-drawn sketch of the Dakota's exterior, to enumerate his latest whims for Fred to fulfil in short order:

1 Book on Cats & Dogs
2 Radio/Tape to Japan (Xmas rush)
3 Smoked Salmon
4 Sean's Photos from FAO Shwartz? [sic]
5 Remind Y. Re: Persian Carpets.
6 Electric clock (Kitchen?)
7 Remind Y Re: MY 'Nightdress' (i.e. being made by some woman)
8 Flowers for Yoko (tell her I sent them!)
9 Cornflakes[112]

Even with a whole raft of staff at his beck and call – including the family's live-in Japanese cook Uneko Uda, known reverentially as Uda-san, and gardener Mike Medeiros, whom John playfully nicknamed Mike Tree – John had come to fancy himself as a kind of "househusband". By contrast, Yoko fulfilled the more traditional role of breadwinner as she wheeled and dealed at all hours of the day and night down in Studio One. At times, John would even come to suggest that his domesticated role as househusband and Sean's chief caregiver served as the impetus for his withdrawal from public life and his recording career.

John often came to define his role in the household in terms of his bread-baking activities, which he perceived to be the *sine qua non* of attending to his home and hearth. He would intentionally liken his work in the kitchen to his former pursuit of excellence in the recording studio: "Bread and babies, as every housewife knows, is a full-time job," he later remarked. "There ain't no space for other projects." John learned his bread-making skills from Rosa, who taught him how to make bread like her ancestors did back in Pontevedra. As Rosa later remembered, "We bought flour, whole wheat, since John really believed in the healthy properties of bran, and we made the kitchen our operation centre. The slow and precise bread-making process was what amazed John the most. He mixed the flour as if it was an old ritual." Which, of course, it was. "It had a real therapeutic effect for John," Rosa recalled.[113]

While he enjoyed the act of baking bread, John was dumbstruck by how quickly the fruits of his labours vanished. "After I had made the loaves, I felt like I had conquered something. But as I watched the bread being eaten, I thought, 'Well, Jesus! Don't I get a gold record or knighted or nothing?'" Although John only baked bread on a scant few occasions in the Dakota's superkitchen, the highly domesticated activity was emblematic of his ongoing desire for self-actualisation. Clearly prone to exaggeration, John's description of his role as baker – and, ultimately, his inability to sustain it, given his easy boredom and ravenous need for variety in his life – offers a vital window into his thinking in the new year:

> I took a Polaroid of my first loaf. I was overjoyed! I was *that* excited by it. I couldn't believe it! It was like an album coming out of the oven. The instantness of it was great. I was so into it, so thrilled with it, that I ended up cooking for the staff! Every day, I was cooking lunch for the drivers, office boys, anybody who was working with us. "Come on up!" I loved it. But then it was beginning to wear me out, you see. I thought, What is this? Screw this for a lark. I'd make two loaves on Friday and they'd be gone by Saturday afternoon. The thrill was wearing off and it became the routine again.

In spite of his inability to sustain his baking activities, John perceived his househusband duties to act as a means for much-needed self-actualisation at this juncture in his and Yoko's lives: "It was more important to face ourselves and face that reality than to continue a life of rock 'n' roll show biz."[114]

As with so many aspects of their lives during this period, elements of John and Yoko's present, more often than not, often collided with key facets from the couple's past. For his part, Fred had discovered one such remnant when he took the seven flights of stairs from Studio One, on the first floor, to the service entrance that led into the superkitchen. There, affixed to the door in the stairwell, was a small brass plate identifying apartment 72 as the NUTOPIAN EMBASSY. Back on April 1, 1973 – April Fool's Day, no less – John and Yoko established a conceptual country that they christened as Nutopia. They announced the founding of Nutopia during a press conference, in which they waved white flags of surrender in the name of peace. The concept of Nutopia had been prompted by the couple's highly improbable hope that the United Nations might recognise Nutopia as an actual country, thus affording the Lennons with diplomatic asylum. On the one hand, it was a brazen attempt to provide John with legal status, hence, circumventing the domain of the US Immigration and National Service and, hence, bringing resolution to his ongoing immigration crisis at the time. John would revisit the formation of Nutopia on his *Mind Games* album, which was released in October 1973 and featured contact information for the Nutopian Embassy, which could mysteriously be reached at 1 White Street in New York City, along with the fictive nation's national anthem, which was, rather appropriately, rendered entirely in silence.

The superkitchen not only served as the daily focal point for the Lennons' family, staff, and pets, but occasionally for their neighbours, with whom they shared a close proximity overlooking the courtyard. Novelist David Marlowe had wistful memories of sitting in his eighth-floor living room on the opposite side of the courtyard from apartment 72. On pleasant days, when Dakotans had their windows open, he would often hear the faint sounds of John playing his acoustic guitar. Looking out of his living room window, Marlowe could see John, sitting at the butcher-block table, his eyes focused in concentration on his fretboard as he strummed his guitar. To his mind, Marlowe discerned a clear contrast between John's Beatles past and the less optimistic tones inherent in his current music. From Marlowe's listening post, "the old Beatles songs, with their wild bursts of melody, which once seemed so exuberantly cheerful ("Yeah, yeah, yeah"), and which were about love as much as anything, now sound sad." They left Marlowe "with a curious feeling of melancholy, a wishful wistfulness for the old days when, it sometimes seems, everything (including people) was a little nicer."[115]

As it turned out, Marlowe hadn't been that far off the mark in terms of John's musical direction across much of the late 1970s. But changes were clearly in the offing. First, John had to exorcise his demons – the "mighty Dylan", for example – in order to find, finally, a sense of forward momentum. At the same time, John hadn't quite freed himself from the sense of dislocation so prevalent in the compositions he had undertaken during his "retirement", or, as he would describe it later in the year, his period of househusbandry. A demo recording of Jimmy Cliff's 'Many Rivers To Cross', which John had turned to on previous occasions, found him playing his electric guitar with a drum machine accompaniment. By the end of the recording, John meanders into fragments of Smokey Robinson's 'My Girl' and, briefly, Dylan's 'I Don't Believe You'. He continued in this nostalgic vein with piano takes of Sam Cooke's 'You Send Me' and the Everly Brothers' 'Cathy's Clown'.

Back in 1974, John had taken a more funereal approach to 'Many Rivers To Cross' when he produced Harry Nilsson's cover version for the *Pussy Cats* LP. During the Nilsson sessions, John, acting in his role as record producer, hastily concocted a string arrangement for 'Many Rivers To Cross'. Later that year, when he needed to devise musical accompaniment for '#9 Dream', a new composition destined for inclusion on his *Walls And Bridges* LP, he lifted his orchestration from Nilsson's 'Many Rivers To Cross' in order to bring '#9 Dream' to fruition. John liked to describe this kind of mechanical approach to songwriting and music production as "craftsmanship", a kind of pragmatic approach, in his own phraseology, for creating work product for the sake of bringing a recording to the marketplace. In 'Glass Onion', a more pointed example from the Beatles' *White Album* days, John elaborated on the inherent difficulty of craftsmanship, which he described as "trying to make a dovetail joint".

By contrast, John preferred songwriting experiences in which lyrics and musical ideas came easily – like bolts out of the blue in moments of pure inspiration:

> I always felt that the best songs were the ones that came to you … I do have the ability to sit down [and] sort of make a song. I wouldn't be thrilled with it, but I can make a song like that. But I find it difficult to do that. But I can do it. I call it craftsmanship, you know? I've had enough years at it to sort of put something together. But I never enjoyed that. I like it to be inspirational – from the spirit.[116]

With the new year only just beginning to unfold, John finally experienced the long-awaited spirit of pure inspiration when it came to composing, of all things, a musical rejoinder to Dylan's 'Gotta Serve Somebody'. It was as if his 1979 line drawing – "in which the spirit moves" – had briskly come to life. John had returned to Dylan with a vengeance. His new song, which he entitled 'Serve Yourself' and performed on the Yamaha piano, burst forth with unchecked savagery as the songwriter ticked off the twisted origins of Dylan's religious awakening. In a vocal torrent, John lambasts Dylan for having "found" and placed his faith in such disparate deities as Jesus Christ, Buddha, Mohammad, and Krishna. Occasionally lapsing into his parodic Dylan voice, John drives homes the chorus with unchecked zeal: you've got to serve yourself, he sings, 'cause "ain't nobody gonna do it for you".

John surely understood – even during the song's explosive composition – that 'Serve Yourself' was about himself, as much or even more than the fiery screed concerned Dylan. During one of the takes, he even goes so far as to dedicate it to "all you phallic worshippers", underscoring the song's onanistic origins. Interestingly, John would often connect Dylan's past songwriterly behaviours with his own need to create something "new" out of the found objects that flitted in and out of his worldview. In short, McCartney and Dylan emerged as his subject matter for the simple reason that they were convenient. In trying to explain his motives vis-à-vis Dylan in 'Serve Yourself', John invoked his treatment of Paul in 'How Do You Sleep?', which, to his mind, "was like Dylan doing 'Like A Rolling Stone', one of his nasty songs. It's using somebody as an object to create something. I wasn't really feeling that vicious at the time, but I was using my resentment towards Paul to create a song," adding that "it was just a mood." And ultimately John's sour mood was directly related to his feelings about himself. If he were really going to make things happen in 1980, it would be up to him to act as the necessary catalyst. "Ain't nobody gonna do it for you."[117]

To Fred's mind, a discernible change was already in the air when his employer began refining 'Serve Yourself'. As John remarked to him at the time, "playing an instrument and writing music is a gift. You give it all you've got – it takes a lot of hard work, a lot of practice – but once you've got those basic skills worked out and you're in the proper frame of mind, then you're in a position to allow yourself to be inspired – by God, by whoever it is. Then the music just flows. When it comes, it's like magic. And when it doesn't, there's nothing you can do to force it."[118]

By this point, John didn't have to force anything. He was all too happy to sit back, guitar in hand, and let the magic flow. During a demo recording for a meandering new song with electric guitar and drum machine accompaniment entitled 'She Runs Them Round In Circles', John sings about an unnamed woman running rings around her society. At one point, he even goes as far as describing them as "magic circles" – perhaps in sly reference to one of the castoff titles for the Beatles' *Revolver* LP. But within moments, he loses the thread of 'She Runs Them 'Round In Circles' and happens upon something much better and even more evocative. Imagining a seafaring scene, John begins singing about a growing happiness that fills his heart with "love and anticipation".

By this juncture, John's new composition has morphed into a father's love song for his son and an innate impulse to protect the boy from life's monsters, metaphorical and otherwise. "Close your eyes, have no fear," John sings. While the lyrics may have been relatively new, the music had been evolving for years; as with so many of his songs, John's lyrics and music would gestate over long periods of time. May Pang would later ascribe the basic melody for 'Darling Boy', as it was currently known, to the soundtrack for a Chinese soap opera that the couple had watched back in 1974. As the demo for 'Darling Boy' comes to an end, John draws his inspiration from a more recent source: as he professed on the caption on one of his line drawings, every day is getting better, in every way. He had also reportedly been inspired by 'Isn't She Lovely', Stevie Wonder's musical celebration of the birth of his daughter Aisha in February 1975. For John, the nascent composition of 'Darling Boy' easily marked the single most hopeful and positive instance among the whole of his "retirement" demo recordings. For the life of him, John can't seem to get 'Darling Boy' out of his mind at this point. In subsequent demos for the song-fragments 'Howling At The Moon' and 'Across The River', John can be heard returning to both the verses and chorus for his evolving composition about his beloved son.[119]

With 'Darling Boy' in progress, John turned to his memories from the Beatles' famous visit to Rishikesh in the company of Maharishi Mahesh Yogi in the spring of 1968, arguably one of the most fertile periods in Lennon's working life as a songwriter. With 'India, India', John invokes his long-ago experience at the Maharishi's ashram like a mantra, singing, "India, India, take me to your heart", and seeking out its ancient mysteries. In 'Help Me To Help Myself', yet another acoustic guitar demo from this period, John shifts from summoning the halcyon days of Rishikesh to the invocation of a Christian god. Lost in a sustained moment of spiritual and aesthetic awakening, he sings, "Lord, help me to help myself."

By this juncture, John's creative impetus found him recycling lyrics and melodies at an increasing rate. It was as if he were testing out each composition via the demo process, grafting various song-fragments onto each other in an effort to discover the most pleasing, effective possible combinations. His composition 'Memories' offered a revelatory case in point. For the song, John freely borrowed musical elements from 'India, India', which he transplanted into lyrics from a variety of sources, including 'Howling At The Moon' and, stranger still, the reference to "driftwood on the sea" from Hank Williams' 1950 release 'May You Never Be Alone'. Williams had exerted a considerable early influence on John, who once recalled that he would imitate the country and western pioneer singing 'Honky Tonk Blues' before he could even play the guitar. With that insanity, John sings in 'Memories', "it's a wonder I survived".[120]

During this same period, 'Real Life' morphed into a new composition entitled 'Girls And Boys'. At this juncture, 'Girls And Boys' was the only composition from *The Ballad of John and Yoko* musical project that was still in circulation. John clearly had a soft spot for the song, with 'Girls And Boys' having been the subject of no fewer than six demo recordings – most recently, in conjunction with a new song-fragment called 'Baby Make Love To You'. In 'Girls And Boys', John sings about youthful diversions, a world where girls and boys busied themselves with toys and merriment, when all they really needed was love.

'I'm Crazy' marked another song that clearly held John's attention during this period. John recorded at least 14 takes of the composition during this period – at one point, he even joked that he was on "take 90". By this juncture, 'I'm Crazy' had easily received the most attention, by far, of any of his compositions during his "retirement"-era recordings. Not only had 'I'm Crazy' undergone numerous iterations, but also several changes in instrumentation, ranging from piano to acoustic guitar – even an electric guitar rendition in the style of the Beatles' 'Revolution' – and back again to John's original piano accompaniment. While the verses had been fairly static over the months since the song's inception, the chorus had been somewhat slower to evolve. When it finally arrived in John's imagination, it found the composer providing a simple explanation, fanciful as it may have seemed in his wistful tune, for his absence from the music industry: "I just had to let it go."

On January 14, the rhythm of the Lennons' daily lives was interrupted when Paul telephoned the Dakota from across the park, where he was relaxing in his suite at the Stanhope Hotel. He and wife Linda, along with their four children Heather, Mary, Stella, and James, were in town in advance of Wings' upcoming Japanese tour, which was set to commence later that week in Tokyo. Paul wanted to stop by, announcing that Linda had "scored some dynamite weed" he wanted to share with John and Yoko. The conversation left the Lennons feeling unsettled. Having declined his offer to visit them at the Dakota, John and Yoko fumed about McCartney's plans to stay in the Hotel Okura's Presidential Suite. "Paul's touring Japan and he called to brag about the fact he's going to be staying in *our* suite at the Hotel Okura. If those two sleep there," said John, "we'll never have peace when we go back to that room. They're going to fuck up our good hotel karma."[121]

But there was more. During his weekly telephone call with Aunt Mimi, John mentioned that he had heard from Paul, who had been complaining about the difficulties of taking Wings back on the road. "Why the hell do you do it, then?" John asked him. "The simple answer is he cannot give up the publicity," John reported back to Mimi. The impulse to stay relevant was surely a need that John could well understand, although he openly mocked it at the time. It was the very same yearning that John summarily rejected at the heart of 'I'm Crazy' – "I had to let it go" – although he, too, had felt the very same pull at times throughout his retirement years.[122]

As was his usual wont, John was of two minds about the desire to maintain artistic relevance, especially when it came to McCartney. "I kind of admire the way Paul started back from scratch," John remarked later that year, "forming a new band and playing in small dance halls, because that's what he wanted to do with the Beatles – he wanted us to go back to the dance halls and experience that again. But I didn't… that was one of the problems, in a way, that he wanted to relive it all or something – I don't know what it was… But I kind of admire the way he got off his pedestal – now he's back on it again, but, I mean, he did what he wanted to do. That's fine, but it's just not what I wanted to do."[123]

Just two days later, McCartney fell off of his pedestal in highly dramatic and very public fashion when he was arrested at Tokyo's Narita International Airport after customs officials discovered nearly eight ounces of marijuana in his baggage. Within a matter of days, the tour had been cancelled. More than 100,000 tickets had been sold for the 11-date tour, accounting for a financial loss of more than 100 million Japanese yen. Back at the Dakota, there were more than a few comments over the next several days about Paul's arrogance, even cultural disrespect for the Japanese. John confided to Fred that "you know, it serves Paul right. I think subconsciously he wanted to get busted" and rebel against his carefully cultivated image of being a "goody-two shoes businessman". To John's mind, "Paul wanted to show the world – particularly the British – that he's still a bit of a bad boy." For her part, the Lennons' housekeeper Rosa recalled that "John was not happy with this incident and he was definitely not glad that his old colleague got arrested. On the contrary, he criticised him and got really angry. I had never heard him talking so sharply." In his ensuing rant, John exclaimed, "If you really need the bloody weed, don't you have people who can carry it for you? You're a Beatle boy. A Beatle. Your face is everywhere. Why did you do something so stupid?"[124]

On January 25, 1980, Paul was released from detention after spending nine days in a Japanese jail cell. In short order, the drug charges were dropped and he was deported back to England. McCartney later confirmed his haughty attitude about bringing marijuana on his flight to Japan when he admitted that he had been briefed in advance about the country's "no-nonsense" approach to drugs. "We were about to fly to Japan and I knew I wouldn't be able to get anything to smoke over there," he later recalled. "This stuff was too good to flush down the toilet, so I thought I'd take it with me." As for John, his old friend's plight in the Far East had left him weary and concerned. At one point, he even sent a good luck card by courier. When he learned that Paul had been released, John quipped, "I'm glad that's over. I feel like I've been keeping a vigil for him. Not that I care, you understand."[125]

By the time that Paul alighted back in England, John and Yoko had continued their real-estate buying spree. With their lawyer David Warmflash in tow, they closed the deal on the purchase of El Solano, a beachside mansion on Florida's Palm Beach island that they had rented the previous March during a family vacation with Julian. Located at 720 South Ocean Boulevard, El Solano was a bona fide legacy property – a white stucco, Spanish-style estate with a terra cotta finish. Built in 1919, the mansion was the brainchild of architect Addison Mizner, whose Spanish Colonial and Mediterranean Revival-style designs pocked the South Florida coast. Mizner christened the estate as El Solano to honour the Northern California county of his youth. For several decades, the estate had served as the vacation getaway for railroad tycoon Harold S. Vanderbilt. The home featured six bedrooms among its 22 rooms, along with a full-sized ballroom, a tennis court, a beach cabana, and saltwater and freshwater pools.

On January 31, John and Yoko purchased El Solano for $550,000 from socialite Mildred "Brownie" McLean, whose family's celebrated holdings once included *The Washington Post* and the Hope Diamond. As they sealed the deal, John prepared tea for McLean's realtor while Yoko hammered out the negotiations. By Saturday, February 2, McLean couldn't contain her excitement any longer and divulged the names of Palm Beach's famous new homeowners to the press. With Yoko's 47th birthday in the offing, the Lennons decided to spend the month lounging around the estate. While John, Yoko, Sean, and Uda-san made the trip by air, Fred loaded up the family car with the ex-Beatle's guitars and began the long southward drive. When he had started working for the Lennons the previous year, they had owned a battered, dark-green Chrysler station wagon. This time around, Fred was driving in the lap of comparative luxury. The new company car was a brand-new, apple-green Mercedes station wagon. With its diesel-powered engine, it was the first of its kind in New York City.

When he arrived in South Florida that winter, John cut a bizarre appearance by any measure. For one thing, he had allowed his hair to run free. As contemporaneous photos would show, it had clearly been a long while since he had visited Viz-à-Viz for a trim. And then there was the issue of the shaggy beard he had been nursing since the family's Thanksgiving jaunt to Cannon Hill back in November. By February 8, the notorious British tabloid the *Daily Mail* had tracked John and Yoko down to Palm Beach, where they managed to capture a shot of John walking along the promenade, his scraggly grooming on full display, and wearing a brand-new full-length fur coat and white straw hat. Smelling a celebrity scoop, *Chicago Tribune* gossip columnist Maggie Daly wrote that John "went walking around town by himself the first day he was there. He dropped in at a posh department store and bought $25,000 in furs in the fur salon during his first 10 minutes in the store. The furs included a black fox coat." John reportedly remarked to the sales staff that "I don't know what my wife is going to use it for, but it will be her breakfast fur."[126]

At El Solano, John and Yoko went about the business of outfitting their new homestead with a full-time staff, which grew to include gardener Dane Worthington, along with his sister Joanne Hochella and her husband John, who worked as caretakers and lived in a cottage behind the estate.

During that first week, the Lennons were joined by their former Dakota neighbours, actor Peter Boyle of *Young Frankenstein* fame and his wife Loraine Alterman, a journalist. The two couples had been friends for the past several years, having met after Loraine interviewed Yoko for *Rolling Stone*. John had even served as Peter's best man at the Boyles' October 1977 wedding. John admired the 44-year-old actor for his rapier-like wit, which he balanced with a kind-hearted demeanour. At the same time, John was fascinated by Peter's lapsed Catholicism, having left the order of the Christian Brotherhood behind to pursue a career in acting. To Fred's mind, "John regarded Peter as a fellow religious renegade." As far as Peter was concerned, their friendship had been a matter of fate. "We were both born under the sign of Libra," Boyle later recalled, "and the rest was history."[127]

By the time that Fred arrived at El Solano, the couples' vacation was in full swing. Although they had rented a red Cadillac Eldorado, which John thought would be inconspicuous as they tooled around Palm Beach, the Lennons and the Boyles opted to keep to the estate, giving John's gnawing fear of being spotted. At first, they enjoyed their time together on the island, lounging around the estate's pools as Uda-san plied them with refreshments, strolling along the beach, and playing with Sean, whom Peter good-naturedly entertained with a succession of madcap facial gestures. But then things began to take a turn for the worse. By this point, John had already grown restless in the Lennons' new home, marooned some 1,200 miles away from his bedroom with its books and music and television – his routine, even – that epitomised his life back at the Dakota. That evening, Peter arranged for an evening out at La Petite Marmite, a trendy French restaurant on the island that not only sported a fancy seasonal menu, but also, in what passed for being *très chic* during that era, individual telephones installed at each table.

Forgoing the Cadillac, Peter arranged for a limousine to ferry the couples to the restaurant in style. Things went downhill quickly from there. When they arrived at La Petite Marmite, John immediately felt besieged in the society haunt, where Palm Beach's finest go to dine and strut their stuff. During the meal, a posse of photographers had taken the couples' picture, which enraged John to no end. When they arrived back at El Solano, John exploded, chastising Peter for "dragging us to second-rate, trendy eateries so you can get your picture taken with us." Boyle flew into his own pique of anger after John described his actions that night as "lame-brained" before realising that he had fallen victim to the Beatle's famous, highly provocative wit.[128]

A few days later, John arranged for the two couples to enjoy a lavish brunch at the Breakers, the Italian Renaissance-style resort hotel just a few miles to the north of El Solano. By this point, the Lennons and the Boyles had clearly recovered from any lingering unpleasantness – or, in Peter's case, embarrassment over having been bested by John. To their surprise, the maître d' refused to seat them without the proper attire. John was wearing his by-now ubiquitous straw hat, along with a leather jacket, while Peter had donned a sweater for the occasion. Not missing a beat, Boyle took the maître d' aside, planted a hefty gratuity in his hands, and made special note that they were in the presence of none other than former Beatle John Lennon.

In short order, the Lennons' party was seated. As Fred recalled, "we were transformed from undesirables into celebrities and seated at a large table near the centre of the dining room." Now ensconced in his central place at the heart of the Breakers, John was suddenly the talk of the restaurant, having captured the attention of nearly everyone there. For his part, Lennon began to engage in one of his favourite pastimes by taking stock of the other diners and making predictions about their behavioural tendencies in the company of someone with his peculiar brand of fame. As Fred recalled:

> He began a running monologue, sizing up the crowd, pointing out those who were most likely to muster the courage to approach our table for autographs. He also pointed out those who "performed" to get his attention: people who pretended not to notice him, all the while behaving very conspicuously, laughing loudly and doing tricks for their wives or girlfriends, as if to say, "Hey, we're having just as much fun over at our table as you are over at your Beatle table." Then there were those sombre diners determined not to notice, who dug deep into their plates, deep into their conversations, their morning Bloody Marys. There were others who stared out of curiosity or boredom, and some who simply gaped in awe – disbelieving, hardcore fans.[129]

During their visit to the Breakers, the *Palm Beach Post* caught wind of John and Yoko's brunch-time activities, and dispatched Patrick

Partington to take their picture. The photograph ran in the *Palm Beach Post* and the *Daily Mail*, and, a few weeks later, was licensed to *Rolling Stone* for the magazine's March announcement about the Lennons' acquisition of El Solano.

After the Boyles' departure, John and Yoko fell back into their daily routine, making headlines yet again for their latest in a long line of extravagant shopping sprees. At one point, the couple had been forced to flee a store on the tony esplanade, where they were browsing the latest furs, after attracting a growing swarm of fans. By this juncture, Yoko had begun bowing out of such daily excursions, telling John and Sean that she was suffering from an extended bout with the flu. Later, she claimed that she was forced to stay home because of Mercury Retrograde, the optical illusion in which the planet seems to be moving backwards from our vantage point on Earth. For astrologers, the backwards motion is often interpreted as a disruptive, mood-altering force.

Undeterred, John and Fred took to exploring the byways and highways of Palm Beach in the rented Caddy. With Fred at the wheel, John came to admire the island's wealth and opulence, along with its well-manicured lawns and "squeaky-clean" streets. But in the same breath, he recoiled at its apparent wholesomeness, suggesting that it needed "a little sleaze" to spice things up. If he were a local businessman, said John, he would open up a "Rent-a-Punk agency" to import bizarre-looking characters with "spikey green or purple hair" to upset "this civilised Palm Beach scene".[130]

During this same period, John managed to indulge in another one of his favourite pastimes, swapping postcards with friends and family – and, in one of the unlikeliest of circumstances – a 14-year-old Brazilian fan named Fernando de Oliveira. Living at the time in Rio de Janeiro, Fernando had recently discovered the music of the 1960s, becoming especially enamoured with the Beatles. When he read in a fan magazine that John hadn't agreed to perform with Paul at the upcoming Concerts for the People of Kampuchea in December 1979, he wrote in a brazen attempt to change Lennon's mind. To his surprise, John answered by postcard, writing, "Fernando! Buenos dias!" Although John had erred by replying in Spanish instead of Portuguese, Fernando could hardly have cared less, hastily posting a Christmas card to the Dakota. In true Liverpudlian form, John replied, complete with one of his signature line drawings: "Haddy grimble and wishy new ear! Love, John Lennon '79". In March, as John lounged in Palm Beach, Fernando wrote to John yet again, asking him to "write me a few words", as the young Brazilian was still learning English. In short order, John replied, scrawling the whole of the alphabet across the back of a postcard for his young correspondent, signing it "John Lennon '80".[131]

On February 15, the *Palm Beach Daily News* began to pick up John's scent, having trailed him to Main Street News, where he and Fred planned to replenish John's flagging stock of reading material: "Loaded down with numerous magazines and newspapers, Lennon darted off in a red Cadillac with a white top bearing Dade County plates." Later that week, John spotted an advertisement for a used bookstore in West Palm Beach. In order to avoid another incident like the one back on the esplanade, John hatched a plan in which they would go to the store in advance and John would dart among the aisles, blitzkrieg-style, pointing out the titles that he wanted Fred to come back and purchase the next day. Back at El Solano, John unpacked his new library of occult classics with unremitting glee. "Look at this, Mother!" he exclaimed, holding up a copy of Madame Blavatsky's 1888 classic *Practical Occultism* for Yoko's inspection. With its chapter entitled "Some Practical Suggestions for Daily Life", *Practical Occultism* proved to be John's favourite book of the lot. "Amazing, isn't it?" a grey-faced Yoko replied, absent-mindedly handing it back to him.[132]

When it came to planning Yoko's 47th-birthday festivities, which were set to commence on February 18, John and Fred experienced their most madcap Palm Beach adventure yet. For their trip into Palm Beach and its environs, John donned his straw hat, a white gabardine jacket, and his favourite T-shirt, a red-and-white number embossed with the image of Marilyn Monroe. "They'll never spot me with this on!" John joked. No sooner had they left the estate in the red Caddy than a carful of stoned teenagers began tailing them. "Fuck a pig," said John, disgusted at being so quickly discovered. With Led Zeppelin's 'Whole Lotta Love' blaring on the car stereo, Fred gunned the engine towards West Palm Beach, where they finally lost the carload of fans.[133]

After picking up a chocolate birthday cake at a nearby supermarket, John hit upon the idea of gathering up a thousand gardenias for his ailing wife. When they returned to El Solano, Fred began calling up local florists, quickly learning that the delicate flowers were out of season. Eventually, Fred located a florist who was willing to provide them with 100 blossoms – at a price, of course. With John screaming "money's no object!" in the background, Fred snatched up his employer's American Express card and arranged for the flowers' midnight delivery to the estate. In the end, John's birthday gambit came off without a hitch – *almost*. "When I woke up on my birthday morning, there was a gardenia beside my bed," said Yoko. "Another one was lying near the door, another one was outside the room, there was a trail of them down the stairs and the whole hallway was full of gardenias. John had bought so many that the local florists had to get in supplies from outside the state. He did that for me because he knew gardenias were my favourite flower."[134]

In truth, Yoko felt terribly guilty over John's Herculean efforts to please her. Unbeknown to her husband, she had recently suffered a heroin relapse of her own. For Yoko, it was the beginning of a personal trauma that would plague her over the next several months as she attempted to go cold turkey. "Thank you for the flowers, Fred," said Yoko, who understood the lengths to which he had gone to round up the flora on John's behalf. "I love the smell. But, you know, they're just not right for the occasion. In Japan, gardenias are the flowers of death. They're used for funerals."[135]

One afternoon a few days later, John and Fred hit the road yet again. For a while, they tooled around the dockside marina that fronts the Intercoastal Canal and separates Palm Beach island from mainland Florida. Suddenly, the ex-Beatle's eyes caught sight of a 41-foot sailing vessel called the *Imagine*. From his place in the passenger's seat of the red Caddy, John gave the boat a quizzical look, wondering aloud if the ship's name had anything to do with his famous peace anthem. With such a personally significant name, the boat's sudden appearance in his life seemed prophetic to John.

CHAPTER 7

Cannon Hill

Later that same day, Fred looked up the boat's owners in the phonebook. Sure enough, the captain and his wife were major-league Beatles fans. Better yet, the *Imagine* was available for lunchtime cruises around the perimeter of Palm Beach island. In short order, Fred booked a charter for the Lennons aboard the vessel under his own name to conceal their identities until the appointed time. For his part, John was giddy with excitement. "I can't wait to blow those fuckers' minds!" he exclaimed.

Still suffering in private from the debilitating throes of heroin withdrawal, Yoko couldn't fathom the idea of taking to the sea, with its ocean winds and choppy waves, on a sailboat. But after John made a rare show of standing his ground and insisting that they book the vessel, Yoko reluctantly agreed to the luncheon cruise. Meanwhile, Sean was jumping up and down with anticipation. As far as he was concerned, the family's extended Palm Beach getaway had been a smashing success, leaving him with a lifetime of memories. "In Florida, the seagulls ate stale bread out of my hand," he later recalled. "I caught lizards in paper cups and watched their discarded tails twitch cryptically on the warm terracotta terrace."[136]

When the appointed day arrived, Fred drove the family to the marina in the Mercedes station wagon. At first, the thirtysomething captain Terry Bosley and his wife Linda didn't seem to recognise their famous passenger, donning his straw hat and sunglasses, along with his scraggily beard and unkempt mane in full bloom. But then they saw the familiar image of Yoko, and the jig was up. "I watched the couple as their faces went through the familiar changes," Fred recalled. "First, they refused to believe. Then they wanted to grab, to possess John, to touch him all over, to ask a thousand questions. But then they saw that, like a rare bird caught out of its habitat, he would fly off if they moved. Soon, they were trying with all their awkward might to pretend that John and Yoko were just another tourist couple out for a spin around Palm Beach."[137]

As for the name of their sailboat, Linda explained that "we were flower children. We grew up with the Beatles." For Terry and Linda, watching *The Dick Cavett Show* back in September 1971 and seeing the video premiere of John performing 'Imagine' on the white baby grand piano at Tittenhurst Park was all she wrote. "That was when we decided that when we got a boat, we'd name it *Imagine*." In addition to Terry and Linda, the sailboat's crew included the couple's teenaged children John and Mimi. As the cruise got underway, John took up a pen and signed the *Imagine*'s guest log. Under the word "date", he sketched one of his patented line drawings of a smiling sign. Under "address" he wrote "here and there" in his distinctive scrawl. The Lennons' voyage on the *Imagine* lasted more than five hours, with Bosley anchoring the boat at lunchtime off Peanut Island. At one point, the captain broke into a sea shanty. Not missing a beat, John served up a spirited rendition of 'Popeye The Sailor Man'.[138]

Not surprisingly, for Yoko, cruising on the *Imagine* around Palm Beach island felt like torture. But for John – with his seafaring Liverpool roots running deep – being aboard the *Imagine* was sheer, unadulterated joy. He was in heaven. The cruise that he had asked Fred to book as a lark had slowly transformed into something much more meaningful and significant. His sulking wife had little effect on him as he sat in the rear of the sailboat with the captain's cat nestled in his lap. As he soaked up the sun and sea, John resolved himself to savour the full measure of his experience that afternoon on the *Imagine*. It was providence that brought him here, John reasoned. As he was fond of saying, in life "there are no accidents."

Meanwhile, working from her tiny galley kitchen, Linda plied the Lennons with a feast of wine, cheese, shrimp cocktail, and freshly baked bread. As the sailboat made its progress around the island, John embroidered the tale that would become familiar throughout the year, telling the captain's wife about his own experiences baking bread back at the Dakota, where he lived as a kind of househusband while his wife looked after the family business. John was so enamoured with the Bosleys and his experience aboard their sailboat that he allowed 14-year-old Mimi to capture a few snapshots of the Lennons, including Sean, in spite of his lingering fear of kidnappers.

As Terry piloted the *Imagine* back into the marina, John asked Fred to take a photo of himself with Yoko in order to memorialise his profound experience that day. Later that week, John and Fred happened upon Terry in a Palm Beach store. As his assistant looked on, John seemed to barely register the captain's presence. For his part, Fred was not really surprised, having already learned on several previous occasions about John's guarded approach to forming friendships of virtually any kind. "He once said that if you give them an autograph, they want a piece of your clothes," Fred recalled. "You give them clothes, they want a lock of your hair. If you give them a lock of your hair, they want to go to bed with you; and if you sleep with them, they devour you."[139]

As the Lennons settled back into their lives at the Dakota, the restlessness that John had experienced during their early days in Palm Beach had returned with a vengeance. With Yoko's mother Isoko "Baba" Ono having flown in from Tokyo for an extended stay, John welcomed the opportunity to travel with Fred back to Cannon Hill, where he could be close to the water in nearby Cold Spring Harbor. As they drove across Long Island, John joked that he was thinking about writing a tell-all book to be entitled *The Real Ballad of John and Yoko*, suggesting that the idea still carried considerable weight in his mindset at this juncture. Even more insistently, he began floating the idea of getting his own boat. After all, Cannon Hill was already outfitted with its own dock.

In early April, with Yoko tending to Baba in the city, John whiled away the hours playing with Sean and noodling around with his new RCA video camera. Clearly missing his wife back at the Dakota and looking forward to her imminent arrival at Cannon Hill, he composed 'Dear Yoko' in a burst of inspiration, as opposed to the hated craftsmanship of practical songwriting. In his early Beatles songs, John often drew on the sound of the early 1960s girl groups to stir his inspiration. With 'Dear Yoko', he updated his approach – in the process, trading on his penchant for disco and turning to Shirley & Company's 1975 dance hit 'Shame, Shame, Shame'.

With his brand-new composition ready for its debut recording, John fired up the video camera on April 11 and captured two takes of 'Dear

Yoko' for posterity, as well as to send via courier to his wife. Still heavily bearded and with his capoed guitar in his lap, he introduced his new song with a reference to 'Oh Yoko!', the *Imagine* album's unabashedly ecstatic closer. "Good evening, Mrs Lennon and your wonderful mother Baba," said John. "Welcome to Cold Spring Harbor. This is a little recitation which you might call 'Oh Yoko! Part 2', circa 1971, -2, or -3. Maybe this time we will get it." Borrowing Buddy Holly's trademark clipped, vocal hiccups, John fashions 'Dear Yoko' into a musical love letter of great sincerity and aplomb: even after so many years, he sings, "I miss you when you're not here".

For the second take, John cracked wise, as was his wont, crediting his video's lighting to Hollywood costume-designing legend Edith Head and, slightly less inexplicably, the song's arrangement to CBS Records executive Saul Rabinowitz. With his encyclopaedic knowledge of early rock 'n' roll, John surely knew of Rabinowitz's involvement in a late 1950s copyright dispute regarding Muddy Waters' Chess Records classic 'Got My Mojo Working', which John referenced, tongue-in-cheek, with the phrase "mojo filter" in the Beatles' 'Come Together'. Lennon had spent the better part of the 1970s in an intellectual-property dispute with Morris Levy, the publisher of Chuck Berry's 'You Can't Catch Me', for which John had lifted a key lyric for 'Come Together'. As with McCartney, who described the Beatles as *"plagiarists extraordinaires"*, John supposedly quipped that "the trick is to steal from the best". When it came to Levy, John was initially forced to settle the lawsuit, only to enjoy the last laugh after the music publisher illegally released the demo recordings for *Rock 'n' Roll* as a mail-order album entitled *Roots: John Lennon Sings The Rock & Roll Hits* in January 1975 on the Adam VIII label. In short order, John launched a countersuit, winning $42,000 in damages from Levy and halting production of the counterfeit LP.[140]

With a second spirited run-through, John brought his demo for 'Dear Yoko' to the finish line. Before switching off the video, he broke into a cockney accent mixed in with a smattering of broken French and German for good measure: "God bless you, Momma, thank you Dad, peace on earth, and good wool to all men, not forgetting the women, of course. This is Long Island Sound, in Cold Spring Harbor, wishing you a *bon* week. Good *nacht*!" As always, John continued to compile his habitual and highly detailed lists of errands for Fred to fulfil. In a late April missive, the typical items were in evidence, including his desire for a fresh batch of reading materials (Nancy Friday's *Men in Love*, which was making headlines at the time for its explicit portrayal of male sexual fantasies, and Pino Turolla's *Beyond the Andes*, a book about the origins of pre-Incan civilisations). In an effort to replicate his setup back in apartment 72, John also wanted a large-screened Sony television set for the living room at Cannon Hill. And when it came to his diet, he made a point of writing "no more yogurt 'balls' and raisins: it's making me sick!" Perhaps most significantly of all, though, he instructed Fred to purchase "a one (1) sail-sailboat – i.e., the 'dumbest' and simplest" vessel that he could find. In short, John wanted to learn how to sail for himself.[141]

Without missing a beat, Fred began seeking out a sailboat for John's personal use. With boatmen hawking their wares up and down the coast of Long Island, Fred had his work cut out for him. Meanwhile, he and John started venturing further and further away from Cannon Hill in the Mercedes in order to "check out the neighbourhood", in John's words. As with their excursions back in Palm Beach in the red Caddy, their leisurely drives offered the opportunity for John to toy with the car radio, scanning up and down the FM dial to catch up on, and often critique, the latest hits or wax nostalgic to the sounds of the golden oldies. He rarely listened to a complete song, save for the instances in which he happened upon something that really caught his fancy. If the Rolling Stones' 'Miss You' made its way across the airwaves, for example, John would smile with delight, singing along and observing that, if nothing else, Mick Jagger had plundered a standout tune from his recent and highly public divorce from wife Bianca. When Beatles songs played on the radio, John frequently changed the dial, complaining that all he could think about were the particular sessions that produced the tracks – and how he felt at the time – rather than being able to sit back and enjoy them.

One afternoon, as Fred drove the station wagon past a shopping mall near West Hills, New York, John heard a familiar voice crackling over the car radio. "Fuck a Pig! It's Paul!" he exclaimed. And sure enough, it was 'Coming Up', which Paul had released as a single at the onset of the same weekend John had concocted 'Dear Yoko'. For John, 'Coming Up' was nothing short of infectious, with its catchy lyrics about love coming back again and again, "like a flower", set against an array of ska-infused electronica.

"Not bad!" John announced from his place in the passenger's seat as 'Coming Up' concluded. While he had tended to dismiss much of Paul's recent work as empty-headed instances of bubblegum pop, this new tune had truly caught his ear. Quite suddenly, John found himself entranced by the staccato beat of Paul's new sound. For the life of him, John couldn't get 'Coming Up' out of his head. "It's driving me crackers!" he said, as he experienced the jarring return of the old competitive energies of his Beatles-era songwriting rivalry with Paul.[142]

At breakfast the next morning, John was still humming the catchy tune. In a July 1980 *Rolling Stone* review, Stephen Holden would describe the song as "a push-button paean to the future," exceeding "Abba in nervous, hook-filled mechanization. Even if you hate it, it's liable to stick to your mind like chewing gum to the bottom of a shoe." John was hooked all right. In short order, he instructed Fred to set up a hi-fi at Cannon Hill so that he could make closer inspection of Paul's latest albums, including *Back To The Egg* and the upcoming *McCartney II*, which was set to be released the following month. But ultimately, it was 'Coming Up', an intentionally over-produced marvel with McCartney playing all of the instrumentation himself, that caught John's ear. For the recording, Paul had treated his voice with a heavy dose of varispeed, the pitch-control tool that George Martin had deployed on Beatles records to pioneering effect on such songs as John's 'In My Life' and 'Strawberry Fields Forever'.[143]

According to Paul, *McCartney II* was completed in a whirlwind following his release from detention in Japan. "In the clink, I had a lot of time to think," he admitted. "I just thought, 'well, before I do anything else, I want to finish up the solo album.'" He was especially excited about the creative process associated with 'Coming Up': "I was working with a machine where you can vary the speed of the tape recorder, so you can speed your voice up or slow it down. I sped my voice up through a sort of echo machine I was playing around with. It's very much like sitting down with lumps of clay. You put one down, and then put another down, and it starts to make itself into a face or something. In this case, it made itself into the song 'Coming Up.'"

McCartney's painstaking efforts to alter his voice undoubtedly struck a chord with John, given Lennon's well-known aversion for the sound of his own vocals. As George Martin later recalled, John "had an inborn dislike of his own voice which I could never understand. He was always saying to me, '*Do* something with my voice! You know, put something on it. Smother it with tomato ketchup or something. Make it different.'"

According to the Beatles' vaunted engineer Geoff Emerick, "That was typical John Lennon. Despite the fact that he was one of the greatest rock 'n' roll singers of all time, he hated the sound of his own voice and was constantly imploring us to make him sound different. 'Can you squeeze that up there?' he would say, or 'Can you make it sound nasally?'" To remedy his issues with his own voice, John would provide Martin and Emerick with metaphors for altering his voice in very specific ways. In one instance, John had asked Martin to imbue his voice with "the feel of James Dean gunning his motorcycle down a highway". Perhaps most famously, when it came to recording 'Tomorrow Never Knows' for the band's *Revolver* LP, John requested that the Beatles' production team "make me sound like the Dalai Lama chanting from a mountaintop".[144]

For John, 'Coming Up' proved to be a watershed moment – an instance in which Paul had surprised his old songwriting partner by pushing the boundaries, by going *too far* in a pop-music environment that had come to expect conventionality from the most successful pop artist among the former Beatles. Over the past several years, Paul's new music had failed to impress John on any level. As it happened, John had been fortunate to hear the "freak" version of Paul's new song on the American airwaves at all. Executives at Paul's new label Columbia Records had a sense that his live version of 'Coming Up', which had been recorded back on December 17 with Wings at Glasgow's Apollo Theatre, would be more appealing to listeners than the LP track, with its hyper-pronounced studio hijinks. To this end, Columbia pressed promotional copies for American DJs, who played the live version of 'Coming Up' in droves, ensuring that the single became McCartney's seventh US chart-topping hit.

In support of 'Coming Up', McCartney concocted a clever video to accompany the LP version of the song, complete with Paul impersonating such artists as Buddy Holly, Frank Zappa, the Shadows' guitarist Hank Marvin, and Sparks' keyboard player Ron Mael. On May 17, McCartney debuted the music video on *Saturday Night Live*. In a timely comedic turn, *SNL* personality Don Novello – in his guise as Father Guido Sarducci – briefly interviewed Paul before the video debut, even hinting that he might ask about a Beatles reunion before taking a very different tack. "This is a question I really hate to ask you," said Novello, "but I'm a journalist, I have to do it, if you don't mind. Paul, if you could be *any* animal, what would it be?" After McCartney replied that he'd be a koala bear, Novello didn't miss a beat, reminding viewers of the pop star's recent unpleasantness back in Japan, saying "Did you hear that? A koala bear – the little animal that eats eucalyptus leaves, getting stoned all of the time!"

For John, hearing 'Coming Up' that afternoon in the station wagon had a revelatory effect on him. "I thought that 'Coming Up' was great," he remarked later that year. "And I like the freak version that he made in his barn better than that live Glasgow one," adding that "if I'd have been with him, I'd have said, '*That's* the one to do.'" Now sitting at the dawn of a new decade, John clearly recognised that he was in a much better psychological space to benefit from the competitive energy that had driven Lennon and McCartney as songwriters at the height of their powers during the Beatles years. By the 1970s, John admitted, "I was so full of meself. Centred. I didn't give a shit what he was doing." Besides, said John, Paul "was putting *so much* stuff out" that it was difficult to keep up. And "sales-wise, *forget it*," as far as John was concerned. Paul "*always* had more fans than me, even in the Cavern. So there's no comparison on that level." As far as artistry goes, said John, it would be like pitting Magritte and Picasso against each other. "How can you compare it?"[145]

Regardless of his personal history with Paul, 'Coming Up' had clearly registered with John on a highly visceral level. "If I'm impressed by a record on the [radio], I immediately want to write [a song]. Warren Beatty said it about movies. 'A great movie is one that makes you want to make a movie.'" For John, catching wind of an exemplary record had the same effect. "I wish I'd made that," John would inevitably think to himself. "Shit, I'd go right out and make it, you know? I don't know what it is, but he [Beatty] is right: when I hear a great record, I want to *make* it."[146]

With his competitive juices flowing at an unprecedented rate, John tasked Fred with getting him up to speed on the contemporary music scene. To accomplish this end, Fred stocked up on cassette releases by such new artists as the Pretenders, Lene Lovich, and Madness. Driving around in the station wagon with Fred at the wheel, John spent hours cruising along the North Shore with the contemporary sounds washing over him from the luxury vehicle's stereo system. While John enjoyed songs like the Pretenders' 'Brass In Pocket' and Lovich's 'Lucky Number', he was particularly taken with Madness, a British ska band that was currently making waves in the UK with tunes like 'One Step Beyond' and 'My Girl'. John had been taken by ska, with its Jamaican, pre-reggae origins, since the 1960s, and he was clearly hungry for more. In short order, Fred rounded up more ska cassettes for the car stereo from the likes of Selecter and the Specials.

A few days later, John and Fred visited a North Shore boat dealership on one of their regular Long Island drives. Coneys Marine, a family owned business, had been in operation since the early 1900s. Sporting the slogan "We've always had at least one foot in the water!", the business was conducted out of a red clapboard building on Route 110 in Huntington, New York, only a few miles away from Cannon Hill. For his starter boat, John purchased an $800 dinghy with a two-horsepower, one-cylinder British Seagull outboard motor. For the boat's maiden voyage, John picked the first sunny afternoon to test it out in Cold Spring Harbor. With Helen and Sean in tow, John and Fred pushed the boat into the shallow water below Cannon Hill and clambered aboard. With a yank of the starter cord, the motor noisily purred to life and John guided the rudder towards Oyster Bay, the headwaters of Long Island Sound.

When the dinghy reached the bay, John turned off the motor so that they could enjoy the sounds of the sea lapping at the boat. Besides an ominous silence, the only other sound emanated from the gulls shrieking in the distance. After a while, Sean asked if he could try one of the oars, and, with Fred taking another oar for ballast, they began slowly rowing back towards Cold Spring Harbor. Eventually, John restarted the motor with a jerk of the cord to speed things along. And that's when it happened: as they shifted around in the small boat to give Sean a turn at piloting the rudder, John inadvertently bumped the head of the motor with his elbow, and the outboard sputtered to a stop. When John and Fred proved unable to restart the motor, they shrugged their shoulders in defeat and began rowing with all of their might back to Cannon Hill. "I'm sure glad Mother wasn't here to see this," John exclaimed. "We'd have never lived it down!"[147]

Later that evening, Yoko made her way to Cannon Hill from the city, with Baba and Yoko's sister Setsuko in tow. No sooner had Yoko returned than she challenged her husband to go on a 10-day vow of silence to cleanse his soul and detoxify his senses from worldly distractions such as current events. Yoko would achieve similar ends by occasionally sending her husband on a series of "directional trips" in order to re-centre himself and reset his place in the universe. John referred to Yoko's tendency to send him on these impromptu journeys as "East meets West". During the Lost Weekend, Yoko had added a directional man, Takashi Yoshikawa, to her standing retinue of psychics, numerologists, and astrologers in order to establish a sense of good luck and happy tidings for her future undertakings. In October 1976, Yoko had sent John on a world tour at Yoshikawa's bidding, believing that a westerly voyage would improve his karma. When Elliot Mintz asked about the necessity of such exercises, John encouraged him to have faith in Yoko's wisdom, just as he had done when he returned to the Dakota in 1975. "Trust her!" he said to Mintz. "Just trust her!" Meanwhile, Ringo came to understand Yoko's motives for the directional trips in a clearer light, recalling that she "used to send him away on his own so he'd grow up. I don't know if he grew up, but he certainly went places without her."[148]

For John, the vow of silence at Cannon Hill was no easy feat, requiring him both to give up talking – a truly difficult undertaking for a person who could speak fluently on a wide range of issues – as well as coffee, one of his most cherished addictions, second only to his beloved Gitanes. Sean and Fred, in particular, were given express instructions not to speak to John. This was especially challenging for Fred, who was still expected to join his employer on their regular errands and their dinghy excursions in the harbour. As for Sean, he had other things on his mind, later recalling that this was the spring when "I learnt to skip stones, to make paper planes, to build a fire, to put a worm on a hook, to draw monkeys, and to steer a sailing boat."[149]

While Yoko forbade John from reading newspapers and magazines, there was no embargo on nonfiction books, so John passed the time rereading G. Gordon Liddy's *Will* up in his Cannon Hill bedroom. One of the central figures in the Watergate scandal and a former FBI agent, Liddy championed the notion of triumphing over adversity through the sheer exertion of human willpower. John was fascinated by the lengths to which Liddy would go in order to demonstrate his will. In one instance, the disgraced former FBI man lashed himself to a tree during an electrical storm. In perhaps the most famous passage from *Will*, Liddy told the story of holding a burning match beneath his palm and refusing to show any outward signs of pain even as the stench of charred flesh began to emanate from his wound.

In the last hours of his vow of silence, John dashed off a spate of notes for Fred. The first concerned Yoko, who had returned to the Dakota, later claiming that she had come down with a case of the Russian flu and that her husband and son should keep their distance to avoid infection. In truth, she had resolved to make yet another attempt at going cold turkey with the assistance of her friend Sam Green, who worked as the Lennons' art dealer. John instructed Fred to arrange for the daily delivery of potted flowers for his wife, adding "make sure that it says from Daddy and Sean (you usually don't tell her who sends them!)" While Liz Smith had been erroneous in her column about a lock-happy Lennon turning his Dakota apartment into a veritable fortress, John had grown concerned about the security at Cannon Hill, writing to Fred and asking him to "explain to ME why we are sleeping here with a front door that any nut can open (it doesn't lock) – people know I'm here – gardeners, painters, etc."[150]

On April 30, John concluded his vow of silence. He also brought his media embargo to an end – and in just the nick of time. When he fired up the television in his Cannon Hill bedroom, he learned about President Jimmy Carter's ill-fated attempt earlier that same week to rescue the American hostages in Iran. Over the past several months, diplomatic negotiations had stilled, prompting President Carter to launch Operation Eagle Claw, a clandestine manoeuvre in the Iranian desert that had resulted in the deaths of eight American serviceman when an American helicopter collided with another aircraft. When they learned about the rescue attempt, the hostage-takers relocated most of the American captives from the embassy to secret locations around Tehran. For Lennon and millions of other concerned viewers around the world, the terrible situation in Iran and the hostages' precarious hope for survival had suddenly been rendered even more bleak.

That same day, John trimmed off the beard he had nursed since the previous autumn. It was in this clean-shaven state that John first laid eyes on the "dumbest" and "simplest" single-mast boat for which he had longed since lounging on the *Imagine* back in Palm Beach. Fulfilling his boss' instructions, Fred had ordered a 14-foot O'Day Javelin sailboat from Coneys Marine. On Thursday, May 1, owner Tyler Coneys piloted the sailboat from Huntington Harbor to the rickety wooden dock below Cannon Hill. John was beside himself with anticipation, standing on the porch of the estate and scanning the horizon for his prized new acquisition. When he saw it come into view, he bounded for the dock, where he and Fred boarded the sailboat for the first time. "All my life I've been dreaming of having my own boat," said John. "I can't wait to learn how to sail!"[151]

In short order, the 24-year-old Coneys took John out into the harbour to show him the ropes. With Fred looking on, John wasted little time in christening his new boat *Isis* in honour of the Egyptian fertility goddess and protector of seafarers. As they tacked the boat around Cold Spring Harbor, John became increasingly comfortable with Coneys, a highly competent sailor who agreed to provide the rock legend with additional instruction as the month progressed. After rigging the boat, Coneys spent the next several weeks schooling John in the fundamentals of sailing. As Coneys later recalled, "We went sailing as many times as I could after work. We spent a lot of time talking together on the boat and going out sailing. We'd just sail around Cold Spring Harbor [and] Oyster Bay." On their furthest trip together, Coneys and Lennon sailed out to the Sand Hole, an inlet on the edge of Caumsett State Park. John shrewdly observed that the most difficult aspect of sailing involved learning to read sudden wind shifts. To Coneys' amusement, John taught himself how to follow the shifts by assessing the direction of the smoke from his ever-present Gitanes.[152]

Meanwhile, John instructed Fred to round up all of the literature that he could about the art of sailing. For John, it was as if all of his reading over the years about Thor Heyerdahl and the Vikings had come vividly to life. Having possession of his own sailboat also forced John to come to terms with his lifelong fantasies about the seafaring lives of his father and grandfather, and his own fear of travelling into the unknown. On the one hand, he longed to put himself at risk on the high seas, while on the other, he simply couldn't fathom the idea of untethering himself from his routine.

With Fred in tow, John tested his emergent skills as a sailor by taking the *Isis* on manoeuvres along the North Shore, all the while continuing his lessons in the company of Coneys. By this point, John had already begun imagining a much larger endeavour for testing his seagoing skills. For the time being, he was content with slowly venturing further and further away from the safety of Cannon Hill's dock and deeper and deeper into Long Island Sound. In one memorable afternoon, John and Fred sailed by the vicinity of singer-songwriter Billy Joel's Cold Spring Harbor manse. Certain that they had moored the *Isis* within sight of the home that had served as the distinctive cover shot for Joel's recent *Glass Houses* LP, John screamed out, "Hey, Billy, I have all of your records!" Indeed, John and Yoko were partial to the Bronx native's work, citing 'Just The Way You Are' as "their song". For his part, Joel idolised the Beatles – John especially – and within a month, he would apply for residence from the Dakota's co-op board. To his dismay, the board rejected Joel's application on June 29, citing the growing number of fans, vis-à-vis the John Lennons, who had begun hanging out in front of the archway.[153]

While John grew more comfortable piloting the *Isis* about the harbour as May progressed, his budding sailing career was not without its mishaps. On one particularly windy afternoon, John and Fred took Sean out for a sail, with Helen and Coneys along for the ride. For Sean, that day in the harbour would emerge as a central memory from his childhood. "I remember that at Cold Spring Harbor there was a green sailboat," he later recalled, "and I think in my mind that I named it *Flower*." At a crucial moment during the excursion, John turned the tiller over to Fred in order to light up a fresh Gitane. In the same instant, a strong gust of wind blew in, causing the boat to pick up speed. Instinctively, Fred pulled hard on the rudder, causing the *Isis* to capsize, spilling everyone into the drink – save for Coneys, an expert sailor to his core, who skilfully managed to position himself on the belly of the boat. Meanwhile, Sean remembered wearing his orange lifejacket and "seeing my flip-flops that I'd got in Japan floating away. I was very upset because I loved those flip-flops, but [John] said, 'Don't worry, we'll get you another pair.' I said, 'Are there any fish in the water?' and he was like, 'Yes,' which really scared me. So I remember my dad protecting me in the water. It's actually a nice memory, just floating around in the ocean with my dad and this capsized boat."[154]

As for Fred, John couldn't help good-naturedly ribbing his assistant after Coneys assisted him in righting the *Isis* and retrieving its soggy passengers from the harbour. "You really disgraced the family name this time, *Seaman*," he joked. For John, the incident that afternoon had left him feeling more confident that he could handle such a "worst-case scenario". Besides, what he really feared wasn't the ocean, but rather, what would happen if Yoko found out about the mishap. "Not a word of this to Mother," he cautioned the others as they made their way ashore.[155]

Not surprisingly, during this same period, John's creative momentum began to pick up steam. As he later recalled, "I got rid of all that self-consciousness about telling myself, 'You can't do that. That song's not good enough. Remember, you're the guy who wrote 'A Day In The Life'. Try again.'" At this point, he began revising a song-fragment entitled 'My Life', which he had been tinkering with on his Ovation acoustic since the late fall months of 1979. A slow number in the style of the Beach Boys' 'Don't Worry Baby', 'My Life' offered a gentle love song for Yoko, who can be heard on some of the demos. Dedicating his very survival and existence to his wife, John entreats Yoko to experience the fullness of their life together, "to share the dreams and nightmares" alike. In sharp contrast with the piano demos for 'My Life' that John had recorded back at the Dakota – with their gospel-tinged, even dirge-like qualities – 'My Life' had begun to assume a more wistful, folkish nature during his acoustic guitar renditions of the song.[156]

As for Yoko, the time away from the city had proven to be very profitable in terms of her own creative renaissance. By this point, with her heroin addiction having lost its hold, Yoko had found herself, like her husband, entering into a new phase of artistic inspiration. Amazingly, she had been able to preserve her relapse from John. Her only confidante, it seemed, was Green, who had assisted her in finally kicking the addiction. To show her gratitude, Yoko presented Green with the gift of an exquisite samurai sword. With summer looming on the horizon, she began to fashion lyrics about her experience, writing "I gave you my knife" in 'Walking On Thin Ice' to memorialise her sense of self-renewal.

The song began to take shape for Yoko on one of the Lennons' car trips between Cold Spring Harbor and New York City. Before long, the lyrics emerged full-flower – in the process, underscoring the terrible risk that her brush with full-on addiction had entailed for her and her family alike. In 'Walking On Thin Ice', she admits to paying a steep interpersonal price for "throwing the dice in the air." With the lyrics in place, Yoko challenged herself to concoct an ambitious new sound to bring the composition's music to fruition. "I wanted to push it a little further, experimentally," she later recalled. "So I was thinking about Alban Berg, in one of his operas, you know, where a drunk is going 'ahaahaahaa'. Just sort of saying things, but in such a way that the emphasis is all wrong, distorted."[157]

For Yoko, the notion of channelling Berg was nothing short of a revelation. The Austrian composer was an early champion of the 12-tone technique, variously known as dodecaphony and 12-note composition, wherein all 12 notes of the chromatic scale receive equal time across a musical composition, thus ensuring that no single note is emphasised to the detriment of another. With 'Walking On Thin Ice', the marriage of Yoko's lyrics with Berg's technique promised to afford the songwriter with the perfect vehicle for her unique brand of vocal performance. In the early 1970s, *Rolling Stone*'s Jonathan Cott described Yoko's singing as the product of a 16-track range. According to Cott, "Yoko's voice enters sound to reveal its most basic frequential characteristics and proposes to the listener that if he wants to hear, he might as well stop trying." To his credit, John had been an early fan of Yoko's vocal stylings. "She becomes her voice," he once observed, "and you get touched." But he also recognised that her approach to songwriting was markedly different from his own. "We're both looking at the same thing from different sides of the table," he remarked. "Mine is literate, hers is revolutionary."[158]

Even still, Yoko knew full well that pulling off such an ambitious structure for 'Walking On Thin Ice' – merging the unusual qualities of her multifarious vocal sound with Berg's innovative compositional form – would be no easy feat. But having bested her addiction and rediscovered her muse, she was more than willing to try.

CHAPTER 8

Megan Jaye

As John continued his training on the *Isis* with Tyler Coneys, he began to imagine a much longer, more adventurous journey to test his seagoing mettle. With his two cousins Ellen and Kevin ready and willing to help out as deckhands, Coneys was prepared to charter a sailing yacht at a moment's notice. When John revealed his master plan to go on an extended voyage, Yoko readily assented, provided, that is, that she could consult Takashi Yoshikawa, her directional man first. With Yoko's blessing, Yoshikawa recommended that John plot his voyage in a southeasterly direction from New York City and that he depart on June 4. Coneys learned about John's plans during one of their sailing trips when his client informed him that "Yoko said I can go to Bermuda, but we gotta do this in, like, 10 days. You gotta get it together right now 'cause we have to go on this date." With the directional man's suggestion in hand, Tyler promptly mapped out a five-day, 635-mile voyage across the Atlantic Ocean from Newport, Rhode Island, to Bermuda.[159]

For John, travelling by sailboat across the Atlantic excited the very same thirst for seafaring adventure that he savoured in the great works of Thor Heyerdahl, especially *Kon-Tiki: Across the Pacific by Raft* (1948) or, more recently, *The Tigris Expedition: In Search of Our Beginnings* (1979), in which Heyerdahl and his fellow travellers burnt their ship, like a modern-day Cortés, at the mouth of the war-torn Red Sea in "protest against the inhuman elements in the world of 1978" – namely, the hi-tech military aeroplanes and warships that swarmed the *Tigris* and refused its landing rights. "To the innocent masses in all industrialized countries, we direct our appeal," Heyerdahl wrote in an open letter to UN Secretary-General Kurt Waldheim. "We must wake up to the insane reality of our time." John would voice a similar sentiment throughout much of his public life. As far back as 1968, he had remarked that "our society is run by insane people for insane objectives. I think we're being run by maniacs for maniacal ends, and I think I'm liable to be put away as insane for expressing that. That's what's insane about it."[160]

John had recently read Heyerdahl's *Early Man and the Ocean: The Beginning of Navigation and Seaborn Civilizations* (1979), but his favourite title, by far, was the explorer's epic *Kon-Tiki*. For John, it was the book that elevated his senses, transporting him into the mysterious world of mystery and adventure associated with seafaring travel. As Heyerdahl wrote in *Kon-Tiki*: "Some people believe in fate, others don't. I do, and I don't. It may seem at times as if invisible fingers move us about like puppets on strings. But for sure, we are not born to be dragged along. We can grab the strings ourselves and adjust our course at every crossroad, or take off at any little trail into the unknown." For John – who had experienced virtually everything that life had to offer and then some – the opportunity to surrender himself to the unknown, to the whimsy of fate, was most welcome, indeed.[161]

But John wouldn't be leaving for Bermuda just yet. Before allowing him free rein to make an ocean voyage – with all of the potential risk that travelling on the high seas entails – Yoko's directional man recommended that John reset his karma and overall psychic alignment with a transatlantic, southeasterly flight to South Africa. As far as John was concerned, making the 7,000-mile flight was a small price to pay to earn his upcoming ocean adventure. Besides, South Africa's mystical, legend-making Table Mountain offered the perfect locale for getting in some thoroughgoing meditation before hitting the high seas.

Meanwhile, Yoko contended with a spate of Beatles-related business. On the eve of John's South African journey, London's *Daily Mirror* reported that John planned to sell his share of Apple Corps, the Beatles' holding company and the epicentre of their business. Apparently, John's recent, fervent interest in sailing had made its way to the media, albeit erroneously. According to the *Daily Mirror*'s report, who seemed to have concocted the article out of whole cloth,

Lennon has just bought a 63-foot yacht. And last night, investors were clamouring to buy his slice of Apple. The 40-year-old [sic] star who lives a quiet life in New York said inquiries from would-be buyers are driving him crazy. "The phone hasn't stopped ringing," he said. But in a rare interview, he revealed he is selling up to concentrate on the artistic life. Yoko explained, "We are both artists and we are really big into being a family. Those are the things that we care about." She added: "We've bought a good-sized boat and we will live comfortably on it."

Not surprisingly, back at the Dakota, the telephone had begun ringing off the hook. As he fielded the calls, Rich DePalma made a joke of confirming John's interest in selling his share of the Beatles. "Make an offer," he said in jest to media inquiries. "I'll pass it along."[162]

For Yoko, Apple business was never far away. That spring, she had contended with one Beatles-related matter after another. On March 24, Capitol Records had released the *Rarities* LP, a compilation of previously unreleased tracks and alternate versions of classic Beatles' songs. Always hungry for new Beatles' content, American fans bought the album in droves, ensuring that the release registered a gold-record showing. Representing John's interests with Apple, Yoko had become embroiled in a lawsuit instigated by the company. Since the previous September, Apple had been in litigation with the producers of *Beatlemania*, the musical that had run for more than two years at Broadway's Winter Garden Theatre before going on a national tour.

Apple director Neil Aspinall was determined to see the lawsuit through – especially after failing to block the release of *Live! At The Star-Club In Hamburg, Germany; 1962* in April 1977. The double-album had been cobbled together from the Beatles' final residency in West Germany in December 1962. The tapes ended up in the hands of Ted "Kingsize" Taylor, who later claimed that John gave him the rights to the live recordings in exchange for a round of drinks. George Harrison had been particularly disgusted by the tapes' 1977 release, describing them as "rubbish" and remarking that "the Star-Club recording was the crummiest recording ever made in our name". Having produced a hit Broadway show, *Beatlemania* offered much higher stakes as far as Aspinall and the Beatles' representatives were concerned. In addition to a soundtrack album, a *Beatlemania* movie was reportedly in the works. In the lawsuit, Apple Corps sued the show's creator Steve Leber and the musical's producer David Krebs for copyright and trademark infringement. By autumn, Aspinall expected Apple Corps lawyers to be conducting depositions – possibly even with the former Beatles themselves going under oath.[163]

On May 23, John's flight touched down at Jan Smuts International Airport before he made his connection to Cape Town, the country's "Mother City" and home of the nearby Robben Island, where political dissident Nelson Mandela had been imprisoned since 1964 for waging his decades-long struggle against apartheid, South Africa's institutionalised system of racial segregation. John checked into the luxurious Mount Nelson Hotel, nestled in the shadows of Table Mountain. At first, he managed to keep his identity a secret, having checked into the hotel as "Mr John Greenwood", a variation on his regular alias, which he variously spelled as "John Green" and "John Greene". Even still, area photographers had caught wind of the ex-Beatle's presence on South African shores not long after his arrival. Working as a stringer for *The Argus* at the time, Ivor Markman joined the chase, hoping, as with Patrick Partington back in Palm Beach, to snap a photo of John for the international wire services.

During the early part of John's stay, the management at the Mount Nelson Hotel narrowly avoided a potentially embarrassing situation involving their famous guest. Still fighting off his jet lag – adhering to South African Standard Time, Cape Town was six hours later than New York City – John paused for a cat nap under a tree in one of the hotel gardens. Mistaking Lennon for a vagrant, another guest had complained to the Mount Nelson staff. In short order, hotel security sprang into action, briefly confronting the unwelcome visitor before belatedly realising his identity.

For John, the main attraction was Table Mountain, the flat-topped sandstone mountain just a few miles to the south, famously capped by its rugged two-mile wide plateau. During his stay, John established a daily routine in which he would wake up, make his own bed (to the surprise of his housekeeper), and rendezvous with John Parker, the taxi driver who had ferried him from the airport to the Mount Nelson Hotel. Back in those apartheid-riven days, his taxi driver would have been known as "Cape-Coloured" for being of mixed European and African descent. Acting as his de facto tour guide, the driver transported his celebrated passenger to and from the mountain vista, where John passed the hours in quiet meditation. At his driver's request, John posed for several pictures – including at least one with Mr Parker himself. With John's permission, he later sold the photos to the Sunday *Cape Times* – provided that he waited until after his famous client had left South Africa.[164]

At one point, John also availed Mr Parker to take him to one of Cape Town's massage parlours. By this point, his abiding need to slake his libidinal desires had become burdensome. Back in September, he had devoted a goodly portion of his audio diary to addressing the issue of human sexuality and its seemingly ceaseless pull on our psyches. The subject had been occasioned by John's reading of an interview with Truman Capote on the eve of the publication of *Music For Chameleons* (1980). In the interview, Capote referenced the experience of British novelist E.M. Forster, who lived into his nineties, always hoping that his sexual urges would finally lose their hold on him, only to discover that they had emerged as an even greater burden during his twilight years. In his audio diary, John likens Forster's dilemma to his own, concluding that the thought of being plagued by erotic tendencies into old age left him feeling "depressed" and wondering about the possibility of his urges following him beyond death and into the afterlife. As John remarked in his audio diary:

> I just thought "shit!" 'cause I was always waiting for them to lessen, but I suppose it's going to go on forever. "Forever" is a bit too strong a word, but say it'll go on until you leave this body anyway. Let's hope. The game is to conquer it, as they say, before you come back for more. And who wants to come back just to come?

For her part, Yoko was no dupe when it came to matters of fidelity. "There was one time when he and another guy went off together to the ocean," she recalled. "Later on, John was showing me photographs of the two of them and I said, 'Wait a minute – someone else had to be there to take the photographs.' He just laughed and said, 'I can never get anything past you.'"[165]

On at least one occasion, Mr Parker drove John up to the Kramat tombs atop Signal Hill, the flat-cropped mountain overlooking nearby Anchor Bay. John was especially interested in the Muslim shrine located on Signal Hill's southern rampart. The picturesque location was dedicated to the city's one-time Muslim slaves, who had been held in captivity on Signal Hill, which formerly served as a means for communicating with ships via semaphore in the harbour about weather-related issues. But for the most part, John kept to himself during his South African adventure. As the housekeeper at the Mount Nelson Hotel later recalled, he ate simple meals, did yoga on the hotel lawn, and, when he wasn't meditating on Table Mountain or lounging in one of the hotel's sumptuous gardens, spent hours on the phone with his wife, whom he was hoping to coax into a Cape Town visit in 1981.[166]

On May 25 – Memorial Day weekend back in the States – John placed yet another transatlantic call – this time, to May Pang in New York City. For May, who hadn't heard from John since December 1978, the call felt like a bolt out of the blue. During their 90-minute call, John admitted that he might have called sooner, but he had secreted her telephone number so effectively that he could no longer locate it for himself. Clearly in much better spirits than their last conversation, John hoped that his one-time assistant might come visit him sometime at Cold Spring Harbor. The two former lovers spoke animatedly about contemporary music, including John's growing interest in new wave – the Pretenders, especially – despite his earlier disdain for the genre. "He told me that he was starting to write again," May later recalled, even hinting that he might be making his return to the studio in the not-so-distant future.[167]

As it turned out, John's directional trip to Cape Town would be decidedly short-lived. Not surprisingly, it was a sudden interest from the media that led him to beat a hasty retreat. It all came about during a bout of inclement weather. Leaving his chauffeur back in the car, John rushed into a clothing store to buy some much-needed rainwear. When it came time to make payment, he handed his American Express credit card to Dennis Dean, a local garment salesman. As Dean later recalled, "a man with a peaked cap bought a raincoat, bemoaning the fact that he had been told one would not be necessary." In short order, Dean tipped off the press about John's presence in South Africa.[168]

On May 28, John decided to cut his trip short and made the long flight back to New York City. During John's absence in South Africa, Tyler Coneys had continued making preparations for the upcoming voyage to Bermuda. He dutifully presented Yoko with a draft listing of 17 potential crew members, along with the dates and time of their births, for consideration by her team of psychics and numerologists. But for Coneys, the real challenge turned out to be landing a charter on short notice, which had proven to be exceedingly difficult with the summer season already off to a steady start. Working with McMichael Yacht Brokers in Newport, Rhode Island, Coneys settled on Hank Halsted, a 30-year-old captain who had just returned from a 10-day tour around the Caribbean. While the burly, shaggy-bearded Halsted had been concerned about sailing to Bermuda with a party of strangers, he agreed to the booking based on Coneys' sterling reputation among boatmen. For his part, Halsted was in charge of the day-to-day operations of the *Megan Jaye*, a 43-foot aft-cockpit, Hinckley centreboard sloop. Owned by Dr Dick Jones, an ear, nose, and throat specialist, the boat had been christened in honour of Jones' daughter. With time quickly running out, Coneys and Cap'n Hank, as he was known among the other yachtsmen, spent a week re-rigging the *Megan Jaye* in advance of their planned departure on Wednesday evening, June 4.

That morning, Fred drove the four crewmates – John and the three Coneys cousins – to Republic Airport in Farmingdale, New York, to make the short plane ride to Newport. To celebrate their upcoming trip, John and the Coneys wore matching sundial T-shirts. "They were really cool," Tyler recalled. "If you leaned back and held out the string hanging from the middle of the T-shirt attached to something like a [sundial] gnomon, then you could tell which was north. John liked that. We all did."[169]

With a teary-eyed Sean waving goodbye on the runway, the chartered Cessna took off for coastal Rhode Island. John had already planned his reunion with his son to occur roughly seven days hence. When the *Megan Jaye* made land in Bermuda, Sean would make the flight along with Fred and Uda-san. But as Cap'n Hank and Tyler well knew, John's ocean trek would be no easy voyage, with the schooner making its way across the Atlantic, passing through storm-ridden Cape Hatteras and into the notorious Bermuda Triangle, with its warm tropical waters acting as the setting for some of the world's busiest shipping lanes.

But before John's journey into the unknown could begin, he had to run a few last-minute errands. As the most inexperienced member of the crew, John was assigned to serve as the boat's galley cook. Before they embarked for Bermuda, he insisted on a visit to a Newport health food store to outfit the boat's larder. With Cap'n Hank looking on, John purchased a selection of vegetables and brown rice, along with nori, the staple of Japanese cuisine that consisted of edible seaweed sheets. At this point, Cap'n Hank – who still hadn't cottoned on to John's Beatles heritage – mentioned that he had a Japanese girlfriend. "Oh, so do I," John deadpanned. Having realised that he had forgotten to bring along his guitar, John requested a side trip to a nearby pawn shop. "Oh, there's always starving musicians," he told his crewmates. "You can always find music equipment at a pawn shop." For their part, John's shipmates contributed a baggie of recreational marijuana, which they smuggled on board the *Megan Jaye*.[170]

At 8 p.m., slightly before sunset, Cap'n Hank steered the schooner away from Murphy's Dock, setting a southeasterly course for Bermuda. As they pulled away, John looked up at the open sky, remarking that "this is cool. I'm moving out of the clouds, moving forward into a clear horizon." As events would show, the calm weather wouldn't last for long. The last land they encountered was Block Island, some nine miles off the coast of Rhode Island and just 14 miles away from Montauk Point, the easternmost end of Long Island. At this juncture, the *Megan Jaye* was nearly 700 miles away from Bermuda. Not long after they passed Block Island, Cap'n Hank figured out the identity of his famous passenger. "Holy shit, you'd better not fuck this one up," he said to himself. "I think you've got valuable cargo."[171]

In terms of navigating the *Megan Jaye*'s journey, Cap'n Hank was a traditionalist, adopting the time-honoured methods of celestial navigation and dead reckoning. John enjoyed observing Cap'n Hank as he plotted the boat's course with a sextant. "That's what Yoko does every night to figure out how we should best be living," he remarked. Hank chuckled to himself, "Yeah, that's the other navigation." To protect the crew and the boat against any sudden changes in the elements, Cap'n Hank had devised a system of ship's watches in which shipmates would serve three hours on watch followed by six hours of rest. The first watch would be carried out by Kevin and Ellen, while John and Tyler would handle the second watch. This left Cap'n Hank taking the solo – or "dog watch" – by himself.[172]

Cap'n Hank was especially concerned about the *Megan Jaye*'s passage through the Gulf Stream, the 62-mile-wide warm-water ocean current in the western region of the North Atlantic. The abrupt temperature contrasts associated with the Gulf Stream would often result in rapid shifts in weather conditions. "It's a weather-maker," said Cap'n Hank. "The Gulf Stream just always puts a big spin on things," adding that "in truth, everything that I was scared might happen did happen, twice over."[173]

After some 30 hours of smooth sailing, the *Megan Jaye* began to encounter cloudy skies on Friday, June 6. As the storm clouds grew darker and the ocean turbulence increased, all of the crew – save for John and

Cap'n Hank – fell victim to seasickness. Suddenly, Cap'n Hank's watch schedule was rendered useless. As Halsted later recalled, it was his own fault. "I was so cheap with the owner's money I'd refused to pay Hinckley's $10,000 for an autopilot, so 24/7 while we were at sea someone had to sit at the steering wheel."[174]

But even still, Cap'n Hank felt that the charter was going well. "It was great sailing," he remembered. "Eighteen hours at the helm for me is a relatively normal drill. I can sit there in bliss, feeling every molecule going across the rudder and just drive a boat offshore. For me, it was no huge thing, and I was 30 years old, so driving the boat was a ball. I kept driving for a long time, getting myself plenty tired. That was part of the dues in those days. It's an interesting thing for a captain because all you have is the ingenuity and strength of your crew." Unfortunately for Cap'n Hank and the *Megan Jaye*, the crew was about to take a turn for the worse.[175]

While the waters had been initially calm, seasickness overtook John and Cap'n Hank's crewmates fairly early as the storm clouds began to stalk the *Megan Jaye*. As Ellen recalled, "Sometimes, you can get what I call 'ocean motion' the first day or two, where your stomach is not quite in tune. I got that way, although I was never seasick; my brother and Tyler were. My brother was put out of commission." Tyler chalked it up to Kevin having eaten too many chocolate-chip cookies before the storm set in. "We lost him pretty quickly. Then Ellen went down. I never normally get seasick, but I was kind of useless. It was the only time I'd been seasick in my life." As everyone else save the captain fell victim to seasickness, John seemed positively immune to the ocean swells. "Most people don't like to be down below in bad weather," Ellen recalled, "they like to be up in fresh air. I remember John could be down there cooking a meal, and everyone else is thinking, 'I can't believe he even wants to cook!'"[176]

With their crewmates having been felled by seasickness, John and Cap'n Hank became fast friends, swapping stories about their lives and times. The two men had enjoyed similar experiences over the years, with Cap'n Hank having worked as a concert promoter for the likes of Janis Joplin's Big Brother and the Holding Company and the Allman Brothers. He had also experienced the darker side of the business, which led him to set up a drug clinic in Colorado before trying his hand at a seafaring life. As the hours wore on, Cap'n Hank came to understand the impetus for John's journey aboard the *Megan Jaye*. "If I'm not wrong," the captain recalled, "this was designed as a psychic cleanse to him. I'm not sure he was expecting all he got. The guy made himself so wide open to experience and growth. It would have been like standing in the middle of a six-lane highway saying 'Come and get me', and that's really the way he approached it."[177]

By the morning of Saturday, June 7, the storm had begun to make its presence known. As Tyler recalled, "It started to get grey and everything busted loose from there. The storm knocked us all apart. It was brutal. The waves were huge. If you could have called a cab, you would have. The sea is so big and the boat is so small. We were on 20 degrees of keel. The massive waves were coming up behind like buildings. We'd be surfing down these liquid mountains. I was like, 'Oh, my God. I hope we live.' It would have been really boring if that hadn't happened because John was looking for adventure. Nobody goes out in a storm, but if you get caught in one, it's something you'll talk about fondly for the rest of your life. While you're there, you wish you were home but he didn't. He *did* not wish he was home. He was in all his glory."[178]

As the day progressed, conditions continued to deteriorate, forcing Cap'n Hank to pilot the boat with the storm jib, which limited the *Megan Jaye*'s progress to just five miles per hour. To make matters worse, the storm had jarred the protective dodger above the hatch, allowing water to cascade through the companionway and into the cabin below, where the Coneys cousins were hunkering down, lost in their seasickness. But there was an even greater challenge in the offing. After spending more than 30 hours at the wheel, Cap'n Hank realised he was teetering on exhaustion. "I got to the point where I knew that I was going to be dangerous – and that's when I looked at John and I said, 'Hey! Come on up here, big boy. You've got to drive this little puppy 'cause I gotta go to sleep.'"[179]

At first, John recoiled at the idea of steering the ship – and particular during such a perilous storm. "Jeez, Hank," said John, "all I've got are these skinny little guitar-playing muscles." For his part, Hank wasn't worried. Tethered to the *Megan Jaye* by a safety harness, John took over the helm at 3 p.m. that Saturday afternoon. "Focus on the horizon, not the compass," Cap'n Hank instructed him. "Try to anticipate what this boat's gonna wanna do. And by the way, there are a couple of things that you absolutely do not do. Don't jibe. Don't let the wind get across the back of the boat. Other than that, John, you really can't hurt us. You might get wet," he added, but "you won't get washed overboard."[180]

When the boat embarked three days earlier, John had settled in for what he expected to be a relatively low-impact, seven-day adventure. Instead, he suddenly found himself treated to the experience of a lifetime in which he was tested in ways that he could never possibly have imagined. As the storm raged on and Cap'n Hank made his way to his bunk below decks, John took the wheel of the *Megan Jaye*, steering the boat to safer seas during a solo shift in which he was forced to brave the elements alone. For John, it was a revelation. Quite suddenly, he was channelling G. Gordon Liddy and struggling to make the universe bend to his will to protect the welfare and safety of his crewmates. As John later recalled,

> I was in a major storm for six hours, driving that boat, you know, and keeping it on the course. And I was buried under water. I was smashed in the face by waves for six solid hours. It's an incredible experience 'cause it won't go away, you know. You can't change your mind. It's like being on stage; once you're on, there's no getting off. And a couple of the waves had me on my knees. I was just hanging on with me hands on the wheel, but I did have the rope around me to the side, but it was very powerful weather. And I was having the time of my life. I was screaming sea shanties and shouting at the gods. I felt like a Viking, you know. Jason and the Golden Fleece.[181]

When Cap'n Hank roused himself from his bunk to relieve John, he was stunned by the change in his shipmate. "I met a different guy. He was totally washed, exuberant, ecstatic." To the captain's mind, John had "went through a full-on catharsis" and "was happy there". As far as Tyler was concerned, the former Beatle had saved the *Megan Jaye* from untold damage at the mercy of the sea. "He was up there at the helm like a madman on an adventure," said Tyler. "What was the choice? If no one was steering, then the boat would have been in worse shape than it was."[182]

All told, the storm had raged for more than 40 hours, battering the *Megan Jaye* with gale-force winds and 20-foot waves. By Monday morning, with the storm finally retreating behind them, Cap'n Hank realised that the *Megan Jaye* had been driven some 70 miles off course, while also suffering damage to its trysail. Having already added galley cook and wheelman to his seafaring résumé, John chipped in and helped with the much-needed repairs. As Ellen recalled, "The sail had torn loose from the main mast. We had to get it sewn back into place because if you just use your engine and you run out of fuel, you really don't have anything to steer the boat, and that's where you can get swamped if a wave hits you the wrong way." It took the crew four hours to make the necessary repairs, but with John's help, they managed to hoist the sail back up the mast.[183]

As the five-person crew made the final leg of their journey to Bermuda, they shared stories about their life's experiences, along with their deepest fears. For his part, John was still rapturous after his fearsome brush with nature at the wheel of the *Megan Jaye*. But he also recognised that the sea, especially during its quietest moments, offered a sort of tranquillity that was virtually impossible to replicate back on land. "We would talk about being in the middle of nowhere," said Ellen. "When it is calm, you do think you are out there in the middle of nowhere." Picking up on this thread of the conversation, Tyler opined that "there's no place like nowhere." Knowing a pithy line when he heard one, John exclaimed, "Write that down! Write that down!" As for his greatest fear, John said that he was deathly afraid that "something would happen to Sean, more than he feared something happening to him."[184]

On Wednesday, June 11, the *Megan Jaye* safely arrived in St George's Harbour in Hamilton, Bermuda. As the schooner made its easterly approach to the island, John and his crewmates caught sight of the greying battlements of Fort St Catherine, followed by the looming expanse of Gate's Bay. The entrance to the harbour itself involved passing through a narrow, majestic cut flanked with tall, forbidding rocks. "It's like going through the gates into never-never land," Cap'n Hank recalled. Meanwhile, there was the small matter of the crew's marijuana stash, which had remained largely unused during the tempest. The last thing anyone needed was a second Beatle falling victim to the drugs squad in the same calendar year. "There was a tiny bit of reefer on the boat," said Cap'n Hank, "and you can never sail into a foreign land with a tiny bit of reefer anywhere, so we had this nice sort of Grolsch bottle, a beer bottle that has one of those caps that you seal, and so we put the reefer in there and we tied it up, and we got about a dozen balloons and tied them around the top. We waited until we were close enough to the island, and we threw it in the water, so hopefully somebody would have a good day." As for the acoustic guitar that he had purchased back at the pawn shop in Newport, John never so much as picked up the instrument during his Atlantic trek.[185]

With customs agents set to board the *Megan Jaye* before the crew disembarked, Cap'n Hank decided to make a last-ditch effort to assist John in concealing his identity during his stay in Bermuda. As the crewmates filled out their customs declaration paperwork, Cap'n Hank slid John's passport in the middle of the others, hoping that his name wouldn't so readily leap out to the customs officers. Even still, the captain realised that keeping his identity was a lost cause. Just before stepping off the *Megan Jaye*, John slid his telltale granny glasses onto his nose. Quite suddenly, he was the spitting image of Beatle John. "Oh, incognito, huh?" Cap'n Hank joked. The only thing left for him to do was sign the sloop's guest book. "Dear Megan," John wrote, "'there's no place like nowhere!' (T.C., 1980) and thanks, Hank."[186]

The next day, John met with Donna Bennett, a local real estate agent, in an effort to book accommodations for Sean and the Dakota staff's upcoming visit. Back in those days, Bermuda lacked the glitz and glamour of contemporary tourism, with its expectations for comfort and luxury. Visitors relied on seasonal home rentals, for the most part, to experience the island's charms. Then as now, Bermuda was perennially mistaken as being part of the Caribbean, which exists some 1,000 miles to the south. John's rented cottage was located six miles away from Hamilton, the capital city of Bermuda, which had been incorporated as a British territory in the 1790s. By 1980, the 21-square-mile island held a population of nearly 55,000 people.

Lennon introduced himself to Bennett as "John Greene", adopting his regular pseudonym for the occasion. In Bennett's memory, "He was a thin man with a straw hat and was kind of sailor-looking with jeans and sneakers. I did not pick up on the accent and he was not wearing his trademark glasses." While it was the height of the tourist season, Bennett managed to find an available rental property overlooking Devil's Hole. Called the "Alexandra", the cosy cottage was located on Knapton Estates, not far from Harrington Sound, and seemed ample enough to accommodate John, Sean, Fred, Uda-san, and the Coneys cousins, who planned to spend a few more days on the island. As he concluded the deal with Bennett, John said, "My nanny's bringing my son down to Bermuda soon." And that's when it hit her. "Is your nanny Yoko?" Bennett asked. Having been found out, John requested that Bennett keep his presence on the island a secret: "Can you give me a couple of weeks?" As Bennett later recalled, "I thought, 'Yeah, I can do that, why not?' You get a request like that, what are you going to do?"[187]

On Friday, June 13, Fred, Sean, and Uda-san flew into Bermuda International Airport. When they arrived at Alexandra, John and Sean enjoyed an emotional reunion. When he caught sight of his Ovation

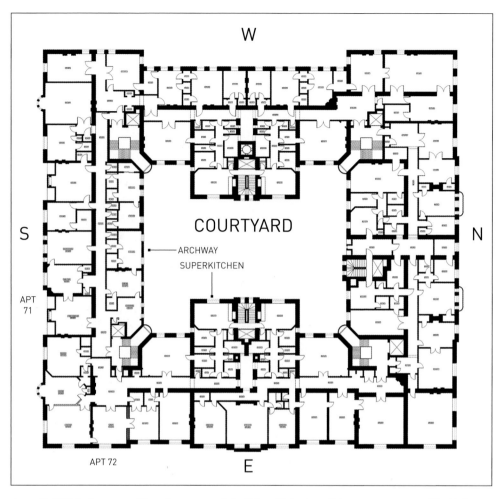

W

S · N

COURTYARD

ARCHWAY

SUPERKITCHEN

APT
71

APT 72

E

Above: By 1980, the Lennons would own five apartments in the Dakota. Their primary living space was apartment 72, with the adjacent apartment 71 acting as the family's storage unit. Apartment 72 is highlighted by the "superkitchen" overlooking the courtyard. Yoko conducted business operations from Studio One, Lenono Music's first-floor offices. [Scott Cardinal]

Above: Purchased by the Lennons in January 1980, El Solano is a beachside mansion on Florida's Palm Beach island, located at 720 South Ocean Boulevard. Built in 1919, the property is a white stucco, Spanish-style estate with a terra cotta finish, and was the brainchild of architect Addison Mizner, whose Spanish Colonial and Mediterranean Revival-style designs pocked the South Florida coast. [Davidoff Studios]

RIGHT: In February 1980, John and Yoko took brunch at the Breakers, Palm Beach island's exclusive resort. The *Palm Beach Post* caught wind of their visit and dispatched Patrick Partington to take their picture. The photograph ran in the *Palm Beach Post* and the *Daily Mail*, and, a few weeks later, was licensed to *Rolling Stone* for the magazine's March announcement about the Lennons' acquisition of El Solano. [Patrick Partington/ Getty]

LEFT: In May 1980, John visited Cape Town, South Africa's Table Mountain, the flat-topped sandstone expanse just a few miles to the south, famously capped by its rugged two-mile wide plateau. He was accompanied by taxi driver John Parker (pictured), who transported his celebrated passenger to and from the mountain vista, where John passed the hours in quiet meditation. [African News Agency]

Above: In June 1980, John sailed to Bermuda from Newport, Rhode Island on the *Megan Jaye*, a 43-foot aft-cockpit, Hinckley centreboard sloop. Owned by Dr Dick Jones, an ear, nose, and throat specialist, the boat had been christened in honour of Jones' daughter. During the voyage, John took over the wheel from Cap'n Hank Halsted for some six hours during a raging storm at sea. [Brian San Souci]

Above: In June 1980, John rented the Villa Undercliff estate, which is nestled in Fairylands, an upscale residential estate in Bermuda. With a commanding view of the Great Sound, the home included a private dock and a bait pool, and, to John's great delight, a Steinway baby grand piano. [Jeff Copeland]

ABOVE: John and Yoko outside the Hit Factory recording studio prior to beginning work on *Double Fantasy*, August 7, 1980.
[Roger D. Farrington]

ABOVE: John playing his Sardonyx 800 D-II guitar on August 7, 1980. Known by John as his "space guitar," the Sardonyx was his primary instrument during the *Double Fantasy* sessions. [Roger D. Farrington]

RIGHT: During the Lennons' six-week stay at Villa Undercliff, New Jersey native Nancy Gosnell painted a father-son portrait that currently hangs in the Lennons' Dakota apartment. Gosnell spent the better part of a week creating the four-foot by five-foot oil rendering of John and Sean reclining together on the pier at Villa Undercliff. During their sitting with Gosnell, John took to calling the portrait-in-progress *The Madonna and Child of 1980.* [Nancy Gosnell Molineux]

ABOVE: John poses with amateur photographer Paul Goresh on November 17, 1980. [Bettmann/Getty]

ABOVE: The flag at the Dakota flies at half-mast to mark the death of John Lennon. December 13, 1980. [David Bookstaver/AP/Shutterstock]

ABOVE: Situated by the Masterworks Museum of Bermuda Art at the northeast corner of the Bermuda Botanical Gardens, the memorial marks the occasion in June 1980 when John found his inspiration for naming the *Double Fantasy* LP. [Verena Matthew/Alamy]

ABOVE: In 1985, Yoko dedicated the Strawberry Fields memorial in John's memory. The Imagine mosaic was designed by a team of artists from Naples, Italy. With the mosaic as its centrepiece, the Strawberry Fields parklet includes the teardrop-shaped portion of Central Park across the street from the Dakota. [Vespasian/Alamy]

ABOVE: John and Yoko were photographed on December 8, 1980, by renowned photographer and Dakota neighbour Annie Leibovitz. "This is it," said John when he saw the polaroid test shot. "This is our relationship." Leibovitz's photo adorned the January 22, 1981 issue of *Rolling Stone* magazine. [Granger Historical Picture Archive/Alamy]

acoustic guitar, which Fred had dutifully brought along from the Dakota, John picked up the instrument and began playing a medley of Liverpool sea shanties as Sean danced around the living room. For his part, Fred was shocked by John's robust appearance. "He had lost the pallor he had acquired over five years at the Dakota," Fred recalled. "Now he was tanned and exuded health and vitality." That night, the *Megan Jaye* crewmates shared a celebratory dinner with Sean and the other Dakotans. All the while, John regaled Sean and Fred with stories about his seafaring adventure. "You can't imagine what it's like when you look around and all you see is water and sky," said John. "You feel both isolated and in communication with the almighty whatever. It's an overwhelming sensation of freedom."[188]

Much later still, John sat on a couch, cross-legged, and performed a new, considerably more raucous version of 'Serve Yourself' for his assistant. With a scathing reference to Dylan as a "'dirty little git", John's lyrics had become even more fierce and biting, if that were possible, and his performance was chock-full of fire and fury. To Fred's mind, the song seemed even more "wicked" and "scorching" than ever before. There was no doubt about it. John was different all right.[189]

The next morning, John and Sean made their way into Hamilton for the traditional birthday parade in honour of Queen Elizabeth II. As a British territory, Bermuda pulled out all of the stops, visiting pomp and circumstance upon its citizenry, parading a pith helmet-wearing honour guard along the avenues, and concluding with a 21-gun salute. John and Sean joined the spectators along Front Street, with father helpfully perching his son atop a nearby windowsill for a better view of the proceedings. For his part, John had to admit that observing the parade from among the thousands of other Brits lining the streets had left him feeling mildly patriotic.

By this point, Cap'n Hank was preparing the *Megan Jaye* for the return voyage to the States. His girlfriend "Fetchin' Gretchen", as he called her, planned to join him. Before they left, Cap'n Hank treated John to one more cruise aboard the yacht. As they tooled their way about the harbour in the *Megan Jaye*, a heavy rain began to fall on Bermuda. "The wind was blowing real hard again, but there was still fun stuff to do," Cap'n Hank recalled. "We got the sails up. Sean got to drive and sailed the boat around the harbour some. We had a marvellous gala afternoon."[190]

By the next day, John had already grown restless, privately instructing Fred to begin making preparations for leaving the Coneys at Alexandra and locating more isolated accommodations on another part of the island. For one thing, John had felt that Tyler was getting too close to him. For Fred, it felt like the scene with Terry Bosley, the captain of the *Imagine*, all over again. "I don't have any friends," John once told Fred. "Friendship is a romantic illusion." But it was more than that. As Fred would shortly learn, John had other things on his mind beyond sun and tourism. Working with real estate agent Bill Lusher, John's assistant discovered a remote property called Villa Undercliff on the outskirts of Hamilton.[191]

With a commanding view of the Great Sound, Villa Undercliff was nestled in an upscale community with manicured gardens and quiet country lanes. The home included a private dock and a bait pool, and, to John's great delight, a Steinway baby grand piano. He would even have access to the estate's tiny Sunfish sailboat. As John had predicted, the splendid home came with an exorbitant cost of $24,000 for a six-week stay, which Yoko had hastily arranged back in Studio One. "I knew we'd end up paying through the nose," said John, "but it'll be worth it." The only problem was that the property was currently occupied by Rolf and Molly Luthi, who informed Lusher that they would need a few days to relocate their young family and make way for John, Sean, Fred, and Uda-san.[192]

For John, a delayed timetable simply wouldn't do. Rolf Luthi eventually agreed to John's terms, provided that he would deliver payment by certified cheque. When it became apparent that the transaction would require several more days to complete, Luthi agreed to accept a personal cheque from John if he could pick it up from the musician in person at Alexandra. "Bloody hell!" John exclaimed. "We're paying a fucking fortune for the place, and now I have to jump through hoops before they let us move in." Later that evening, Luthi met with John at the cottage. Coming face to face with the Beatle, he began plying him with invitations to society parties and boat cruises. But John wasn't hearing of it. As he wrote out the cheque, John curtly announced that he had come to Bermuda expressly to work, not to socialise.[193]

And so it was that during the early morning hours of Wednesday, June 18 – his old mate Paul McCartney's 38th birthday – that John quietly slipped out of Alexandra with Sean, Fred, and Uda-san in tow. Leaving the Coneys cousins behind in their slumber, they made their way across the island to the relative remoteness of Villa Undercliff, nestled as it was in the much beloved – some even say "magical" – residential estate known as Fairylands.

CHAPTER 9

Fairylands

John wasted little time in settling down to work in his new digs. The unflinching determination that he had revealed during his brief meeting with Rolf Luthi had been a hint of things to come. At Fairylands, John's voyage of self-renewal kicked into an even higher gear. In preparation, he had brought along his trusty shoulder bag from the Dakota. Inside were dozens of cassette tapes of his compositions over the past decade, including many of the unfinished song-fragments that he'd performed on the Yamaha keyboard.

On Thursday, June 19, having been ensconced at Villa Undercliff for little more than a day, John was determined to outfit the estate to his liking. In addition to asking Fred to replicate his usual TV setup in his Villa Undercliff bedroom, he sent his assistant on an errand to buy a "ghetto blaster" – in the parlance of the era – along with some new music to get his creative juices flowing. He also suggested that his assistant round up some bongos and a tambourine at a musical instrument store. For Fred, the best bet turned out to be Stuart's Electronics on Reid Street in downtown Hamilton, where he purchased a Sony CF-6500II boom box. Retailing for around $275 at the time, the top-of-the-line portable cassette player was a classic AM/FM stereo unit with four built-in speakers. At the time, tech geeks often referred to the player by its nickname, the ZILBA'P, which the Japanese multinational company had intentionally created by stamping the unusual word on the body of the unit. Denoting the phrase "Zoo Intelligence Learning Body Action Playing", the ZILBA'P was powered by a whopping eight D cell batteries and featured a built-in stereo microphone, as well as a host of inputs for external mics, speakers, and power components.

During his shopping spree, Fred also managed to round up a cassette version of the Wailers' 1973 reggae classic *Burnin'*, which included such gems as the anthemic 'Get Up, Stand Up' and 'I Shot The Sheriff'. As they listened to the LP on the veranda at Villa Undercliff – a wide expanse overlooking the Great Sound – *Burnin'* brought back fond memories for John, who recalled listening to the album back in his Lost Weekend days. After a while, 'Hallelujah Time' played over the speakers on the ZILBA'P. During the sombre mid-tempo number, John sat rapt as Bob Marley affected a falsetto voice and sang about "living on borrowed time". After listening to the song yet again, John suddenly announced, "That's it!" As Fred looked on, John could hardly contain himself. "'Living on borrowed time'," said John. "That's the phrase I've been looking for! I've had this song in my head for ages. It'll have a reggae beat, and I'll write the words around the theme of living on borrowed time, which is exactly what I've been doing. Or, come to think of it, what we're all doing, even though most of us don't like to face it. And that includes you and me, my dear."[194]

In the flush of inspiration, John began crafting lyrics for his new song. By dinnertime, he had completed a rough draft of 'Borrowed Time', which he debuted for Fred on his Ovation acoustic guitar, singing that his "future is brighter", now that he's older. In short order, John had Fred sent for the Roland CompuRhythm drum machine back at the Dakota. For the first demo recording of his new composition, John exclaimed "Welcome to Bermuda!" as he cued up the tape. While continuing to refine 'Borrowed Time', John recorded three more demos on the ZILBA'P – even trying the tune out on the Steinway for good measure – before returning to 'I Don't Wanna Face It', one of the numerous song-fragments strewn among the cassettes in his ever-present tan leather bag. In its latest manifestation, the song had taken on more hard-rocking pretensions.

By this point, John had begun fantasising about when and where he might begin recording a new album. Speaking on the telephone with Yoko at the time, he had begun to discuss the possibility of a comeback, with his wife countering that perhaps he should consider a more tentative step at this juncture – an EP (extended play) record instead of a full-fledged long-player. After listening to Bob Marley and the Wailers' *Survival* (1979)

LP, he floated the notion of producing his new work at one of the reggae singer's regular Jamaican studios. For John, Marley had emerged as the one true giant on the 1970s music scene – a lyrical poet, like himself, who championed peace in the face of adversity. In 1976, John had the opportunity to experience Marley's talents for himself when he and Ringo took in the Wailers' performance at the Roxy in Los Angeles during a break from working on Starr's *Ringo's Rotogravure* album. Meanwhile, John entertained Fred with stories about Marley's life and times, including the instance in the late 1970s when a gunman broke into his home, determined to assassinate the musician for his outspoken political beliefs. Marley refused to back down, narrowly escaping with his life, and – in spite of his brush with death – continuing his political activism.

That Friday, John and Fred sailed around the Great Sound in the Sunfish. John had been eager to return to the sea almost as soon as he had disembarked the *Megan Jaye* with Sean. Later that evening, John suggested they visit one of the local discotheques. When he had first arrived on the island, John had asked Donna Bennett about Hamilton nightlife, and the realtor recommended Disco 40. But John had also heard about another hot spot called Flavors, which he was eager to visit, figuring that it catered to a hipper crowd. When they arrived at Flavors, John and Fred were greeted by the blaring sounds of Diana Ross' 'I'm Coming Out'. Quickly deducing that Flavors was little more than a hangout for tourists and bland music lovers, John reluctantly suggested that they move their party, such as it was, to Disco 40.

In sharp contrast with Flavors, Disco 40 was a veritable hive of activity. After passing through a sea of mopeds outside the nightclub's entrance, the two found themselves at the edge of a crowded dance floor populated, for the most part, by twentysomethings and teenagers. At first, John tried his hand at finding a dance partner, although all of the young women he asked had flatly turned him down. "They must think I'm weird or something," John told Fred. Later, as they drank one convivial beer after another, the house DJ cued up the B-52's 'Rock Lobster'. John couldn't believe his ears. During the song's introduction, band member Kate Pierson sang a series of high-pitched, yodelling-like vocals. To John, her vocals sounded exactly like Yoko's unconventional performance stylings – the "16-track voice" that Jonathan Cott had lauded all those years ago in *Rolling Stone*. "Can you believe it?" John exclaimed to Fred. "They're doing Yoko!" As he listened to the new wave band, John couldn't contain himself. "Mother will love it!" he continued. "She's always complaining that nobody takes her seriously as a rock singer. I can't wait to tell her she's finally arrived!"[195]

By the time they left the nightclub, John was feeling the full effects of the alcohol. Adhering to a strict health-conscious diet had rendered him a lightweight in comparison to his hard-drinking days during the Lost Weekend. When they arrived back at Villa Undercliff, he promptly threw up in the front yard. But he was on a mission, and he wouldn't be deterred. As he told Gerry Hunt, a local reporter for *The Royal Gazette* who spotted him at Disco 40, "The wife sent me here on a working vacation." Once more, he fully intended to tackle the unfinished wares in his leather carryall. The next morning, he rolled out of bed, and, in spite of his raging hangover, revisited his song-fragments for 'Real Life' and 'That's The Way The World Is'. Refashioned as a livelier tune entitled 'I'm Stepping Out', John updated the lyrics to reflect his more carefree state-of-mind in contrast with his gloomier outlook the previous fall. With his Ovation acoustic guitar at the ready, he fired up the ZILBA'P, singing of lighting a cigarette and blowing "my worries to the sky".

By the next day, June 22, John's hangover was long gone, but his energy and inspiration were in full flower. Indeed, as a songwriter, John may have enjoyed his most productive period in years. But first, he decided to treat his housemates – which included Sean, Fred, Uda-san, and Helen, who had arrived from New York City the previous afternoon – to lunch at a restaurant in the Bermuda Botanical Gardens. A few miles outside of Hamilton and just to the north of Hungry Bay on the island's southern shores, the gardens featured flora from around the world, along with rolling lawns and stately Camden House, the official residence of Bermuda's premier. Il Chianti, an Italian restaurant, operated out of a nearby cottage at the time. As John later recalled, they went to Il Chianti so that "I could get some espresso and Sean could get some junk food." After the meal, John obligingly signed some autographs for the waitstaff before taking a stroll in the gardens.[196]

And that's when it happened. "I was just walking in, and I looked down," John remembered, and a tiny sign under a cedar tree read FREESIA, DOUBLE FANTASY. John was thunderstruck by the phrase. "I just thought, 'Double Fantasy' – that's a great title! 'Cause it has so many meanings that you couldn't even begin to think what it meant. So it means anything you can think of. It means double-couple." He was so ecstatic that he didn't even notice that there was no freesia in evidence, with the flower having gone dormant for the season. What he likely saw was a hibiscus that had been recently planted in its place. "The Double Fantasy hibiscus is gorgeous," said Mary Lodge, who frequented the botanical gardens. "It is as big as a dinner plate." Freesia or hibiscus – it hardly mattered to John. It was the phrase itself that had caught his eye. "It just sort of says it all," John recalled. "Without really saying anything, it says everything."[197]

Back at the Villa Undercliff, John had set up a makeshift recording studio in the sun room that consisted of the ZILBA'P and the CompuRhythm drum machine. During a second visit to Stuart's Electronics, John had purchased a National Panasonic RS-4360 DFT tape recorder, some blank cassette tapes, a pair of headphones, and a microphone. With the second recorder, he planned to "double-track" his demos. To accomplish this end, he would record a basic track with vocals and guitar on the ZILBA'P, then playback the original recording while capturing additional instrumentation with the Panasonic. At this point, he was ready to take another pass at 'Darling Boy', the love song he had written for Sean earlier that year. At John's instruction, Fred tried his hand at performing a reggae accompaniment on the bongos. As he took up his acoustic guitar and positioned himself in front of the ZILBA'P, John could sense his assistant's fraying nerves. "Just play it by ear, Fred," he said. As he activated the ZILBA'P, John introduced the song as "'Darling Boy', now known as 'Beautiful Boy'." For the second take, Fred took up the bongos again, playing along as John worked out the song's finer points. As John cued up the tape, he announced, "Fritz and Heinz, take 2 of the singing lullabies!" Later, he asked Fred to try tapping out a basic rhythm with a pen or, on another pass at the song, by handclapping a reggae rhythm. While his assistant's performance was often off-beat, John didn't mind. He was clearly thrilled with the results, even in their crudest form.[198]

As the June 22 demos of 'Beautiful Boy' reveal, the song's lyrics had evolved in subtle, yet significant ways since its earlier gestation. John was still attempting to work out a third verse for the song, which he double-tracked using the Panasonic later that same evening. In 'Beautiful Boy', John had begun singing a memorable lyric about the fleeting nature of human existence. As it happened, the maxim "life is what happens while you are busy making other plans" had originally been published by Allen Saunders in a 1957 issue of *Reader's Digest*. It was very likely that John, always the voracious reader, had happened upon the line more recently in William Gaddis' 1975 novel *J R*. Published shortly after John's 35th birthday, *J R* had been highly anticipated among the New York literary set. As the first novel released by Gaddis since 1955's *The Recognitions*, the hoopla associated with its publication could hardly have escaped John's attention. In *J R*, Gaddis makes light of the saying, deriding it as mindless fodder for the walls of a dentist's office. Lennon powerfully reclaims the phrase in 'Beautiful Boy', deploying it with a hint of sentimentality to create an earnest and eminently hopeful effect. While John had originally used the lyric during the piano takes associated with his 'My Life' song-fragments, the adage made perfect sense in 'Beautiful Boy' as sage-like advice from father to son in a song about growing up and growing older.[199]

With 'Beautiful Boy' having taken flight, John wasn't done quite yet. With Fred playing the bongos again, he returned to 'Borrowed Time'. "Ready for a little reggae?" John exclaimed as he cued up the ZILBA'P. After double-tracking a new demo of the song in his sun room studio, John returned to 'Dear Yoko' for the first time since April back at Cannon Hill. As with 'Beautiful Boy', 'Dear Yoko' had taken on clear lyrical shifts after his voyage aboard the *Megan Jaye*. In a newly penned verse, John sings about being out at sea, where, in Coneys' words, "nowhere is the place to be." Flush with the full-on resumption of his musical powers, John returned to 'I Don't Wanna Face It' yet again. During the recording, John performs the song in double-time, remarking that it "should be slower and probably for Ringo." All the while, as John worked later and later into the night, the sound of the tree frogs that pocked the Fairylands estate can occasionally be heard in the background, affording John's songs with arguably the most unusual vocal accompaniment across his entire career. For the composer, it was as if nature, quite literally, had become aligned with his reinvigorated muse.

Having created double-tracked demo recordings for 'Beautiful Boy', 'Borrowed Time', 'Dear Yoko', and 'I Don't Wanna Face It', John was clearly on a roll. The next morning, he debuted 'Beautiful Boy' for Sean, who danced around the sun room with pure joy, ecstatic that his father had written a song for him. Sean was already having the time of his life, roaming the estate with Helen and playing in the water with his dad. "It was in Bermuda that I learnt to swim the sidestroke," said Sean. "I remember splashing vigorously with one eye submerged, the other searching for my father's approval, his slender frame obscured by blinking rivulets."[200]

Enjoying this newfound head of steam, John reached into his leather bag, grabbed some of his cassettes, and began the process of bringing several of his longstanding song-fragments to fruition. For John, this would have been a fairly painstaking activity, given the sheer number of compositions that remained unfinished over the past few years. Up first was 'Girls And Boys', for which he fashioned a double-tracked version using his sun room recording setup. In this case, he deployed the earlier, original take of the song as the basic track, overdubbing acoustic guitar and backing vocals on the Panasonic. His efforts over the coming days suggest that 'Girls And Boys' had captured his attention, that it was one of the compositions – as with 'Beautiful Boy' – among his small, but growing list of favourites.

In the meantime, John's presence on the island finally made the newspapers, thanks to Gerry Hunt, whom John had met back at Disco 40. In exchange for a loosely orchestrated interview over drinks, John asked Hunt to constrain any reportage during his time in Bermuda to a short article. True to his word, Hunt published a brief piece in the June 27 morning edition of *The Royal Gazette* entitled "Holiday in the Sun for John and Yoko", tracking the couple's alleged movements from Hamilton to St George. At this juncture, Yoko had not arrived on the island, occupying herself with Lenono business – namely, the record-breaking Holstein cow story, which would be dominating the entertainment headlines around the world in a week's time. As for John, Hunt kept things short and sweet, as promised, writing that the ex-Beatle was enjoying his time in the sun, which indeed he was. As he told Hunt back at Disco 40, "Bermuda's really great."[201]

Unbeknownst to Hunt, Yoko finally joined her family in Bermuda later that same day, although not without great consternation on everyone's part. That Friday, Rich DePalma provided John with regular updates about Yoko's progress, as she missed one flight after another, only to rebook a later plane. After a while, it seemed that she might not even make the trip at all. Eventually, her flight from New York City was set to arrive that evening at 9.30 p.m., and John was determined to meet her at the gate. After dinner, John and Fred went to a bar near the airport, the Swizzle Inn, to pass the time. Over drinks and Gitanes, John went into a long diatribe about his sexual past, while stressing the fact that he was feeling amorous at the thought of his upcoming reunion with his wife, when he could "jump Mother's bones". As Fred listened, John spoke disparagingly about his past behaviours with women, his sexual obsessions and fantasies. He chalked it up to being "a weird, psychotic kid covering up my insecurity with a macho façade." He credited Yoko with helping him to tame his aggression and embrace his tender side. And that's when Fred happened to look down at his watch. Leaping up from his barstool with a start, he chillingly informed John that Yoko's plane was arriving from New York City at that very moment.[202]

John and Fred frantically made their way to the airport, but they were too late. Rushing to the gate, they happened upon a janitor, who regaled them with an anecdote about a tiny Japanese woman who had been wandering around and seemed lost and confused. John could only begin to imagine Yoko's rage at having been abandoned by her husband in a faraway locale. In his haste, Fred called Villa Undercliff to confirm the terrible truth. "Better come quick," Uda-san informed him. During their mad taxi ride back to Fairylands, John announced that "there's only one way out of this. You'll have to take the blame. Tell her that you talked me into having a couple of beers. She'll want to fire you, of course, but don't worry, I'll save your ass."[203]

To their surprise and delight, Fred's hide didn't need to be rescued after all. In spite of her ordeal back at the airport, Yoko was fairly tranquil. Leading his wife into the sun room, John recorded a boisterous demo of 'Serve Yourself' in her presence, ratcheting up the expletive-laden song to great effect. Pleased with Yoko's reaction, John launched into a performance of his latest and growing repertoire. Working his Ovation acoustic guitar with obvious Dylanesque stylings, he performed his newest version of 'I'm Crazy' – now going under a revised working title of 'Watching The Wheels' – with the tape running. At this juncture, John had become increasingly smitten with his folksy acoustic guitar take, although he maintained a fondness for his slower, rolling-piano version of the song.

In addition to plying her with the latest incarnation of 'Beautiful Boy', he reached even further back to 'Everybody's Talkin', Nobody's Talkin'', which was known by this juncture as 'Nobody Told Me', thanks to the composition's chorus, which found its roots in the time-honoured catchphrase "My mother told me there'd be days like these". Over the past few days, he'd been refining the song. At one point, he prepared a double-tracked demo with his original Dakota piano take, which he adorned with new vocals and maracas, courtesy of Fred. For one of his acoustic guitar takes, John can be heard offering his usual proviso, "This one's gotta be for Ringo." With the CompuRhythm keeping time in the background and John strumming his Ovation with all his might, he tackles the chorus with uncharacteristic vim and vigour. During this same period, John also resuscitated his song-fragment for 'Memories', for which he double-tracked his lead vocal and supplemented his original Dakota piano instrumentation with an improvisational acoustic guitar part.

Yoko's island sojourn would be decidedly brief. Consumed with Lenono business, she spent much of her short stay at Fairylands on the telephone. By Sunday, she announced that she was ready to make her return to New York City. Afterwards, John and Fred returned to the botanical gardens, where they sipped cappuccinos at Il Chianti. In his assistant's recollection, John was especially miffed about his wife's seeming disinterest about his musical renaissance, not to mention his growing catalogue of, for the most part, fully realised compositions. In particular, he was concerned that Yoko wasn't properly gearing up for his planned return to the recording studio, although they had discussed potential producers that they might tap for the enviable role of helming a new Lennon project after his five-year hiatus. Yoko had already expressed a preference for Jack Douglas, given their past experience with him, as well as his recent successes with Aerosmith and Cheap Trick. When they left Il Chianti, John slipped into the garden for one more glimpse of the DOUBLE FANTASY sign and its attendant flowers – whatever they were, freesia or hibiscus – before heading back to Fairylands.

As John and Yoko resumed their regular transatlantic phone calls, he began setting down the receiver and performing his new compositions for her in a blatant effort to encourage her interest in his project, even hoping that she would begin composing new material of her own. At one point in early July – only a few days after her departure from Bermuda – John failed to raise her on the telephone. No one answered his calls up in apartment 72, and when he dialled her private line in Studio One, the phone was busy, staying that way for hours. In a full-fledged panic, he coped with the situation by chain-smoking Gitanes, gathering up his acoustic guitar, and firing up the drum machine.

Taking full advantage of his desperation, John returned to his demo for 'Stranger's Room', borrowing the earlier song's structure to create 'I'm Losing You', one of the composer's most chilling works of excoriation and self-contempt. During Yoko's brief stay at Fairylands, the couple had argued several times in the privacy of their bedroom. 'I'm Losing You' offers a chilling glimpse into the heart of their recent marital impasse. But for John, his inability to speak with his wife on the phone served as a mere introduction to the larger issues that they faced. As John later recalled, the genesis of his

131

new song "literally started when I tried to call from Bermuda and I couldn't get through. I was mad as hell and feeling lost in space and it's just as much a description of the separation period in the early Seventies as that occasion when I physically couldn't get through on the phone," adding that "Yoko has an incredible memory. You know, wives will bring back past things."[204]

Pouring his emotional distress into this latest composition, John concocted one of the most unnerving middle-eights among his storied career. Making a sly reference to the 1945 film *The Valley of Decision*, directed by Tay Garnett, John sings about his inability to act juxtaposed with an increasing feeling that his wife's love for him has slipped beyond his grasp. As his demo recording unfolds, John strikes at the heart of the matter, Yoko's growing sense of carnal frustration, counterpoised by her sometime disinterest in her husband because he reminds her of "all that bad, bad, bad stuff" inherent in their shared sexual past – namely, John's numerous infidelities. While he ostensibly takes ownership for the emotional damage he wrought – clearly referring to the Lost Weekend and his many other infelicities – he places the onus back on his wife, asking her to stop berating him about behaviour that occurred "way back when".

With 'I'm Losing You', John had concocted a micro-narrative about the Lennons' marital strife at this juncture. But it was much more than that. With a stroke, his lyrics on the demo recording illustrate the seemingly implacable nature of the masculine ego. At first, he delivers a veiled apology only to surrender to his own insatiable need for transferring the blame back onto his wife. In this way, 'I'm Losing You' – even in its unvarnished state – stands with John's finest moments of confessional songwriting, a roster of compositions that includes the likes of *Plastic Ono Band*'s 'God', 'Isolation', and 'Look At Me'. Not surprisingly, the song's traumatic psychological portrayal was not lost on Yoko, who later remarked that "'I'm Losing You' is an incredible song. When I hear that, it makes me almost faint. It's so beautifully written and the emotion is so powerful. I feel guilty, of course, as a woman, because he was scared he was gonna lose me."[205]

Although John managed to reconnect with Yoko in a matter of a few hours, he remained flummoxed by the desperation he experienced while trying in vain to reach her on the telephone and ultimately while composing 'I'm Losing You'. In short order, he hatched a plan to dispatch Fred on a lightning trip to New York City. For the errand that he had in mind, no simple courier service would do. John instructed his assistant to personally deliver a few gifts to his wife. He prepared a special mix-tape comprised of the songs he had completed during his Bermuda holiday. In a particularly meaningful gesture, he also acquired a cedarwood box. Cutting off a lock of his hair, he wrapped it in a handkerchief and placed it inside. Handing the box to Fred, John explained that he had prepared the gift in accordance with an ancient Japanese custom, cautioning his assistant that under no circumstances should the box be opened, lest the magic of the romantic ritual be spoiled.

Meanwhile, Yoko had taken John's concerns about making a new record to heart in more ways than one. First, she made clandestine contact with Douglas in order to gauge his interest in the project. Yoko recognised that connecting with the producer was the initial step in a process fraught with trepidation. While she and her husband may not have been on the same page in terms of their private life, she knew full well that the stakes had never been higher as they plotted his return to the recording studio. For her part, she was all too cognisant of the inherent risks, knowing that John desperately wanted to effect his return to music-making, but also understanding that any hint of failure or unwanted publicity – no matter how slight – might send him beating a hasty retreat back to his bedroom in the secluded Dakota skies above Central Park West. As the summer progressed, it was a burden that Yoko would feel ever more acutely. And then there was the matter of igniting her muse, which had experienced its own state of dormancy over the past several years, leaving Yoko with a protracted sense of artistic frustration. The solution, it turned out, had been right in front of her all that time. Perhaps John's renaissance might dovetail with her own?

For Douglas, hearing from Yoko after lo so many years seemed like a bolt out of the blue. And to top things off, there was a cloak-and-dagger feel to their initial interactions. In July, her office called him, asking the producer to go to the 34th Street pier and board a seaplane, which ferried him to Cannon Hill. As Jack later recalled, "The seaplane landed right onto the beach. It was hush-hush." As they went into the house, Yoko handed him an envelope marked "for Jack's ears only". Inside were the demo recordings that Fred had recently delivered to Yoko. "John's gonna call you now," Yoko told him. "But I just want to tell you he's going to ask you to do a record," which "you would produce for us." And that's when she added that "I'm going to have a few songs on it, and John doesn't know yet." Then she handed Jack a sheaf of her own compositions.[206]

And that's when John called from Bermuda. "He told me he felt he couldn't write a song anymore," Jack recalled, "and that these songs were really shitty." Later, after he had an opportunity to listen to the cassette, Jack was speechless. "The feel and intimacy of the demos was so great," Douglas recalled. "Afterward, I got a call from John, who asked me what I thought of the material and I told him it was incredible. I told him, 'I don't know if I can beat this stuff. It's so good.' And he cracked up." Later, when Yoko and the Lennons' attorney David Warmflash met with Jack and his Waterfront Productions business partner Stan Vincent, she outlined a process for moving forward with the project. "Listen," said Yoko, "I don't want to interfere with this album, this is John's baby, this is John's album."[207]

By this juncture, Jack had come to understand the reasoning behind John and Yoko's overarching secrecy: "What he made clear to me was that when I did this whole process of preproduction – putting a band together, booking a studio – it had to be done in complete secrecy because he was damned if he was gonna let the press know he tried to do a record and fell on his ass." Indeed, it was the selfsame dilemma that left Yoko frightened to the hilt on her husband's behalf. Hence, she had carefully built in safeguards to avoid going public until the time was right. "John didn't know if he could do it," Jack recalled, "and he didn't want to be made a fool in the press. If anyone found out that this was going on, the project would stop." It was that simple.[208]

As John became increasingly aware of Yoko's intentions to participate in the album, it seemed like manna from heaven as far as he was concerned. As Fred later recalled, he jumped at the chance to work with her, believing that a mutual recording project might be just the thing to revive their flagging relationship. In terms of the couple's collaboration, things began once and truly to unfold when Yoko shared a new song, 'Let Me Count The Ways', which she had based on Number 43 ('How Do I Love Thee?') from Elizabeth Barrett Browning's *Sonnets from the Portuguese* (1850), her collection of love poems dedicated to her husband Robert, who nicknamed his wife "my little Portuguese". As Yoko later explained, "I woke up with 'Let Me Count The Ways' ringing in my head. I called John, who was then in Bermuda, and played it over the phone." As John listened, she catalogued the many ways in which she loves her husband with a gentle piano cadence, describing her romantic feelings as being "like that gentle wind" felt at dawn. Hearing that her husband had been deeply stirred by her gesture, Yoko suggested that he compose something in return, channelling Robert Browning as if they were the spiritual rebirth of the great Victorian poets. As Yoko recalled, "Back when we were living in England in Ascot, John was reading this book about them. He said, 'We're just a reincarnation of Robert and Elizabeth Browning.' I said, 'Maybe.' It was very funny because Elizabeth was older than Robert and I was older than John."[209]

The thought-experiment might have ended there had John not watched *A Love Affair: The Eleanor and Lou Gehrig Story* (1978) later that same day at Villa Undercliff. A made-for-television movie based on Eleanor Gehrig's autobiography *My Luke and I* (1976), the programme starred Blythe Danner and Edward Herrmann as Eleanor and Lou Gehrig. Known as "The Iron Horse" during his playing days, Gehrig had been felled during the prime of his career by the disease (amyotrophic lateral sclerosis) that would one day bear his name. In July 1939, he famously delivered a farewell speech to his fans at Yankee Stadium. "Today I consider myself the luckiest man on earth," he remarked, adding that "when you have a wife who has been a tower of strength and shown more courage than you dreamed existed – that's the finest I know." For decades afterwards, television networks would run Gehrig-related fare – most often *The Pride of the Yankees* (1942) to commemorate Gehrig's famous speech. In July 1980, the US-based NBC television affiliate in Bermuda had selected *A Love Affair* to mark the famous episode in American history.

Watching the heartbreaking film that day in Bermuda, John must have been struck by the scene when Eleanor (Danner) reads a letter from her future husband Lou (Herrmann): "Thanks very much for sending me that book of poems," he writes. "I especially liked the one by Robert Browning that goes, 'grow old along with me, the best is yet to be'." Quite suddenly, the movie held John's full attention – both because of the coincidence of his earlier conversation with Yoko, as well as his longtime fascination with the literary arts. Originally published as 'Rabbi Ben Ezra' in *Dramatis Personae* (1864), Browning's poem afforded John with a wellspring of inspiration:

> Grow old along with me!
> The best is yet to be,
> The last of life, for which the first was made:
> Our times are in His hand
> Who saith, "A whole I planned,
> Youth shows but half; trust God: see all, nor be afraid!"

For John, it was nothing short of pure kismet. Better still, authoring his latest composition was the result of sheer inspiration, as opposed to the rote sort of craftsmanship he so often derided. The lyrics came to him in a flash, which he borrowed almost verbatim from Browning and played with a gently rolling acoustic guitar accompaniment. For the melody, he drew on the concluding cadence for 'Memories', which he had recently polished in his sun room recording studio. As Yoko later recalled, "John proudly played his song over the phone. That's how our two songs happened."[210]

Particularly taken with his new song, John tried variously playing 'Grow Old With Me' on his acoustic guitar and, later at the Dakota, with piano and drum machine accompaniment. He was especially enamoured with the religiosity inherent in the middle-eight, singing about a "world without end" in which he and Yoko would spend their livelong days as "man and wife together". With this aspect in mind, the Lennons began imagining a greater life for 'Grow Old With Me' beyond their project, that it might become a wedding-hall standard which couples would play in church on the occasion of their marriages – possibly even with a full symphony orchestra providing a grand accompaniment.

By this point, John had taken to creating signed manuscripts of his lyrics, as if he were intent on drawing every last bit of inspiration from the estate's enchantment. For 'Grow Old With Me', he printed out the lyrics by hand, signing and dating them "Fairylands, Bermuda, July 5, 1980, JL". As the sun began to set that evening, John and Fred took their usual place on the veranda at Villa Undercliff. During a break from listening to Bob Marley on the ZILBA'P, they caught the sounds of bagpipes wafting across the water from nearby Bluck Point. With a little sleuthing, John and Fred learned from Rolf Luthi that the player was 23-year-old John Sinclair. As Luthi recalled, "The Sinclairs used to live across the water, and at sundown he would go out to the point and play, and the sound would drift across and everyone loved it. John said what a beautiful sound it was." That summer, Sinclair had been working on "Struan Robertson's 'Salute', a category of bagpipe music called piobaireachd, which is also known as 'ceol mor' or 'The Great Music'," the musician recalled. "It's probably as close to Scotland as one could experience in Bermuda."[211]

And all the while, the songs kept on coming. Over the next several days, John attempted several more demos, including 'Mr. Hyde's Gone (Don't Be Afraid)'. With a bouncy piano part reminiscent of the Beatles' 'You Know My Name (Look Up The Number)', the whimsical number has the sound and feel of a father's gentle caution for his son at bedtime by way of Robert Louis Stevenson's Gothic-laden *Strange Case of Dr Jekyll and Mr Hyde* (1886). John also took up his acoustic guitar for 'The Happy Rishikesh Song' and a bluesy tune called 'Something Is Wrong'. For the former, he appeared to be drawing yet again upon the Beatles' 1968 sojourn with the Maharishi, as well as the melody of George Harrison's 1979 hit 'Blow Away'. John's wistfulness is balanced by a realisation of the absurdity of unconsidered chastity in the name of religion: if anything's missing in God's almighty plan, is it that "you need a woman?", he sings against the driving rhythm of the Villa Undercliff baby grand.

At the same time, John returned to 'Girls And Boys', which he had refashioned in a succession of piano takes as 'Real Love (Waiting For You)'. Over the course of five passes at the song, which had been ruminating in the songwriter's mind since as early as 1976, John made several refinements, scuttling the song's middle-eight and adding a sweet piano interlude. By take 4, John had 'Real Love' well in hand, playfully remarking "Okay, start again, silly boy" for his introduction. In the composition, he sings about all his "little plans and schemes", which, in truth, had diverted him from realising that all he was doing was "waiting for you". As if to underscore the finished nature of 'Real Love', John carefully printed out another manuscript, signing it from "Fairylands, Bermuda, July 9, 1980, JL".

Meanwhile, John had become entranced by the artwork that adorned the walls at Villa Undercliff, particularly a large portrait of the Luthi family. When he learned that the painter, American artist Nancy Gosnell, lived nearby, he commissioned a portrait of himself and Sean, which she painted over the next several days. Each morning, father and son would sit for Gosnell, who painstakingly created a four-foot by five-foot oil rendering of John and Sean reclining together on the pier at Villa Undercliff. In the portrait, Gosnell depicted them with their matching long hair, tank tops, and shorts. John's only stipulation was that she make sure to include the pendant around his neck in the painting. For his part, John enjoyed conversing with the worldly and intelligent Gosnell. He was particularly taken with her teenaged daughter Hannah after hearing that she had learned about the Beatles back at her high school in New Jersey. "You're studying *us*?" he asked. "You're kidding!"[212]

John took to calling the portrait-in-progress *The Madonna and Child of 1980*. For her part, Gosnell recalled John's excitement about his island holiday. "He was enchanted with the fact that the house was situated in an area of Bermuda called Fairylands," she remembered. At the same time, he was open about his reason for being there, that it was a working vacation designed to afford him with the headspace to compose a raft of new material. "He was tired of writing songs for kids," she observed. "He wanted to write music for adults and couldn't wait to get back in the studio and start recording." Gosnell fondly remembered John's affable nature, from his warm-hearted relationship with Sean to the songs he played for her on the piano. "He was funny and entertaining," said Gosnell. "He could do impressions of famous people. His Henry Kissinger was quite amazing."[213]

As July wore on, John's vast stores of American currency had begun to run low. In a breakneck effort to replenish his cash, Rich DePalma swung into action back at Studio One. Short on staff at the Dakota, he dispatched Mike Tree, the tall, bespectacled gardener who tended to the plants strewn about apartment 72, to act as courier and provide John with a parcel of American dollars to get him through the rest of his trip. As it turned out, John didn't bother to wait. On July 14, he carried out one of his legendary shopping sprees, haunting the antique shops and clothiers on Hamilton's Front Street. With his American Express card at the ready, he charged $5,250 and $14,882.25 at Heritage Antiques and Bluck's, respectively, later ordering a grey flannel suit from the English Sports Shop for good measure. Having flashed his credit card in public, John had suddenly put his much-valued privacy at risk. Sure enough, an article detailing his extravagance appeared in the *Mid-Ocean News* a few days later. For the first time during his island visit, John was revisited by the paranoia that he had seemingly left behind in New York City.[214]

In a final burst of creativity, John composed a final trio of new compositions in Bermuda. Up first was 'Cleanup Time', which had emerged directly from a conversation with Jack Douglas on July 20 as they made preparations for their August recording sessions. "We were talking about the 70s and that. We were talking about cleaning up and getting out of drugs and alcohol and those kinds of things – not me personally, but people in general. He said, 'Well, it's cleanup time right?' I said, 'It sure is', and that was the end of the conversation. I went straight to the piano and started boogying, and 'Cleanup Time' came out." During the same telephone call, John vacillated about which version of 'Watching The Wheels' he wanted to perform in the recording studio with Douglas. Would it be the acoustic guitar version – which Jack later described as having a "fast", "almost Dylany" "boom-jang, boom-jang" cadence – or the statelier piano take?[215]

As it happened, 'Cleanup Time' wasn't entirely new. John borrowed a lyric from 'Memories' – "no friends and yet no enemies", which he had derived from shipping magnate Aristotle Onassis, who famously said, "I have no friends and no enemies, only competitors." As with the Beatles' 'Cry Baby Cry' from *The White Album*, 'Cleanup Time' found John expressing his lifelong fascination with nursery rhymes – only this time, the traditional gender roles had been reversed with the queen toiling in the "counting house" to earn the family's keep. Meanwhile, the king spends his workaday life in the kitchen "making bread and honey". Recognising the self-referential nature of the song, John described his musical domestic drama as "sort of a description of John and Yoko and their little palace, the Palace of Versailles – the Dakota." In his composition, the Lennons' world is ruled by Yoko's cadre of psychics and fortune-tellers who ensure that the couple casts "the perfect spell".[216]

With 'Cleanup Time', John demonstrated the Lennons' progressive cultural fluency with second-wave feminism, which they espoused, to their minds, via their reversal of traditionally masculine and feminine domestic roles. At this juncture, the concept of males as homemakers had enjoyed considerable media play. Insatiable reader that he was, John had no doubt read John's Irving's *The World According to Garp*, the 1978 runaway bestseller about a writer-husband who tends the home, while his wife works as a college professor. Meanwhile, Garp befriends a transsexual former NFL football player, while his mother emerges as an international feminist icon – not unlike the Lennons' Upper West Side neighbour Susan Sontag.

When he finished 'Cleanup Time', John once again printed out a manuscript of the lyrics, which he signed from "Fairylands, Bermuda, July 20, 1980, JL".

Working in a similar vein as 'Cleanup Time', John completed 'Woman' in brisk fashion. In many ways, the composition continued John's line of thinking back at the Swizzle Inn with Fred about his sexual past, particularly in terms of behaviours that he had come to deeply regret. During his Beatles days, John had penned a key lyric for *Sgt. Pepper*'s 'Getting Better', admitting that he used to be cruel to his woman, beating her and keeping her away "from the things that she loved". For John, it had been a very public reckoning of his one-time penchant for expressing himself through violence. As he later explained:

I used to be cruel to my woman, and physically – any woman. I was a hitter. I couldn't express myself and I hit. I fought men and I hit women. That is why I am always on about peace, you see. It is the most violent people who go for love and peace. Everything's the opposite. But I sincerely believe in love and peace. I am a violent man who has learned not to be violent and regrets his violence. I will have to be a lot older before I can face in public how I treated women as a youngster.[217]

With 'Woman', John made an express effort to pay homage to the subjects of his youthful violence. "'Woman' came about because, one sunny afternoon in Bermuda, it suddenly hit me," said John. "I saw what women do for us. Not just what my Yoko does for me, although I was thinking in those personal terms. Any truth is universal." Working in the sun room with his acoustic guitar and ever-present drum machine, John announced, "take 1 of the new one". With a buoyant strum of his Ovation, John sings that he can "hardly express" his "mixed emotions" at his thoughtlessness.[218]

While the song came quickly for John, 'Woman' went through numerous takes as he perfected the composition. At one point, he even lost track of how many takes he had compiled. At yet another, he seems to be on the verge of frustration, announcing that the latest version is "positively *the* take, take 9". As with previous Villa Undercliff demo recordings, John overdubbed a double-tracked version of 'Woman', joyfully singing along with himself in the process.

He would attempt one last demo recording to cap off his fabled two-month sojourn in Bermuda. Entitled '(Forgive Me) My Little Flower Princess', he attempted three takes of the lively composition in his Villa Undercliff studio. In contrast with such fully realised tunes as 'Watching The Wheels', 'Woman', 'Cleanup Time', and 'Beautiful Boy (Darling Boy)', as it came to be titled, '(Forgive Me) My Little Flower Princess' remained largely unfinished. But no matter. John's summer odyssey had been an unqualified success.

For his part, Fred was left in a state of near-ecstasy. Since that very first day back in February 1979, he had worked as a glorified gofer, performing mindless errands for the outlandishly rich and famous while running himself ragged in the process. But life with John in Bermuda had been something altogether different. It had been scarcely four months since that signal moment back on Long Island when John heard Paul's

'Coming Up' blaring across the station wagon's radio and felt a spark – it may have been out of creativity or competition or even idle curiosity, but it was a spark nonetheless. And now, with his working retreat in Bermuda entering its final days, John had amassed a repertoire of no fewer than a dozen studio-ready songs.

More than a year earlier, John had likened himself to a phantom who only existed inside of people's minds. With a clutch of new, top-drawer compositions in hand, that selfsame phantom was ready to make his grand return to the corporeal world beyond the imagination.

CHAPTER 10

Hit Factory

On July 24, as John prepared to take his leave from his island getaway, he was crushed to learn that actor Peter Sellers had died at age 54 having perished from a heart attack in London. Sellers had exerted an enormous influence on John, who idolised the zany British funnyman for his work on *The Goon Show*, a satirical BBC radio programme. Like so many of his countrymen, John had become enrapt with the side-splitting antics of Sellers' pioneering comedy albums with George Martin during the producer's formative years before working with the Beatles.

Struggling to make sense of his grief, John sent Fred into Hamilton to buy all of the American and British newspapers he could find so that he could digest the obituaries and tributes. When he returned to Villa Undercliff, Fred was surprised to discover that John's funk had worsened. John had been especially taken with Sellers' recent Academy Award-nominated performance in director Hal Ashby's *Being There* (1979). Based on a novel by Jerzy Kosiński, *Being There* told the story of Chance the gardener (Sellers), a simple-minded servant whose entire life experience has been created by what he observes on television.

For John, Sellers' life trajectory eerily reminded him of his own experiences, particularly in terms of handling psychosocial issues. "If Sellers hadn't made it in show business," John told Fred, "he would have died in the nutty bin. If you're a nobody and are as crazy as he was, they lock you up. But if you're famous, then you're simply considered eccentric." But for

John, Sellers' late-career comeback with *Being There* after a decade of *Pink Panther* B-movie retreads was a matter of deep personal significance. "At least he went out with a hit," John said. "It sure beats fading from public view with a whimper", adding that nothing could be worse than dying in obscurity after having experienced the professional heights and accolades of his earlier triumphs.[219]

Over the next few days, John and Fred began packing up their belongings at Villa Undercliff, breaking down the recording studio in the sun room, and readying themselves for the short flight back to New York City. Yoko's directional man had spoken, advising that Monday, July 28 offered the best tidings for making a safe journey home. A few days before their planned departure, John made a point of dispatching Fred to the Sinclairs' Bluck Point residence to deliver a gift to the musician who had serenaded them with the sound of bagpipes over the past several weeks. In addition to a 21-year-old bottle of Chivas Regal Royal Salute Scotch whisky, John included a typewritten note saying, "thank you for the beautiful music and memories of Scotland. Here's a little something for the piper." After reading the letter, John Sinclair was pleased to discover one of Lennon's famous line drawings to boot.[220]

During their last full day on the island, John and Fred made one final sightseeing tour. They spent several hours exploring the building and grounds of Their Majesties Chappell, a seventeenth-century Anglican church on Queen Street. John had been especially interested in strolling through the graveyard at the rear of the church. As they made their rounds that day, John informed his assistant that he and Yoko had already settled on *Double Fantasy* as the name of their new long-player. The couple had decided it would be a "concept album". John added "we'll probably alternate tracks and create a kind of dialogue. It'll be the first vinyl soap opera."[221]

Back at Villa Undercliff, they took a final walk around the grounds of the estate. As Fred looked on, John began to share a deeply foreboding tale. For his part, the assistant felt a sudden chill, while John remained "very serious, very impersonal, and spoke without any visible feelings," Fred later recalled. "It was as if he were thinking out loud." As they walked along the shore, John described a recent series of "'weird' recurring dreams in which he suffered a violent death." Worse yet, he explained that he understood the genesis of these visions. "Because he had lived a life filled with violence, both in thought and in deed," John explained, "he was destined to die a violent death," adding that "he often fantasised about getting shot, which, he said, was a modern form of crucifixion, a rather elegant means of moving on to the next life with a clean karmic slate."[222]

Fred found himself bewildered by John's stunning revelation, reminding John that he was just 39 years old, a husband and father in the prime of life – not to mention, having just written a slew of well-wrought songs. With Sean, Helen, and Uda-san packed and ready to make the journey home, John remarked that "I guess it's time to say goodbye to paradise", flicking the butt of his Gitane into the waters that abutted Fairylands.[223]

When it came to selecting a recording studio for staging the Lennons' comeback LP, Yoko afforded Jack Douglas and his business partner Stan Vincent with a wide berth, stipulating that "you can do it anywhere in the world except for the Record Plant, and no California." Douglas and Vincent reasoned that Yoko's ongoing dispute with Roy Cicala must be at the heart of her embargo on working at the Record Plant. While the studio head had carried out the engineering duties associated with such albums as *Plastic Ono Band* and *Imagine*, Cicala's relationship with Yoko had apparently soured over the years. Yoko had supposedly come to resent Cicala's palpable deference to John's creative perspectives over her own. Meanwhile, Yoko's West Coast embargo was easy to understand, given its obvious roots in John's Lost Weekend activities in the Golden State during the early 1970s.[224]

To Jack's mind, the Record Plant didn't make any sense anyway. "The Record Plant was so visible," said Jack. "That's where they would *expect* him to be. I just couldn't do the record there." That's when Douglas and Vincent settled on the Hit Factory, which was neutral territory as far as they could ascertain. Better yet, it was off the beaten track. With Yoko's mandate for absolute privacy in mind, the Times Square location seemed like the perfect fit, all things considered. As Jack recalled, "The studio was located way over on the West Side at 10th Avenue and 48th Street in a building that no one would think to camp out in front of. No one would know. We could go in and out of there without ever being seen." Vincent saw an added bonus in the Hit Factory's private key-operated elevator that went directly to the sixth-floor studio where Jack planned to produce the album. To ensure what they hoped would be absolute secrecy, Rich DePalma block-booked the sessions at the studio in his own name.[225]

The Hit Factory was founded in 1968 by American songwriter Jerry Ragovoy, the composer behind the Rolling Stones' 'Time Is On My Side' and Janis Joplin's 'Piece Of My Heart'. Purchased by Ed Germano in 1975, it was a state-of-the-art recording studio by the summer of 1980, with Germano and his son Troy carrying out several refurbishments and modifications. As with the most cutting-edge facilities in the industry at the time, the Hit Factory featured a 24-track machine, along with a 10-channel rotary fader console. But Jack had other things in mind. Working with engineer Lee DeCarlo and assistant engineer Jon Smith, he modified the setup in the sixth-floor studio by outfitting it with two 16-track Ampex analogue machines. The idea, as Smith later recalled, was to deploy 16-track recording in order to improve the signal-to-noise ratio, which afforded the tape with more recording space and, in turn, decreased the amount of hiss. Although the vast majority of the Beatles' albums were recorded on comparatively primitive four-track machines, John was eminently familiar with 16-track technology, having deployed it for his *Mind Games* and *Walls And Bridges* albums.[226]

Wasting little time, Vincent enlisted Tony Davilio to begin creating arrangements for John's Bermuda demo tapes. In the 1960s, Davilio played guitar with the Stingrays and, later, the Silver Caboose. Since the early 1970s, he had made a steady living as an arranger, preparing notation for legacy acts and newcomers alike. He had also worked for a lengthy stint on behalf of Vincent's production company. As with the other personnel who would be selected for the project, Davilio was required to provide his astrological data in advance.

In terms of his contributions to *Double Fantasy*, the most important thing as far as Stan was concerned was that Davilio worked quickly and that his transcriptions were first-rate. In order to maintain the veil of secrecy that Yoko expected, Davilio was only allowed to listen to the recordings at Vincent's Upper East Side condo, where he put in 10-hour stints creating "lead sheets", the process via which arrangers transcribe a composition's melody and define its chord structure. Working with his acoustic guitar, Davilio compiled the lead sheets in Vincent's kitchen, drinking pots of coffee to keep his attention sharp. All in all, Davilio arranged some 30 compositions by John and Yoko.

To protect the Lennons' artistic interests, Vincent secured copyrights for all of the songs in advance of any rehearsals or recording sessions. He also handled the voluminous union paperwork associated with the project.

Without a standing recording contract, John and Yoko planned to handle all of the production costs out-of-pocket – from the expenses associated with Douglas and the studio musicians down to booking the Hit Factory and paying for food and beverages. As Vincent recalled, "One thing [John] hated was we had tons of contracts to sign. For every session, we had to submit contracts to the union and they had to be paid in a specific time. I had so many contracts and John had to sign every single one of them."[227]

Meanwhile, Douglas was forced to assemble a top-drawer backing band on short notice. John told Jack that "the most important thing to him was that the musicians on the date would be his contemporaries. So if John made a reference about a particular song that may have come from the Fifties or the Sixties, they would understand what he was talking about. He didn't want to talk to kids." On August 1, Jack sealed his production deal in the company of Yoko and David Warmflash, who agreed to provide Douglas with the handsome reward of five percentage points on top of the LP's gross profit. To mark the occasion, Yoko instructed Fred Seaman to write out a $25,000 advance to Douglas and Vincent's Waterfront Productions. That same afternoon, Douglas auditioned keyboard player George Small at the Record Plant. Vincent had recommended that Douglas consider the veteran session man for *Double Fantasy*, given Small's talent for moving easily among Broadway, television, and rock 'n' roll projects. For the audition, Small recalled, "I knew one of the things I was gonna have to play convincingly was stride-style piano like Fats Waller, where you have to play all the notes on the piano and use all the fingers on both hands. The upright piano I auditioned on was missing about a third of the keys, so it was an interesting piano to play. Right next to that piano in a very cramped storeroom was the actual mellotron that was used for *Sgt. Pepper*." To his great relief, Small passed the audition, and Douglas set an appointment to meet with the keyboard player the next day, Saturday, August 2, at the corner of West 72nd Street and Central Park West.[228]

Douglas, Small, and Davilio would shortly be joined by ace guitar player Hugh McCracken, who had previously worked on 'Happy Xmas (War Is Over)' with John and Yoko. In the interim, McCracken had emerged as one of the most sought-after session men in the business. He had also played on the sessions for Paul and Linda McCartney's *Ram* LP and briefly considered joining Wings in the early 1970s. John took the guitarist's association with McCartney in stride, once quipping, "Oh, so you were just auditioning on *Ram*, were you?" As with Small, McCracken had been carefully selected for the pre-production meetings at the Dakota. McCracken held the distinction of being the only player specifically chosen by John to perform on *Double Fantasy*.[229]

The pre-production meeting at the Dakota turned out to be a marvel, with John revelling in the opportunity to play his new songs for an audience of top-notch musicians. In preparation, John asked Fred to round up copies of 'Magic', Olivia Newton-John's hit single from the *Xanadu* soundtrack (1980), and Kate Bush's *Never For Ever* LP (1980), with its haunting, quirky introductory cut 'Babooshka'. That afternoon, he warmed up for his visitors by listening to Noël Coward's 'The Party's Over Now'. John was entranced by Coward's evocative, emotional falsetto. "Listen," said John. "He's crying." When his guests arrived that night, John announced, "Welcome to our humble abode, my dears. I've been waiting for you for five years!"[230]

As Yoko continued refining her lyrics that evening in apartment 72, the bandmates tried their hand at Davilio's transcriptions, which Fred had helpfully photocopied down in Studio One, performing rudimentary versions of such songs as 'Borrowed Time' and, as it had now come to be known, 'Beautiful Boy (Darling Boy)'. As they worked that night, the musicians took notes on Davilio's scratch sheets for reference during the upcoming Hit Factory sessions. The arranger recalled that John "was like a kid, he was very excited". At one point, Davilio and McCracken even found themselves in a good-natured fracas over one of the chords from John's Bermuda demos. "I thought it was an A chord," said Davilio, but McCracken "thought it was an E chord. John overheard us arguing and came over and said, 'Hey hey, boys, what's going on?' We asked him, 'What's the chord you use on that part of the song?' He played it, and Hugh and I looked at each other sheepishly and realised we were both wrong."[231]

With Davilio, McCracken, and Small in the know as far as their famous clients were concerned, Douglas filled out the rest of the *Double Fantasy* band with a host of crack players, including bassist Tony Levin, whose wide-ranging credentials included his work on Buddy Rich's jazz recordings, Paul Simon's bestselling LP *Still Crazy After All These Years* (1975), and Peter Gabriel's recent solo work. Standout bassist Willie Weeks had originally been considered for the project, although he proved to be unavailable, having already been booked, somewhat ironically, for a George Harrison session. As for the band's drummer, Douglas tapped

Andy Newmark, the veteran performer on such albums as Carly Simon's *No Secrets* (1972) and Gary Wright's *The Dream Weaver* (1975), as well as the touring drummer for George Harrison's 1974 "Dark Horse" American tour. To fill out the percussion, Douglas recruited Bronx-native Arthur Jenkins, who had played with Lennon's idol Bob Marley, Calypso king Harry Belafonte, and Johnny Nash, for whom Jenkins served up percussion on the global smash hit 'I Can See Clearly Now'. Jenkins was a known quantity to Lennon, having provided percussion on *Walls And Bridges* and *Rock 'n' Roll*.

When it came to landing a lead guitarist for the project, Douglas had something altogether different in mind. While the other players sported long, distinguished résumés, he wanted a slightly younger musician to fill out the band. To his mind, 27-year-old Earl Slick suited the role perfectly. He would come to describe Slick as *Double Fantasy*'s "wild card", as an edgier sort of player who could infuse the coterie of veteran players with a different kind of energy and spunk. At this juncture, Slick's most significant credential involved his service as a member of David Bowie's touring band, especially his guitar work on the *Young Americans* (1975) album. John had made key contributions to that record in the form of a cover version of the Beatles' 'Across The Universe' and 'Fame', which he had co-written with Bowie and Carlos Alomar. Although he had been kept in the dark like the other recently drafted members of the *Double Fantasy* band, Slick already deduced the identity of his bandleader. "I'm a pretty good detective," Slick later observed, "and I figured that if Jack was the producer then it had to be Aerosmith, Cheap Trick, or John Lennon. And only John made sense, given the top secret way we were doing things."[232]

Douglas held rehearsals with the musicians at New York City's SIR Studios, which was nestled inside a loft in Chelsea's gallery district. Working with Davilio's charts, the band members began the laborious work of perfecting the arrangements. To their credit, McCracken and Small maintained the veil of secrecy, well aware of John's dictum that if anyone broke confidence, he would scuttle the entire project. As the band required a singer to conduct their rehearsals, Douglas performed rough takes of John's vocals during their run-throughs. When he sang lead, Jack later recalled, the band would break out into laughter. With his deeper register, Jack's vocals often required the group to play the song in a lower key.

With Davilio, McCracken, and Small in tow, Jack conducted one last rehearsal with John and Yoko for the project on Tuesday, August 5, in apartment 72. That night, they played through several numbers in the Lennons' living room, furnished in all white with the baby grand white piano as its centrepiece. For John, the rehearsal had found him to be truly in his element, energised by the simple act of hearing his latest repertoire beginning to come to life. After a dinner break, John rejoined the rehearsal with a futurist-looking guitar strapped about his neck. It was the Sardonyx – the strange contraption with the two stainless-steel outrigger bars that he stored in apartment 71 with his vast inventory of guitars. As the musicians looked on, John plugged in the Sardonyx and began violently strumming the instrument, which emitted a fusillade of metallic sound. At one point, his playing wandered into a strange key, leaving Davilio and McCracken baffled as they attempted to figure out which one of the songs he was rehearsing. John quickly grew bored with the musicians as they analysed the intricacies of his performance. "You should explain it to her," he said, pointing towards Yoko, who possessed formal music training. "She understands this stuff much better than I do." Not missing a beat, McCracken began playing the opening riff to the Beatles' 'I Want You (She's So Heavy)', and John suddenly perked up. "That's the first song I wrote about her!" he exclaimed. "Most of my songs are about her, you know!"[233]

Of all of the instruments that would come to adorn the musical palette of *Double Fantasy*, none was more unusual and eccentric than John's Sardonyx, which he had taken to calling his "space guitar". Built by luthier Jeff Levin and outfitted with custom electronics by Ken Schaffer, the Sardonyx 800 D II guitar was virtually unknown at the time. Having produced some two-dozen Sardonyx guitars over the years, Levin and Schaffer worked out of Matt Umanov's renowned New York City guitar shop. Schaffer later recalled that John had purchased the instrument himself, having been a regular customer at Umanov's Lower Manhattan store when he and Yoko lived in the Village in the early 1970s. Levin fashioned the body of the guitar out of wood, with the guitar strap attached to the upper aluminium tubing. The upscale version of the Sardonyx John bought included a complex of electronics that Schaffer had designed around two output channels, which the player could toggle in a series, in parallel, or in and out of phase with each other to produce myriad sounds. At one point, Levin built a bass version of the Sardonyx.[234]

Prior to Lennon's work on *Double Fantasy*, the instrument saw its most visible action in the hands of Howard Leese, the lead guitarist for Heart, who deployed the instrument, which he described as being straight out of *Star Trek*, during the band's late 1970s concerts. Not surprisingly, it was the talk of the Hit Factory. When he first laid eyes on it, Slick said that it looked "like a fucking ski rack for a car!" For his part, Douglas playfully called it the "Sardonicus". During his run with the guitar, Leese praised the instrument's "big, thick tone", adding that "it really gets some unusual sounds". As for his concert performances, Leese would never forget the audience response. "It was fun to play, and people constantly asked, 'What *is* that?'"[235]

As Jack later recalled, the last Dakota rehearsal would end on a most unforgettable and fortuitous note. While the musicians were packing up their equipment, John paused near a Fender Rhodes electric piano by the door of apartment 72 and began playing a composition that hadn't been included on the Bermuda tapes. "Where'd that come from?" Jack asked, astonished at the mysterious new tune. "Oh, I dunno," John replied. "It just kinda came. You think it'll make it to this record?" Douglas couldn't believe his luck. "Make it?" he answered. "It's gonna be the first single. It's gotta be the first song on the record. You know, come on, it's perfect."[236]

Known by this juncture as 'Starting Over', John's latest number was hardly new, having evolved over a period of months. As the product of no fewer than three different song-fragments, it had begun life as 'My Life', one of the fall 1979 demo recordings that John had performed on the Yamaha. For a short while, he sustained the tune as 'I Watch Your Face', with musical overtones of Buddy Holly's 'Raining In My Heart' and possibly the Applejacks' 'Tell Me When'. In perhaps its most poignant moment, 'I Watch Your Face' refers lovingly to Sean; as his son sleeps, John sings that no one told him that "life was so worth keeping".

In the days since John's return from Bermuda, the song had morphed into 'Don't Be Crazy', which formed the verse foundation for the song that would eventually become 'Starting Over'. In 'Don't Be Crazy', John calls to be left alone, singing that they can't "paint the empty skies for you", in obvious reference to legions of fans and critics clamouring for his return to the stage. To fill out the verses, he took to singing Holly's 'It's So Easy' with his piano arrayed against his usual drum machine accompaniment: "the lessons have been learned", he sings. Throughout his demo recordings for 'Don't Be Crazy', John quotes liberally from the musical bridge of the Carpenters' 1970 worldwide smash hit '(They Long

To Be) Close to You', penned by the legendary songwriting team of Burt Bacharach and Hal David.

As John consolidated 'My Life' and 'Don't Be Crazy', a bevy of older songs were clearly on his mind, if not the spirit itself of rock legends like Holly and Elvis Presley. With inspiration at hand, John concocted 'The Worst Is Over', which formed the eventual chorus for 'Starting Over'. By early August 1980, 'My Life', 'I Watch Your Face', 'Don't Be Crazy', and 'The Worst Is Over' had made their steady progress into becoming 'Starting Over'. John recorded three demos for the tune, singing along with his acoustic guitar and with his ever-faithful CompuRhythm by his side. By this juncture, the lyrics were nearly in place, save for a pair of guide vocals that John presented as place-savers. For the bridge, John sings about taking off on a getaway weekend – a second honeymoon in a phoneless "old hotel" far away from the madding crowd. At another point, he returned to his old literary favourite Lewis Carroll to fill out the verses, borrowing "the time has come, the walrus said" from *The Walrus and the Carpenter* (1872) as part of his guide vocal.

As John readied 'Starting Over' for the studio, he was surely aware that the pop music marketplace had been overrun with the title, especially in the country music sector, throughout the past several months. Up first was Tammy Wynette's 'Starting Over', which had been composed by prolific country crossover songwriter Bob McDill. The song had become a Top 20 country hit that spring for Wynette, the country music stalwart behind such classics as 'Stand By Your Man' and 'D-I-V-O-R-C-E'. And then there was 'Starting Over Again', which had originally been penned by disco queen Donna Summer and her husband Bruce Sudano. In the hands of entertainer Dolly Parton, 'Starting Over Again' had topped the country charts in May 1980. To separate John's song from the increasingly crowded herd, Lennon and Douglas opted to retitle his eventual release as '(Just Like) Starting Over'.

As the Lennons' inaugural date at the Hit Factory grew ever near, John's muse – which he had jumpstarted in fine style back in Bermuda – simply wouldn't quit. Returning to 'Help Me To Help Myself', he began reshaping the composition into a gospel-tinged number on the Dakota's baby grand piano. The recording is briefly interrupted at the outset by a sticky sustain pedal. In a mock-German accent, John says, "What's the matter with this thing? It is sticking on my feets here. That's why we are having these interruptions. It's very bad." With the pedal back

151

in order, John sings about his attempts to "stay alive" in spite of "the angel of destruction", which seems to hound him endlessly in spite of his earnest and concerted efforts to find his way. One of the most promising compositions of the year – which was truly saying a lot, in John's case – 'Help Me To Help Myself' finds the composer summoning quasi-spiritual forces in the service of his art, perhaps even in the service of his talent on the eve of making his return to the recording studio.

At this same juncture, John took yet another pass at landing a solid demo of 'Serve Yourself'. By this point, the lyrics had evolved considerably, with John eschewing some of his Dylan-oriented vitriol in favour of a larger religious critique that was seemingly at odds with the spiritual acceptance of 'Help Me To Help Myself'. In a single stanza, he manages to grapple with the whole of Christianity and evolutionary science in nearly the same breath. For John, the notion of blindly accepting the results of apparently settled questions – whether they hail from the scientific perspective of evolutionary theory or the blind faith of organised religion – was a bridge too far. "I don't believe in the evolution of fish to monkeys to men," John remarked that September. "Why aren't monkeys changing into men now? It's absolute garbage. It's absolutely irrational garbage, as mad as the ones who believe the world was made only 4,000 years ago, the fundamentalists. That and the monkey thing are both as insane as the other."[237]

For John and Yoko's *Double Fantasy*, the big day finally arrived on Thursday, August 7. For his part, John had not recorded any new original music at a professional recording studio since July 1974, when he began working on *Walls And Bridges* at the Record Plant. Although they were separated at the time, Yoko had also completed her most recent turn in the studio during that same period, when she recorded 'Yume O Moutou (Let's Have A Dream)'. Recognising the historic nature of the moment, Yoko had retained a Boston publicity agent, Charles J. Cohen, to capture the couple's triumphant return to the recording studio on that hot August day. To mark the occasion, Cohen dispatched photographer Roger Farrington to meet the Lennons at the Dakota and accompany them to the Hit Factory. "My job," Farrington recalled, "was to get one photo of them to document their return to the music business."[238]

When he arrived that afternoon, Farrington was instructed to wait in the room outside Yoko's Studio One office. The first thing he heard was the sound of John's voice as he made his way downstairs – presumably from the superkitchen six floors above. For his part, Farrington was nervous, having not received much in the way of instructions for carrying out the photo shoot that day. Dressed in a summer suit, he was perspiring slightly when John entered the room, wearing a black cowboy outfit that included an embroidered shirt and wide-brimmed hat. In his hand was a black attaché case. Over his shoulder was his tan leather bag of demos and other attendant paraphernalia. John was joined by Yoko, who emerged from the inner office wearing an ensemble comprised of a blue hot-pants playsuit, heeled mules, and a baseball cap. As they prepared to leave Studio One, Farrington could make out light-coloured food stains on her outfit. It was a truly odd occurrence for a woman who had seemed so pulled together, so tautly arrayed in terms of her clothing and demeanour over the years.

As they made their way through the *porte-cochère* and onto the sidewalk that fronted West 72nd Street, Farrington jockeyed for position in front of the couple so that he could document the occasion. Standing nearby was Paul Goresh. With his ever-present Minolta XG1, he captured a shot of the couple exiting the archway, with John's eyes fixed squarely on the portly fan. As the Lennons climbed into a waiting limousine, Farrington couldn't help noticing that Yoko was overrun with anxiety. Looking furtively up and down the streetscape, there was a sense of fear in her eyes, in the seriousness of her expression. In that moment, Farrington wondered if the aloofness that she seemed to project in public life had been mistaken all along. For her part, Yoko seemed positively nervous – far more nervous than Farrington even, with his strange assignment – that something might go wrong right there outside the Dakota and catapult John back into exile in his bedroom. There was no doubt about it: she was concerned for her husband.[239]

As the limo pulled away, Farrington realised he didn't have a ride to the studio. And that's when Fred pulled up in the station wagon, filled with John's guitars and other assorted equipment, and offered the cameraman a lift. After they made the short trip to the Hit Factory, Farrington hopped out onto West 48th Street so that he could photograph John and Yoko as they made their way towards the building's entrance. Of the 31 shots he captured that day, Farrington knew that Yoko would most likely select the photo of the Lennons entering the Hit Factory just below the studio's awning. After taking the elevator with John and Yoko to the private sixth-floor studio, Farrington noted that John's sense of humour seemed to grow in direct relation to Yoko's anxiety. As they stood in the lobby beside the studio's elaborate logo, he snapped several pictures. "Are we doing PR for the Hit Factory?" John joked.[240]

When they made their way inside the studio, John's running commentary continued. "The photographer was me wife's idea," John quipped, as Fred began setting up the guitars, which included the electronic Sardonyx, his Ovation acoustic, and the Gibson Hummingbird from Manny's Music. Farrington followed John into the control booth, where John carefully opened up the attaché case, only to discover that he had unclasped it upside down, nearly spilling reams of sheet music onto the floor. After he righted himself, he carefully removed a photograph of Sean, which he affixed inside the control booth above the mixing desk. As John later recalled, "I was guilty all through the making of *Double Fantasy*. We had his picture pinned in the studio 'cause I didn't want to lose contact with what I'd got. We had the picture up there all the time in between the speakers so whenever you're checking the stereo, he was looking at me all the time."[241]

Back on the studio floor, John began to strap on the Sardonyx. As he snapped photographs of the musician, Farrington caught sight of a scar on John's neck, the result of a July 1969 automobile accident that he and Yoko, along with their young children Julian and Kyoko, had suffered during a break from the production of the Beatles' *Abbey Road* LP. As he waited for John to begin playing the strange electric guitar around his neck, Farrington attempted to make conversation with Yoko. "So how's the record going to work?" he asked. "We're not sure yet," she curtly answered. "One side might be his, the other mine. Or we might alternate songs." And that's when John began strumming the Sardonyx, which emitted an explosive, howling fusillade of electronic sound. As he snapped a few more pictures, Farrington watched as John threw up his arms to greet Earl Slick, who had just strolled into the studio. For his part, Slick had big plans that day, hoping to be the first to arrive at the studio in a display of earnestness and responsibility. But he had been shown up by John, of all people – the very person whom he had most hoped to impress that day.[242]

"I couldn't believe it!" said Slick, having seen his plans thwarted so quickly. As he walked up to introduce himself to John, he was stunned by Lennon's warm-hearted, ebullient greeting. "Nice to see you again!" John exclaimed. "I was like, 'nice to see you, too, but we haven't met'," Slick recalled. John assured the young guitarist that his memory must be faulty, that they had in point of fact met during the sessions for Bowie's *Young Americans* LP. "Trust me," Slick laughed. "You're a Beatle. If we'd worked together before, I would have remembered it." As for the Bowie sessions, "we must have recorded at different times", Slick added. "No," said John, "we were there together." For Slick there was only one possibility. "Maybe I was fucking stoned," he replied. "Well," said John, "that's a possibility." If Slick thought that the matter had suddenly concluded in John's mind, he would shortly learn that he was sorely mistaken. As a joke throughout the *Double Fantasy* sessions, John frequently asked "remember me now?" to Earl as an ongoing jibe.[243]

As the other musicians began to arrive, Farrington realised his assignment was over, that it was time to hurry back to Boston, develop the photographs, and meet his deadline with Cohen. To his surprise, Yoko paused to offer him lodging that night at the Dakota, although he politely declined, knowing he had to make his flight later that afternoon at LaGuardia Airport.[244]

So far, Yoko's veil of secrecy seemed to be coming off with nary a hitch – that is, for everyone except Davilio, who hadn't even gone to the right studio that day. Eager to begin the first day of recording sessions, Davilio had left his apartment, accidentally going to the Record Plant instead of the Hit Factory. Absent-mindedly walking up to the front desk at the Record Plant's 44th Street location, the arranger covertly informed the receptionist that he was there for "the Lennon project". And that's when he realised his mistake. As Davilio later recalled, "She looked at me in utter disbelief and whispered, 'I think you want the Hit Factory.'"[245]

Apparently, the new John and Yoko album hadn't been that much of a secret after all.

CHAPTER 11

A Heart Play

As the musicians quickly learned, John planned to make decidedly short work of the recording process for *Double Fantasy*. To ensure that he was ready for virtually anything, he instructed Fred to haul his guitar inventory over from the Dakota. "John brought all of his guitars to the studio," Douglas remembered. "Every Beatle guitar that you ever saw him with was in the room – his Rickenbacker 325, his Epiphone Casino. There were about 20 guitars in the room – beautiful old Strats, Les Pauls, 335s and other things like that." Within half an hour, John was poised and ready to launch into the first song. As Andy Newmark remembered, "John showed up, he said hello, had a cup of coffee, made some small talk for a few minutes, and then said, 'Okay, let me show you guys a tune.'" Up first, rather fittingly, was 'Borrowed Time'.[246]

As Douglas later recalled, "everyone was a little nervous" that first day – even the folks in the control booth. The technical side of *Double Fantasy* was overseen by engineer Lee DeCarlo, whose recent credits included Aerosmith's *Live! Bootleg* (1978), Chicago's *Hot Streets* (1978), and Aretha Franklin's *La Diva* (1979), along with assistant engineers Jon Smith and Julie Last. Realising the historical significance of the *Double Fantasy* sessions, Douglas instructed his production team to record them in their entirety, including background chatter between takes. As Smith recalled, "Jack said we were to record John whenever he was on mic." To accomplish this end, the production team set up a Studer B67 two-track machine in the control booth. Occasionally, John would notice the surreptitious machine running in the background and enquire about its purpose. Jack's production team would gently brush him off, explaining that the Studer was for "tape echo". Over the course of the sessions, Jack's ruse would allow for the accumulation of some 115 hours' worth of studio conversation and outtakes.[247]

Out on the studio floor, the bandmates had already begun to feel each other out. "I was basically a loose-cannon, rock 'n' roll guitar player," said Slick. "That's what John liked about me. Everybody else in the band were organised session guys who had their shit together." To Slick's mind, veteran players like Tony Levin and Hugh McCracken were eminently more sophisticated in their approach than he could ever be. "I would come into the studio hungover and beat up, but I still got it done."[248]

Even though he had been to the private rehearsals with John at the Dakota, George Small still found himself star-struck by the experience of working with Lennon in the studio. "John would get in the vocal booth and count it off and start singing. Man, that voice would be enough to galvanise you into playing in the proper spirit. I couldn't always see him, but the presence of his voice was in your headphones, it was inside your brain. I mean, there were times I just had to pinch myself, 'Am I here?'" Remarkably, even veteran sidemen like Newmark – who had performed with many of popular music's most vaunted names – had difficulty coming to grips with the special import of the unique opportunity to play with Lennon. As Tony Davilio later recalled, nearly every time Newmark made a mistake, he would say, "Uh oh, they're gonna call Russ Kunkel", referring to the ace session drummer who had worked with such luminaries as Jackson Browne and James Taylor. Finally, John got fed up, saying "Dammit, Andy, if I wanted Russ Kunkel, I would have gotten Russ Kunkel." And that was that.[249]

For 'I'm Stepping Out', John put the band through their paces, quickly establishing each player's role in the song, and set the stage for Jack to lay down the track in the booth. A work-process soon developed in which John would briefly take the musicians aside to go over their parts – sometimes, after playing one of his Bermuda demos to set the mood. To keep things moving briskly in the studio, John developed a shorthand for referring to the players, calling out "you, drummer!" in reference to Newmark or "hey, Kojak!" to bassist Tony Levin, who had recently shaved his head in the style of TV star Telly Savalas. When he felt that Newmark had begun doing too many drum fills, he'd tell him to "play like Ringo". By the same token, when he didn't like something, John would announce, without a hint of anger or distress, "that sucks, guys", and the bandmates would launch into another take. Jack's production team positioned the vocal isolation booth on the studio floor so that John could sing his vocals live along with the group's performance, which imbued each track with deeper levels of energy and emotion.[250]

During one of the takes for 'I'm Stepping Out', John prefaced the song with a spoken-word introduction, saying "This here is the story about a househusband who, you know, just has to get out of the house, he's been looking at the, you know, the kids for days and days, he's been watching the kitchen and screwing around watching *Sesame Street* till he's going crazy!" After knocking out several high-octane takes of 'I'm Stepping Out', the band turned to Yoko's 'Forgive Me, My Love', a relatively new song that she had composed after scanning the lyrics to '(Forgive Me) My Little Flower Princess'. During the recording sessions for John's songs, Yoko would often sit in the booth with Jack's production team, either knitting or reading to pass the time. In some cases, she would relax in the nearby green room that Ed Germano had set aside for the Lennons' private use during their time at the Hit Factory. During Yoko's recordings, John would often sit beside Jack at the console, offering up words of encouragement for his wife over the studio's talkback system.

In short order, the group of musicians and studio personnel developed a working routine, beginning each day's sessions at 2 p.m. As fellow Upper West Siders, Jack and John would meet at 9 a.m. outside the Dakota and make the short walk over to Café La Fortuna, where they would have breakfast and discuss the previous evening's session. As Jack later recalled, "We'd sit in the back garden and have chocolate iced cappuccinos and talk over what happened last night, what was gonna happen, what was going on with Yoko, everything." Not surprisingly, they would frequently discuss John's concerns about the quality of his performance after his five-year hiatus. He also worried that the musicians didn't cotton to his more contemporary, grown-up sound. Jack was always ready to allay his fears. "There were moments at La Fortuna," Jack remembered, "where I had to say, 'John, really, I swear, it's good. You sound great.'"[251]

On Friday, August 8, Sean joined his parents at the session, taking a tour of the control booth with his father, and observing the band's rehearsal for 'Borrowed Time', the next song on the docket. John took special delight in showing off the control room to Sean. "It's a funny place, right? Like a spaceship, isn't it?" John asked his son. "Did you see your picture?" With Sean looking on, John captured 'Borrowed Time' in a few short takes. To set the stage, he suggested that the group imagine the song in the style of the Isley Brothers' 'Twist And Shout' or the instrumental 'Spanish Twist'. From the first take, 'Borrowed Time' prominently featured Arthur Jenkins' percussion, with his bongo part affording the song with the tropical island sound of its Bermuda origins. With 'Borrowed Time' under their belts, the band turned to Yoko's 'Kiss Kiss Kiss', a high energy, danceable ode to uninhibited female eroticism. Yoko performed the song with unchecked, salacious abandon. As she remarked a few weeks later, on 'Kiss Kiss Kiss', "there is the sound of a woman coming to a climax on it, and she is crying out to be held, to be touched. It will be controversial, because people still feel it's less natural to hear the sounds of a woman's lovemaking than, say, the sound of a Concorde, killing the atmosphere and polluting nature. But the lovemaking is the sound that will make us survive."[252]

Although many of the musicians were unfamiliar with Yoko's style, they quickly took a liking to her avant-garde compositions. As Slick later recalled, "I really enjoyed playing on 'Kiss Kiss Kiss'. I got to do some really wacked-out feedback stuff." To his mind, "Yoko was so ahead of what everyone was thinking at the time." When it came to performing on her songs, Slick and McCracken would decide which of the two guitarists would be featured, given their different playing styles. As Slick remembered, on "'Kiss Kiss Kiss', John, Yoko, and I worked on it together because this was a little edgier and off the wall." Meanwhile, "Hughie did the more intricate, melodic stuff."[253]

At the conclusion of 'Kiss Kiss Kiss', Yoko transformed her vocals into a series of highly suggestive, orgasmic sounds. "I was lying down on the floor in the studio to sing that part at the end so I was able to have some privacy," she recalled. "It was pretty funny." With Davilio contributing an eerie keyboard part to accompany the song's "great punk energy", in McCracken's words, she performed the "Yokogasm" while everyone else piled into the control booth with their "jaws hanging open". As for John, he was thrilled with his wife's effort. When she was finished, John jumped out of his seat, shouting, "Yeah, Mother!"[254]

As the Friday night session wore into the wee hours, John and the band tried their hands at 'Nobody Told Me'. By this time, the musicians were nearing exhaustion, although John was determined to capture a take of the four-year-old song. As they gathered for take 1, John's guitarists were still making their way back to the studio floor after taking a short break. Thanks to Jack's Studer recorders, the studio chatter survives, underscoring both the breakneck pace of John's work style, as well as the manner in which he balanced his home and professional lives during his time at the Hit Factory:

John: Slick's not here. Where's Hugh? Okay, well, whoever's here, let's play it then! And if they're not, good, we'll take it without 'em! … Okay, okay, let's do it… Leave four bars and I'll come in, or just play until I come in, whatever…

Yoko: John, Sean wants to say goodnight.

John: Okay, put the phone up to the speakers… What time is it? He should be in bed already… Goodnight, Sean, see you in the morning. Goodnight, Sean, I love you. Sweet dreams. See you for breakfast!

Yoko: He said, "I love you, too."

John: Well, I hope he does. I'm the only dad he's got!

And with that, John and the band launched into their first, rough take of 'Nobody Told Me'. In the nick of time, Slick managed to return to his place on the studio floor, where he picked up his vintage 1965 Gibson SG Jr, which, along with his black-lacquered Les Paul, was his guitar of choice during the *Double Fantasy* sessions.

By Saturday afternoon, they were back at the Hit Factory with another trio of songs to compile. They completed two standout Yoko compositions on the day, including 'Nobody Sees Me Like You Do' and 'Don't Be Scared'. For 'Nobody Sees Me Like You Do', the band adopted a smooth, medium-tempo sound as Yoko sang about growing old together with her husband, "rocking away in our walnut chairs". For John and Yoko, the image of old age was a frequent motif in their conversations. As he neared his 40th birthday – and Sean's fifth – John had begun to worry that their son's childhood had been whizzing by, that the precocious boy would soon be needing them less and less – no more lullabies or bath time. "When we're 80," said John, "we'll be in rocking-chairs, waiting for Sean's postcards." For 'Don't Be Scared', the band adopted a gentle reggae sound, as Yoko explores the anxiety of commitment and the age-old reality that to love is better than to "never love at all".[255]

But the main event that Saturday was clearly John's '(Just Like) Starting Over', which Jack had confidently slated to be *Double Fantasy*'s lead track. In many ways, the song acted as the thematic centrepiece of John and Yoko's entire project – the notion of taking a leap of faith, both in themselves and their audience, and allowing themselves to become vulnerable to whatever the fates had in store. In his self-consciousness about the song, John began reading far too much into his own lyrics, including the phrase "spread our wings and fly". At one point, he recalled, "I nearly took the word 'wings' out because I thought, Oh, God! They'll all be saying, 'What's this about Wings?'"[256]

With his usual lightning-quick recording style, John led the band through three takes of '(Just Like) Starting Over'. Before performing the first take, John asked DeCarlo to attempt to engineer a 1950s-era sound. "Make me magnificent, Lee, make me the man of my dreams. I want Elvis Vincent." As he geared up for the first run-through, John dedicated the track to "Gene and Eddie and Elvis… and Buddy!" For John, the song's essential nature drew him back to his musical roots, a lost world without irony or judgement in contrast with the present. "I'd done that music and identified with it – that was my period – but I'd never written a song that sounded like that period," said John. "So I just thought, 'Why the hell not?' In the Beatles days that would have been taken as a joke. One avoided clichés. Course now clichés are not clichés anymore."[257]

With a studio full of crack professionals, the band rose to the occasion, adorning '(Just Like) Starting Over' with energy and finesse. From Small's piano triplets and Levin's galloping bass to Newmark's steady backbeat and Slick and McCracken's soaring guitars, the recording was a marvel. John fired up the band in between takes with quick stabs at Roy Orbison's 'Crying' and 'Only The Lonely (Know How I Feel)', as well as a new original composition called 'Gone From This Place'. John relished his role as bandleader, enjoying the give-and-take of the camaraderie that was developing among the musicians. At one point, he chides McCracken for not wearing his headphones during the rehearsal that evening, with the guitarist answering in perfect deadpan:

John: Hugh, get on the phones and you wouldn't play so fucking loud.

Hugh: I can't hear. I don't have my phones on.

*   *   *

As he crafted his voice for '(Just Like) Starting Over', John came to describe his vocal stylings as a kind of "Elvis Orbison". In so doing, he recalled the key influences of his rock 'n' roll youth. By contrast, the song's lyrics held far more significance for John in the present day, a place where encroaching middle-age finds him reaching back for one more shot at greatness – not merely in his professional life, but in terms of his relationship with Yoko. With his vocal gusto on full display, John sings of falling in love again: "It'll be just like starting over."

In just three short days, John and Yoko had already cut eight tracks. Working at such a pace required everyone to be in top form. On several occasions, John ensured that he was treated by a masseuse before laying down his vocals, believing that a back massage helped to open up his vocal cords. Meanwhile, Jack ensured that the studio piano was tuned before every session. With John and Yoko footing the bill – and still without a contract, no less – every aspect of the recording process seemed to be magnified. At one point, Jack finally asked the question that had been on his mind since he had climbed aboard the seaplane back in July: "Why am I doing this record with you?" John didn't miss a beat, answering "because you have good antenna, and that works for me because you always can read me." Most importantly, John told him, "you know what this is about." Jack was content with John's reply, having felt that communication was one of his strong points as a producer. But he also knew that John was the ideal client as far as he was concerned. "He was so without ego when he was working," Jack recalled. "He would just take a direction. If I told John, 'for this vocal, I need you to stand on your head', he'd say, 'if you think that's better, I'll do it.' I mean, he was like that." Knowing his friend as well as he did, Jack made sure to treat John's voice with slap-echo – the sound associated with Elvis Presley's 1950s-era productions with Sun Records – in order to address Lennon's longstanding concern over the quality of his vocals.[258]

After taking a much-deserved day off, John and Yoko resumed their work at the Hit Factory on Monday, August 11. Up first was 'Woman', which was already an unqualified favourite for Douglas, who felt that the Bermuda demo, even in its unvarnished form, was ready for release. From the moment he heard it, Jack thought it "was gonna be a pop classic because it said everything about how a man feels about his wife or girlfriend." John had taken to calling 'Woman' the "Beatle track" for obvious reasons, given its throwback sound. To prepare the band, he suggested that they think of the song as an "early Motown circa '64 ballad".[259]

John was clearly in a playful mood that afternoon, improvising an instrumental called 'Let's Get Peculiar'. As was their practice by this comparatively early date in the *Double Fantasy* sessions, John and the band captured 'Woman' in an economical four takes. While the band recorded their musical accompaniment – which included well-timed, sonically uplifting key changes during its latter stages – John sang his lead vocal in the isolation booth on the studio floor. During a break, he remarked that "I feel like I'm still in the fucking Beatles with this track." In subsequent interviews, he cast 'Woman' as a "grown-up" version of the Beatles' 'Girl', a standout track from *Rubber Soul*. In the earlier song, which John penned at age 25, the speaker was in love with a girl who was largely cold, if not aggressively mean to him. By contrast, 'Woman' found John celebrating the vitality of mature, healthy human relationships.[260]

Not surprisingly, the music of the Beatles came up fairly often during the Hit Factory sessions. And inevitably, John would follow up with a story or two about his days in the Fab Four. As assistant engineer Julie Last recalled, "When he started reminiscing, everything would stop and we would all be like a bunch of kids sitting at an elder's knee; just hanging on every word." The musicians would often draw John out by playing a Beatles riff to get things rolling. As Davilio recalled, "A few days into the sessions, during a break in recording, Hugh broke into the riff from 'I Feel Fine'. He started playing the verses and John started singing it. Then, after a few bars, John stopped and said to Hugh, 'Is that the original key?' Hughie goes, 'Yeah', and John says, 'Jesus, it's that high?'"[261]

On another occasion, John confided in Davilio that he wanted to re-record 'Strawberry Fields Forever' for his next album. As with his superkitchen conversation with George Martin the previous December, John was deadset on reimagining one of his most famous compositions. As Davilio looked on, "John started playing the whole song to me. He told me he always wanted to redo that song and make it less psychedelic. The version he played me had a chugging, rhythmic feel. It was real powerful. I was blown away. I'm sitting there, and here's John singing one of the greatest Beatles songs to me; it was like my own mini-concert." Eventually, the musicians got around to the most prevalent question among music fans the world over. It was engineer Lee DeCarlo who broke the ice: "I asked him one day, 'John, what broke up the Beatles?' He said, 'Maxwell's Silver Hammer'". I sat in the studio for three weeks while McCartney did the vocals, and, by the time we were done, I hated him.'" John was speaking tongue-in-cheek, of course. There were many reasons why they disbanded. But in John's mind, the recording of 'Maxwell's Silver Hammer' was "the straw that broke the camel's back".[262]

After 'Woman', the band turned to Yoko's 'Yes, I'm Your Angel' – which went under the working title of 'I'm Your Angel'. As with 'Woman', it was a throwback composition of sorts, albeit in this case, it was highly unoriginal in nature. Over his long career in the music business, John had been fond of making light of his occasional songwriterly bits of petty theft. McCartney recalled that he and Lennon developed this perspective out of sheer naïveté: "John and I didn't know you could own songs. We thought they just existed in the air. We could not see how it was possible to own them. We could see owning a house, a guitar or a car – they were physical objects." But after Harrison's legal fracas over 'My Sweet Lord', the global smash hit from his *All Things Must Pass* (1970) LP, the concept that a song might have a passing resemblance to another (in this case, 'My Sweet Lord' vis-à-vis the Chiffons' 'He's So Fine') was no longer moot.[263]

During their rehearsals back at the Dakota, John had openly worried that Yoko's song had far more than a passing acquaintance with 'Makin' Whoopee', the jazz standard composed by Gus Kahn and Walter Donaldson, later popularised by such luminaries as Eddie Cantor and Marlene Dietrich. If nothing else, the clear evocation of 'Makin' Whoopee' inherent in 'Yes, I'm Your Angel' afforded Yoko's song with a ready form of Jazz Age-era charm. For her part, Yoko perceived ths song as a sort of in-joke with her husband. "Oh, it's a big put-on thing," she recalled. "But at the same time, the lyrics are really not a put-on. It's presented in a put-on way." The sound of Yoko singing "tra, la, la, la, la" only scant days after simulating an in-studio orgasm created a jarring aural effect, while also considerably widening the album-in-progress' stylistic range in the process.[264]

The following afternoon, Douglas opted to shake things up a bit, having invited members of Cheap Trick, for whom he had served as executive producer on several recent top-selling efforts, to try their luck as the Lennons' backup band. For Jack, it seemed like an experiment worth trying – especially since the members of Cheap Trick were diehard Beatles aficionados. In June, they had released an EP entitled *Found All The Parts*, which featured a live cover version of the Beatles' 'Day Tripper' that was enjoying strong radio airplay. Earlier that same summer, Cheap

Trick had been working with legendary Beatles producer George Martin at AIR Studios on the Caribbean island of Montserrat, where they were recording their *All Shook Up* LP. Jack telephoned Martin to see if guitarist Rick Nielsen and drummer Bun E. Carlos might be interested in backing John and Yoko at the Hit Factory. "I had to call Martin at his island studio to book my players," Douglas later recalled. "I called him and said, 'Can I borrow some of my guys to play with your guy?'" Without missing a beat, Nielsen and Carlos hitched a ride on the next plane to New York City.[265]

On Tuesday afternoon, John took his first pass at 'I'm Losing You' in the Hit Factory, with Nielsen and Carlos joining Levin on fretless bass and Small on piano among the Lennons' supporting cast. Well known for his onstage antics as much as for his massive collection of guitars, Nielsen was mesmerised by the sight of John's Beatles-era guitars arrayed about the studio. "He showed me his Rickenbacker 325," said Nielsen. "I'm a guitar collector, so that was the coolest." For the session, Nielsen had "brought a Les Paul and Hamer and a Fender Telecaster with a B-string bender on it. John had never seen one of those. So I ended up giving him that guitar."[266]

John quickly walked the musicians through the song, as was his wont, assigning parts and affording the players with plenty of wiggle room to make the song their own. At one point, Carlos remembered saying "We're just trying to give it a Plastic Ono Band feel", which was fine as far as the two outsiders were concerned. "That's where we were coming from because Cheap Trick were big Plastic Ono Band fans," Carlos said. As the session unfolded, they recorded the song live, with John singing and working his Sardonyx. As Carlos recalled, "With those two guys and Lennon, the road was paved for us musically. Those guys were all top dogs and it was really a pleasure to do. John was like Chuck Berry, he was the perfect rhythm guitar player."[267]

The result was a hard-rocking, bone-crunching version of 'I'm Losing You'. After a few passes at the basic structure, Nielsen developed the song's central guitar riff and Carlos established the tempo. "What speed do you want this?" the drummer asked John. "Oh, whatever speed you think it should be," he replied. For his part, Carlos was surprised by the level of freedom that John had afforded them. "They just kind of let me and Rick take the lead on it. We did a few takes and that was it." Nielsen performed the solo for 'I'm Losing You' live, later doubling his guitar part as the others observed from the control booth. "Man, I wish I'd had you on 'Cold Turkey'," said John. "We had [Eric] Clapton on that and he froze up and could only play this one riff."[268]

After taking a break, the musicians turned to Yoko's 'I'm Moving On'. To get things rolling, Jack suggested that Carlos recycle an unused drum part from Cheap Trick's debut album. Having studied Davilio's lead sheets, Nielsen hastily concocted a guitar riff. At this point, Carlos recalled, "John got on the mike and said, 'Mother, dear, why don't you do Tony's first verse and then do the boys' arrangement', 'cause he was calling me and Rick 'the boys'." Without missing a beat, Yoko offered a fiery retort: "Fuck you very much, John", and the studio exploded with laughter. "We just cracked up with that, 'cause it was pretty obvious, you know, they were a team," Carlos said. "Our playing wasn't great on Yoko's track, the feel never quite coalesced. But there were things like, Yoko'd be in the booth and say, 'Does anyone want some granola?' or whatever she had, and it looked like animal feed. And John would be, like, down the hall with the roadies, you know, sneaking a slice of pizza."[269]

Later that night, after Nielsen and Carlos had departed, the full *Double Fantasy* band regrouped to take their first pass at 'Beautiful Boy (Darling Boy)'. Interestingly, John and the band recorded his lullaby for Sean in the same room where Stevie Wonder had recorded 'Isn't She Lovely', later included on his *Songs In The Key Of Life* (1976) album, for his daughter. As the band performed the gentle tune that evening, it became apparent that the SIR Studios rehearsals had really paid off. The musicians had become so familiar with the songs that they were able to afford even greater nuance to Davilio's charts. By this juncture, the band's trio of guitarists – Lennon, McCracken, and Slick – were in exquisite form. As Slick recalled, "John and I played acoustic guitar on 'Beautiful Boy' and Hughie played electric," adding that "I played John's black Yamaha acoustic guitar with a dragon on it." As always, John couldn't wait to move from rehearsal to recording. "Let's get a take before I have to go for a pee!" John announced. "Hugh, for Christ's sake you know this song backwards. Put your fucking headphones on and listen. He's reading them bits of paper, man. There's three chords. Come on, let's go!"[270]

When it came to the lead vocal for 'Beautiful Boy (Darling Boy)', John took great pains to capture his remarkable depth of feeling for his four-year-old son. After a while, Jack got in on the act, talking John through the vocals – particularly the segment where he sings, "it's getting better and better". When Jack questioned him about his pronunciation of the word "better", John harkened back to drummer Jimmie Nicol, who briefly sat in for an ailing Ringo during the Beatles' June 1964 Australian tour. As John explained to Jack, Nicol kept saying, "it's getting better all the time" – the phrase that inspired the Beatles' 'Getting Better' and, in its own small way, 'Beautiful Boy (Darling Boy)'. As they got back to work, John attributed his random reminiscence to "another memory lane from Jock O'Flynn". When it came to the conclusion of the song, John had taken to singing "darling, darling, darling, darling boy". He originally planned to end the tune by telling the listener to "fill in your own child's name". And that's when it hit him. "I should've said 'Sean' instead of 'boy'," he mumbled to himself. Fittingly, on the next pass at his lead vocal, John altered the outro for the song, singing "darling, darling, darling, darling Sean".

The next afternoon, the Lennons continued apace, with Yoko's 'Silver Horse' and John's 'Cleanup Time' on the docket. But the real story that day was the wide dissemination of Cohen's press release. As Roger Farrington had predicted, Yoko and the publicity agent had selected the photo of the Lennons standing below the awning of the Hit Factory's 48th Street entrance. United Press International carried the press release, which announced that "former Beatle John Lennon and his wife Yoko Ono have started recording their first record in seven years." In addition to reporting that "a label has not yet been selected, but a release date is set for early fall," the statement added that "the musicians are all excited over the new Lennon material," which "is the best of Lennon to date." By the next day, the London *Evening News* had hyped the story even further, claiming that the Lennons' "comeback album" and a "British concert tour" were in the offing, adding that a bidding war was likely to unfold for the chance to distribute John and Yoko's new record.

As news about the Lennons' work in the recording studio spread, the Dakota was flooded with well-wishes from across the globe. Having dispatched a bouquet of flowers to the Hit Factory, Paul McCartney sent his regards from London, where he was preparing to work on a new solo album with George Martin at the helm. Meanwhile, George Harrison placed a call to the Dakota from his Friar Park estate. When he learned that Harrison had telephoned, John refused to return his old friend's call. "Well, it's kind of George to call after forgetting to mention me in his book," John remarked to Fred. Earlier that month, Harrison had published *I Me Mine*, his lavishly produced autobiography, which came out in a limited edition of 2,000 signed copies. John's name was referenced a mere

11 times. In September, John made his feelings plainly known during the press blitz for *Double Fantasy*. "George put a book out privately and I was hurt by it," said John, "so this message will go out to him. By glaring omission in the book, my influence on his life is absolutely zilch and nil. Not mentioned. In his book, which is purportedly this clarity of vision of each song he wrote and its influences, he remembers every two-bit sax player or guitarist he met in subsequent years. I'm not in the book."[271]

By the time he and Yoko returned to the studio that afternoon, John was all business. Up first was 'Silver Horse', a dreamlike guitar fusion about Yoko's vision of a silvery steed. "I thought he might take me to that somewhere high," she sang against Slick and McCracken's warm bed of electric guitars. "I thought he might take me to that deep blue sky." The sombre mood of 'Silver Horse' was shortly supplanted by the raw ebullience of 'Cleanup Time'. Working around a spirited riff from Tony Levin, the rehearsal developed quickly, with Lennon trying out his guide vocal as McCracken and Slick performed soaring guitar work in the foreground. The evening concluded with the superimposition of a steel-drum part on 'Beautiful Boy (Darling Boy)'. Originally, John and Yoko had toyed with the idea of commissioning an entire steel-drum orchestra for the song, but eventually settled on one player when they realised the exorbitant expense – more than $20,000 for a single session – of bringing in so many highly specialised players. Instead, they settled on Jamaican musician Robert Greenidge, who performed admirably on the song's musical bridge and coda, adorning 'Beautiful Boy (Darling Boy)' with a tropical island air. In an inspired and genuinely charming instance, Sean was recorded saying "goodnight" in Japanese as a spoken-word coda for the song.

On the morning of Thursday, August 14, John prepared for the day's recording sessions by asking Fred to round up some LPs by Tito Puente, Ray Barretto, and other Latin performers. He also placed his weekly call to Aunt Mimi, where the conversation turned to the holiday season. When she inquired about ideas for Christmas gifts, her nephew allowed that he might be interested in copies of Shakespeare's *Sonnets* or Lord Byron's collected poems. With the sound of the Mambo King roiling around in his head, John led the band through several takes of 'I Don't Wanna Face It' that afternoon, later recording a rough version of '(Forgive Me) My Little Flower Princess'. The most straightforward rock 'n' roll tune from the *Double Fantasy* sessions, 'I Don't Wanna Face It', found Slick and

McCracken in solid form, with the former breaking off a spirited solo. For the lead guitarist, hearing John call out his name before the solo – "Earl Slick!" – was a career-making moment, by any measure. Several days later, John and Slick overdubbed a new guitar solo for the song. As Slick recalled, "It's kind of a double-stop thing. We did it live in the studio in something John called an 'old Beatle trick', where we had two little Princetons or something facing each other, with a stereo mic on the amps, and we just did it facing each other in like two takes."[272]

But the clear highlight that day was Yoko and the band's first pass at 'Walking On Thin Ice'. Recorded in seven takes, 'Walking On Thin Ice' featured some wicked guitar runs from Slick, backed by Levin's galloping bass and Yoko's dance-club vocal turn. After one of the takes, John suggested that McCracken restrict his playing to the backbeats. "That's great, really funky," said Yoko, and the guitarist tried out the new playing style. For his part, John was jazzed about Yoko and the band's progress on the song, which was still relatively simple at this juncture, save for Slick's ambient guitar sounds. When Yoko and the group finished the last take, John couldn't wait for her to join him in the control booth for the playback. "Come and listen before I break your neck!" he said to his wife, anxious for her to hear what he had been experiencing in the booth with Jack. After they listened to the most recent run-through, John couldn't contain himself any longer. "I think you just cut your first number one, Yoko," he announced, borrowing the phraseology, if not the intuition, of George Martin's proclamation to the Beatles nearly 18 years earlier. On that day back in November 1962 at EMI's Abbey Road Studios, Martin activated the studio PA and announced, "Gentlemen, you've just made your first number-one record" after witnessing the band's performance of 'Please Please Me'.[273]

While it may have seemed strange to compare the emergence of the Beatles' first chart-topping hit with 'Walking On Thin Ice', which was still in its infancy at this point, John was absolutely sincere in his pronouncement. He was clearly entranced by the song, perceiving it to be the precipice for a new kind of musical style in the still-young decade. John had also begun imagining potential music videos for his new songs, having recently watched a promotional clip for David Bowie's new single 'Ashes To Ashes', which had been released earlier in the month. Having participated in pioneering film shoots for such Beatles songs as 'Strawberry Fields Forever' and 'Penny Lane', John was ready to join pop music's nascent video revolution. At the time, Bowie's video, co-directed with David Mallet, set the high-water mark for production costs, given the promo's elaborate sets and costumery. John was mesmerised as he watched the video for 'Ashes To Ashes', remarking to Fred that "he's doing what I should be doing." As he brainstormed about potential promo films of his own, he dreamt up a video concept with the image of himself soaring around the landscape as a flying monster.[274]

During that same session, the couple began to discuss cover ideas for *Double Fantasy*. John had already sketched out a few different concepts, which he referred to as the "face one" and the "lying down one". In both concepts, John imagined the Lennons' faces would be juxtaposed with a floral motif that depicted the image of freesia that had delivered the album's title for him back in the Bermuda botanical gardens. For the "face" cover, John suggested they hire Richard Bernstein, "who does the [Andy] Warhol *Interview* covers. He invented that style." At one point, George Small recalled hearing about a variation on the "face" cover that would have featured a painting of Robert Browning and Elizabeth Barrett Browning with their faces cut out and the Lennons' superimposed over them. "It was gonna have that sepia, early photography kind of look," said Small. In any event, John's plan was to have both covers prepared – the "face one" and the "lying down one" – and "whichever stands out to be the cover will be the front." The couple had also given serious thought to the album's liner notes, which they wanted to be relatively sparse – at least, for *Double Fantasy*'s exterior. They had even concocted a subtitle for the LP, which they had cast as "A Heart Play starring John and Yoko".[275]

That Friday, John and Yoko were forced to work without Slick available. As the guitarist later recalled, "I was so fucking hungover and sick that day that I didn't show up at the studio. I called, but I didn't play on it. I was so fucked up that I couldn't get to the studio. This is part of who I was at the time. That was one of the very few times in all the years, even when I was out of control, that I ever did something like that and of course I did it on a Lennon record." John took Slick's absence in stride, although he couldn't help imagining a newspaper headline to account for the guitarist's absence: "THE MUSICIANS ARE DYING DURING LENNON SESSIONS". As Slick remembered, "John used to think it was quite funny when I'd crawl into the studio the next day after being out all night and fucked up. He'd just laugh and say, 'You've had a night out!' I think he got a kick out of me because he was seeing a bit of himself in the old days and living vicariously through my dysfunction."[276]

When John and the band began work on 'Dear Yoko', they retained much of the composer's original intent during his demo back in April. As Douglas noted at the time, "It had an early Fifties feel to it that John was so good at because he was good at that rhythm. I thought it was the lightest, funniest track on the record." The same bouncy, old-time rock 'n' roll sound was in evidence, as was John's nifty, Buddy Holly-inspired lead vocal. John reverently mimicked the Texas phenom's hiccup-singing style throughout 'Dear Yoko', especially evident in the bravura intro, when he sings, "A-wella-hella-hella even after all these years". Not surprisingly, Slick's absence exerted an effect on the basic tracks, with McCracken understandably dominating the song's musical direction. "Because Earl wasn't there, that was Hughie's track in terms of how the guitars are structured," said Douglas. "Hughie really took over the musical part of that song." With McCracken taking the lead, Yoko's 'Beautiful Boys' – her answer, during the husband-and-wife songwriters' give-and-take, to 'Beautiful Boy (Darling Boy)' – experienced a similar fate, with a comparatively stark guitar landscape affording the track with an eerie quality.[277]

By Monday, August 18 – a mere 11 days after John and Yoko had begun work at the Hit Factory – there were only a handful of songs left to commit to tape. Up first was 'Watching The Wheels', the long-gestating composition that had begun life as 'Emotional Wreck'. The basic track featured Lennon and Small on piano. As Small later recalled, "That's the most keyboard-oriented song on the record. It's not so guitar-driven as much of the other material. That's me on piano and John played a Yamaha electric grand." As with the other initial recordings of the *Double Fantasy* tracks, Lennon performed his lead vocals with the intention of refining them later when he planned to superimpose additional tracks onto the songs. As the band attempted various takes, John's delight at being back in the studio was evident at nearly every turn. After one take, he playfully remarked that "we'd like to change the tempo now and do a little foxtrot for Mrs Higgins of Darwin, Australia." Earlier, during the rehearsal for 'Watching The Wheels', John offered a comic send-up of the Beatles' 'I Am The Walrus'. With his parodic Dylan voice in its full glory, he sang, "I am he as you are he as we are thee and you are all together", before the band dissolved in laughter.[278]

Meanwhile, John had hit upon the notion of appending a barroom ambience to the conclusion of 'Watching The Wheels', which Small executed perfectly. As the keyboard player remembered, "On the ending part – where John sings, 'I just had to let it go' – he really made a big point of making sure that I had played that romantic piano line on the tag exactly that way. He told me he was in a bar one night and was listening to a piano player and that riff just stuck in his head. So he had to have that riff on the end of it."[279]

Up next was Yoko's 'Give Me Something', another avant-garde dance mix from among her evolving repertoire. In only a matter of days, her contributions to *Double Fantasy* had already shifted her profile from an almost purely experimental artist into a songwriter with a growing pop sensibility. John's prophecy about his wife's changing musical fortunes back at Bermuda's Disco 40 was continuing to ring true. After making short work of 'Give Me Something', John and the band shifted their attentions to remaking 'I'm Losing You'. During the scant few days since Cheap Trick's departure, John and Yoko had begun to sour on their contribution to the album. Things began to unravel when the band's manager presented Lenono Music with a $3,000 invoice for Nielsen and Carlos' services. By this point, Douglas could see the writing on the wall as far as the band from Rockford, Illinois, was concerned. "Yoko decided Cheap Trick would be riding on Lennon's coattails," said Jack. "Her attitude was 'Who are these people, I've never heard of them! We're not gonna give these guys a free ride.'"[280]

When it came to remaking 'I'm Losing You', the band members happily accepted the challenge. For their part, Slick and Newmark admired Cheap Trick's versions of 'I'm Losing You' and 'I'm Moving On', although Slick could see a logic for not including them on *Double Fantasy*. "Now, I've heard the Cheap Trick version of 'I'm Losing You', and I love it," said Slick, "and I think Rick [Nielsen] did a monster job on it." But "I think the reason John didn't want to use it was because Cheap Trick's sound is so identifiable – he didn't want his stuff to sound like it was a Cheap Trick record."[281]

Douglas would later recall playing the Cheap Trick versions of 'I'm Losing You' and 'I'm Moving On' through the bandmates' headphones in an effort to acclimate them to the musical arrangements from the August 12 session, although Slick pointedly remembered things differently: "'I'm Losing You' was really cool because John, Hughie McCracken, and I went in the control room, and John divided up our parts: 'Slick, you play the first bit; Hughie, you play the second; Slick, you play the third; and then Hughie, you finish up with the fourth.' So I came up with my two ideas, and Hughie came up with his two, and we did them together. There must be, like, four tracks of guitars going on there." All the while, John played along on his Sardonyx. His performance was aided by his deployment of the Eventide Harmonizer, a pioneering audio-effects device that allowed him to manipulate the levels of feedback, pitch, and delay. As engineer Jon Smith recalled, "There was a specific setting that he loved, and he didn't mess with it too much. You can really hear it wailing on the end of 'I'm Losing You'."[282]

As it happened, the August 18 session was memorable for more than the basic tracks for 'Watching The Wheels' and 'I'm Losing You'. By this point, the band had found their groove, easily shifting among John and Yoko's new compositions and outtakes of such rock classics as the Beatles' 'She's A Woman' and Eddie Cochran's 'C'mon Everybody'. That evening, a video crew led by Jay Dubin had been on hand, filming the session for 'I'm Losing You', for which John plied his Sardonyx with unchecked abandon. Afterwards, he refused to watch the playback, saying that "I know what I look like – like a fucking bird!" To cap things off, the sessions had briefly fallen into a mild panic when Ahmet Ertegun, the acclaimed co-founder and president of Atlantic Records, managed to slip into the private elevator and make his way to the sixth floor of the Hit Factory, where he was clearly hoping to register his interest in landing the Lennons' comeback album. Fortunately, the studio's security personnel managed to corral him before he could accost John and Yoko.[283]

Incredibly, by the next evening, phase one of the recording sessions associated with *Double Fantasy* had concluded with the basic tracks for Yoko's disco-tinged 'Every Man Has A Woman Who Loves Him' and the gospel dirge 'Hard Times Are Over'. Later that evening, John and Yoko sat for Bob Gruen's group portrait of the band, followed by a sumptuous dinner at Mr Chow where a festive banquet table had been readied for the occasion. And that's when Stan Vincent said what was on everybody else's mind. As Vincent later recalled, "I turned to John and said, 'Listen, look what you've just finished. You've got to go on the road with this band and play live.'" At first, John politely answered, "No, I don't wanna go on tour." But Vincent wouldn't back down. "I kept on him and he said, 'All right, I only want to do one night in major cities.' I had my martini in front of me and said, 'Are you gonna do it?' And he said, 'Yeah, yeah, yeah' in this kind of wanting-to-do-it-but-disgruntled way. I got up in front of the musicians, held my martini glass up and said, 'Gentleman, we're going on tour!' And everybody rose up, saluted and clinked glasses."

The Lennons were understandably elated that night – and deservedly so. In a mere 10 days of work at the Hit Factory, John and Yoko had succeeded in laying down basic tracks for 22 songs.

CHAPTER 12

Stepping Out

The phantom was back.

By Wednesday, August 20, any pretence of keeping the *Double Fantasy* project under wraps was over. Cohen's press release had done its work, and *Rolling Stone* had picked up the baton. Quoting an unnamed source who turned out to be none other than Hugh McCracken, *Rolling Stone* reported that "John's songs are really catchy, even more so than before. He was smoking Gitanes and singing some of the lyrics in French. He seemed to have all the effects he needed built into this custom-built Sardonyx guitar he was playing. Yoko was eating sushi and drinking green tea, and singing very melodically. They seemed nervous, but really excited." The article was illustrated with Roger Farrington's photograph of the couple at the Hit Factory back on August 7.[284]

That Wednesday, Jack and his production team began compiling rough mixes of the 22 extant John and Yoko songs. After a series of listening sessions, Jack and the Lennons had evaluated the recordings and begun sketching out a rough sequence, along with the songs' working titles, for the contents of the *Double Fantasy* LP:

Side A:
Starting Over
I'm Your Angel

Side B:
Walking On Thin Ice
Dear Yoko

175

Beautiful Boy (w/'Sean's Goodnight')	Beautiful Boys
Gimme Something	Woman
Watching The Wheels	I'm Moving On (Cheap Trick version)
Every Man Has A Woman	Cleanup Time
I'm Losing You (remake)	Hard Times Are Over[285]

On Monday, August 25, John and Yoko began carrying out extensive overdubbing sessions for *Double Fantasy*. In preparation, Jack and his production team had spent Sunday evening linking two 16-track multitrack analogue machines, which were synchronised using SMPTE (Society of Motion Picture and Television Engineers) striping to afford them with maximum transferral and overdubbing capabilities. As it turned out, their work had paid off, given the myriad ideas that the Lennons had dreamt up in order to enhance the basic recordings. This was both a product of their fertile imaginations, as well as John's anxiety – understandable, under the circumstances – about making his highly public return to an industry that was on the verge of going digital; indeed, the first fully digitally recorded album had already hit the marketplace with Ry Cooder's *Bop Till You Drop*, which had been released in July 1979. As John had confided in Fred as they entered this latter phase of the recording process, "the more insecure I am, the more I put on a track."[286]

Fittingly, John began the day superimposing additional instrumentation onto '(Just Like) Starting Over'. After overdubbing an acoustic guitar part for the song's intro, he joined Douglas and Davilio on the studio floor to superimpose a series of handclaps onto the recording in order to enhance the song's energy and forward momentum. George Martin and the Beatles had experimented with adding handclaps to a number of standout tracks in the early 1960s, including 'I Saw Her Standing There' and 'I Want To Hold Your Hand', among a host of other tunes. Back in his Beatle days, John and the other Beatles had taken advantage of such moments as excuses for tomfoolery, and '(Just Like) Starting Over' was no different. Davilio would never forget the image of John carrying out this otherwise monotonous activity at the Hit Factory: "We were doing handclaps on a song. John came out and started shadow boxing and swinging his arms. He was like, 'Come on, Tony, show me what ya got!' So I went into a boxer's stance and John's jumping around, real animated. We were kind of throwing punches around, but not hitting each other. He was a playful guy. We started laughing, and I turned around, and he slapped me in the back of the head and ran into the control room."[287]

After a visit from Sean and his Dakota neighbour and friend Max LeRoy, Yoko remade her lead vocal for 'Every Man Has A Woman Who Loves Him', which John jokingly referred to as 'Every Man Has A Wombat Who Loves Him' between takes. For the song, John later doubled her lead vocal with a harmony vocal of his own. For 'Dear Yoko', Hugh McCracken overdubbed a series of harmonica takes, which he doubled, in some instances, with a slide guitar part. In the end, Hugh had adorned the song with four different harmonica overdubs, affording the song with a light-hearted, funky ambience. Later, John added some spirited, spoken-word chitchat as a coda to the song: "When you come over next time, don't sell a cow", he remarks, in reference to Yoko's prized Holsteins. "Spend some time with me and Sean. You'll like it!"[288]

The next day, John and Yoko – in a moment of grand ambition and resolve – brought the full *Double Fantasy* band back to the Hit Factory to remake 'I'm Losing You' (for the second time, no less), 'I'm Moving On', and 'Kiss Kiss Kiss'. At this point, it had become clear that both of the Cheap Trick recordings would be left on the cutting room floor, at least for the time being. Still hoping that Cheap Trick might be of use, Jack asked Carlos and Nielsen to return at a later date, although John kindly rebuffed them with autographs and heartfelt thanks. For his part, Nielsen gifted Lennon with a personalised Hamer guitar. During his previous visit to the Hit Factory, Nielsen had covertly measured the short-scale neck of John's Rickenbacker 325 to customise his new Hamer guitar. Nielsen had the new guitar's headstock inscribed with the words "Rick N Hamer" in reference to the famous guitar that had seen the launch of John's Beatle years.

After cutting a satisfying remake of 'I'm Losing You', the band took its first pass at 'I'm Moving On'. During a break in the session, John turned to the musicians and said, "Remember, the guy [in the song] is losing her and she is moving on. Keep it sneaky." Not missing a beat, Yoko playfully added, "No, no, no, we girls don't get heavy." Over the next few days, McCracken would add a series of guitar overdubs to 'I'm Losing You' and 'I'm Moving On', imbuing both songs with edgier textures. Small would close out the week with the superimposition of a series of Prophet 5 synthesizer parts on 'Every Man Has A Woman Who Loves Him',

'Woman', and 'Dear Yoko'. For 'Woman', in particular, Small fashioned the synthesized sound of a French horn, affording the song's later passages with a stately air.[289]

Working that Saturday at the Hit Factory, Yoko remade her lead vocal for 'Don't Be Scared'. The remainder of the session was devoted to 'Yes, I'm Your Angel'. With Smith in the control room, Davilio tested out his arrangement for the tune. His original plan called for bringing in a spate of woodwind players to support Yoko's composition. Working instead with an electric guitar, Davilio recorded each of the individual horn parts, christening the resulting mix as a "guitar orchestra". As Chip Madinger and Scott Raile observe, Davilio's arrangement for guitars "was evocative of an early Les Paul multitracked recording and offered a unique voice to the arrangement (which had been scored using clarinets, saxophones, and flutes in the style of a 1930s big band)."[290]

Earlier that day, German photographer Lilo Raymond joined John and Yoko for a photo shoot beginning along the Upper West Side, where they enjoyed the late summer sun in the back garden of Café La Fortuna, and concluding at the Plaza Hotel's luxurious Palm Court. In many ways, Raymond's appearance marked the onset of the next stage of the Lennons' media blitz, as John and Yoko prepared to land a record deal and, ultimately, loose *Double Fantasy* upon a waiting world. For the occasion, John donned a suitcoat along with his Quarry Bank tie – arguably, his most treasured accessory outside of his signature eyeglasses. John liked to describe the outfit – black coat, white shirt, white trousers, and dark tie – as his "space suit", having recently memorialised the outfit in 'Stepping Out', in which he sings of putting "on my space suit" in order to look his best.

For the Lennons, Tuesday, September 2, began with a stroll through Central Park. Back in July, photography student Stuart Zolotorow had mentioned to Helen Seaman, whom he had met during John's immigration fight, that he would soon be graduating from college and was interested in growing his artistic portfolio. When he arrived at the Dakota that morning from Baltimore, he informed the doorman he was there, and in short order, Helen was notified that Stuart was downstairs. Some 10 minutes later, the Lennons emerged from the archway. "Where's the guy from Baltimore?" John asked. When he laid eyes on Stuart, John began to good-naturedly razz the college grad, who was suddenly overcome with nerves.[291]

"Come on now, Mr All-the-Way-from-Baltimore, you can do this!" said John. "Come on now, you've got one of those Olympus cameras.

All you have to do is focus and press the button!" By this point, Stuart managed to meekly release the shutter. "Great. There, take another one! And go ahead, take another *just* to be sure – always take extra. Do ya think ya gotta good one?" John asked. "I think so," Stuart answered. "Let's go take a walk!" said John, with Yoko and Stuart following him up Central Park West for a few blocks. Stuart couldn't help noticing John and Yoko offering friendly nods to passersby as they made their way along the sidewalk. After thanking the Lennons profusely, Stuart prepared to go on his way. "Let's do this again later!" John sang out, as he and his wife disappeared into Central Park.[292]

Later that afternoon, John and Yoko returned to the studio, where they continued to refine the sequencing for *Double Fantasy* with Douglas. Yoko suggested that "we all throw our sequences into this hat and somewhere between the three of us we'll come up with the right one." John and Jack's suggestions were remarkably similar, having arranged all of John's songs on side A and all of Yoko's on side B. For her part, Yoko wasn't having it, saying, "No way. If you wanna listen to John, you've gotta hear Yoko." John said, "She's right," and Jack quickly fell into line. As he recalled, the album "was sequenced so that a John song would be followed by a Yoko song. If the album wasn't sequenced that way, what would have happened is people would have only listened to John's songs and not have given her songs a chance." If *Double Fantasy* were truly going to be a play, Jack admitted, then John and Yoko's songs needed to exist in dialogue with one another.[293]

Having agreed to this shared approach, the trio continued to reshape the running order. To this end, Jack's production team prepared a new compilation entitled *Double Fantasy – New Composite – Ruff Mixes 9/2/80*:

Side A:	*Side B:*
Kiss Kiss Kiss	Every Man Has A Woman Who Loves Him
Watching The Wheels	Beautiful Boys
I'm Your Angel	I'm Losing You
Starting Over	I'm Moving On
Don't Be Scared	Hard Times Are Over
Gimme Something	Woman
Cleanup Time	Dear Yoko
Beautiful Boy (w/'Sean's Goodnight')[294]	

To accommodate the inclusion of 'Kiss Kiss Kiss', 'Walking On Thin Ice' had been omitted from the latest sequence. By Thursday, a new compilation had been drafted. Entitled *John & Yoko 9/4 (Jack's Sequence)*, the contents had shifted yet again:

Side A:	Side B:
Starting Over	Cleanup Time
Beautiful Boy	Woman
Gimme Something	Beautiful Boys
Watching The Wheels	Dear Yoko
I'm Losing You	Kiss Kiss Kiss
I'm Moving On	Hard Times Are Over
Don't Be Scared	Every Man Has A Woman Who Loves Him[295]

On Friday, September 5, Jack and the Lennons began conducting overdubbing sessions in earnest. Up first was a series of horn arrangements, scored by Davilio, for 'I'm Losing You', 'Cleanup Time', '(Just Like) Starting Over', and 'Yes, I'm Your Angel'. The session players included Howard Johnson, Grant Hungerford, J.D. Parran, Seldon Powell, Roger Rosenberg, Dave Tofani, Ron Tooley, and George Young. As the musicians warmed up that day, John joked that the musicians should "play with no clothes on". In short order, they replied "we'll have to check the union rules!"[296]

By the following week, John and Yoko were balancing three initiatives, including the overdubbing sessions at the Hit Factory, a media blitz in order to create additional buzz for their new album, and a shadow campaign to land a record deal with the right suitor: the very kind of record executive who understood the value of the Lennons as a musical team, rather than as disparate solo acts. On the afternoon of September 8, Yoko met with 24-year-old David Sheff in order to discuss the possibility of a wide-ranging interview in *Playboy* magazine. In nearly the same instant, Yoko met with journalist Barbara Graustark, an associate editor with *Newsweek* magazine, on the recommendation of Bob Gruen.

That evening, the *Double Fantasy* band gathered to take another pass at 'Yes, I'm Your Angel', which they recorded in ¾ time. Yoko later remade her vocal for 'Hard Times Are Over'. The session concluded with another group picture – this time, with photographer David Spindel capturing the images of John, Yoko and the musicians for posterity. The overdubbing sessions would continue well into the next week, including the work of keyboard player Ed Walsh, who would add Oberheim synthesizer parts to 'I'm Losing You', 'Watching The Wheels', and 'Woman'.

On Thursday, September 11, Sheff began his multipart interviews with John and Yoko. In addition to questioning them about their latest album, he planned to ask John about his memories of the Beatles, even suggesting that they go song-by-song in an innovative exploration of his songwriting history. As Sheff later recalled:

> I looked at the two of them, waiting intently, and began. "The word is out: John Lennon and Yoko Ono are back—" John interrupted immediately, and laughingly nudged Yoko. "Oh, really?" he joked. "From where?" I smiled and continued: "—in the studio, recording again for the first time since 1975, when they vanished from public view. What have you been doing?" John turned playfully to Yoko. "Do you want to start, or should I start?" he asked. "You should start," she replied firmly. "I should? Really? Okay."

At one point during the interview, a shrill scream emanated from the streetscape below. "Oh," John ad-libbed, "another murder at rue Dakota." With Sheff in tow, the Lennons left for a 2 p.m. recording session at A&R Recording Studios on West 54th Street, where they worked with the Benny Cummings Singers and the Kings Temple Choir to complete 'Hard Times Are Over'. For John, the session was pure magic:

> They were beautiful. Just before the take, they suddenly all took each other's hands, and Yoko was really crying, and I was emotional because it's right up our alley – whether it's Jesus or Buddha, for us it's all right, either one will do, any of them are all right by us. So there they were, holding hands before the take, and they were singing, "Thank you, Jesus, thank you, Lord", and I was like, "Put the tape on! Are you getting this?" And that's what you hear, exactly as it happened – "Thank you, Jesus, thank you, Lord" – and then they go right into singing the song.[297]

As it happened, the choirs had something special in mind for John and Yoko that afternoon. After completing work on 'Hard Times Are Over',

Douglas supervised two takes of the singers changing "one world, one people" as a potential ending (ultimately unused) for the LP. For the Lennons, "one world, one people" was the logical extension of the concept behind 'Imagine' that they had shared nearly a decade earlier – the idea of imagining a world without boundaries, without restrictions, without prejudice. "We're one world, one people whether we like it or not. Aren't we?" John asked. "I mean, we can *pretend* we're divided into races and countries and we can carry on pretending that until we stop doing it. But the reality is that it is one world, and it is one people."[298]

After they completed the take, the choral leader announced, "Mr Lennon, we have something we would like to give you." And that's when the choirs erupted in a hymn, 'It Is Well With My Soul', that they had prepared just for the Lennons. "God came to the session," said Jack. "He did, or *She* did," Yoko replied. Later that night, after a playback session at the Hit Factory, Sheff joined the couple back at the Dakota, where John explained their plans for *Double Fantasy* and beyond. To his mind, the new LP was "the dialogue between a man and a woman, which is what it is, and this album is part one of at least two, that's for sure. And we were originally calling it an Ear Play. It went to Heart Play, which still contains the word 'ear', as a kind of radio play."[299]

On Friday, John and Yoko continued their media parade, including an interview with *The New York Times*' Robert Palmer, as well as additional conversation with Sheff. They cut the interviews short in the early afternoon, when John realised they were needed at the "little wooden box", his shorthand for the Hit Factory, given its distinctive wood-panelled design motif. That afternoon, John and Davilio supervised the Ritchie Family, a group of singers comprised of Cassandra Wooten, Michelle Simpson, and Cheryl Mason Jacks, who fashioned themselves as "Cas Mijac" for their work on *Double Fantasy*. The session proved to be a gruelling affair, as Davilio had planned to have the singers, who didn't read music, double the existing horn parts on '(Just Like) Starting Over'. In the end, Jack and the Lennons scrapped the horn overdubs, while retaining Cas Mijac's backing vocals.

That weekend, John and Yoko's search for a record label took a very promising turn in the form of maverick music executive David Geffen. In the previous few weeks, they had been approached by several record execs, many of whom were only interested in signing John as a client, rather than Yoko. The experience of trying to land a record deal had its share of comedic moments, including the time that the head of Stiff Records sent a telegram to John about signing with his label, whose motto was "if it ain't stiff, it ain't worth a fuck". The message to the ex-Beatle was simple and to the point: "Heard you are recording. We're prepared to offer you $5,000 to sign with us." John asked Lee DeCarlo, "who the hell is Stiff Records?" When the engineer gave him the rundown on the low-budget label, John replied, "Jeez, that's funny."[300]

As for Geffen, the West Coast record executive was a horse of a very different colour. As with John, he had taken a leave-of-absence from the record business in 1977 after successful stints as co-founder of Asylum Records, on the advice of Ahmet Ertegun, no less, and with Warner Bros. film studios. Geffen had left the industry after experiencing a cancer scare at age 34 and began teaching part-time courses at Yale University, only to discover he had been misdiagnosed. In 1980, he received a clean bill of health and returned to the business with a vengeance, founding Geffen Records and naming Warner Bros. executive Ed Rosenblatt to serve as the new company's president. In short order, Geffen inked disco superstar Donna Summer and pop stalwart Elton John. Summer's LP *The Wanderer* was slated for an October release, with Elton's *The Fox* scheduled for May 1981.

On September 13, Geffen contacted Yoko via telegram and requested a meeting about distributing the Lennons' new album. When John saw the telegram, he was immediately impressed, saying, "That's the guy." For her part, Yoko agreed: "You see, David's a very clever guy. He immediately knew that he had to get in touch with me, whether he liked that or not. David didn't act like the president of a record company, he was like us." Later, when they spoke on the phone, Yoko told the record executive that she would have to run his numbers before holding a face-to-face meeting. "Are you worried?" she asked. "No," he replied, "because my life is too good for my numbers not to be good." That same day, Elton John performed a concert in Central Park for an audience of several 100,000 people. As part of his set, a typically gaudily costumed Elton played 'Imagine', which he introduced as "a song written by a friend of mine. He only just lives over the road. He hasn't done a record for ages, but he's doing one at the moment."[301]

That Thursday, Yoko invited Japanese photographer Kishin Shinoyama to join the Lennons for a photo session. They posed for several shots near Central Park's Bow Bridge near the mouth of Wagner Cove. Dating back to the 1860s, the cast-iron bridge created a pedestrian walkway over the lake, the body of water only a few hundred feet away from the Dakota. As Shinoyama remembered, "We went into Central Park to shoot those photos in the glow of sunset. I was watching their loving attitude, so I proposed to them the idea of the kiss." Leaning against a park bench, the Lennons embraced, with the San Remo apartment building's twin towers rising in the distance against the sunset. Shinoyama also photographed John and Yoko standing in the shadows of the Dakota at the corner of West 72nd Street and Central Park West. At first, the Lennons weren't convinced about using Shinoyama's pictures for the cover art. "We shot that photo with us kissing, and we thought it looked great," said Yoko, "but we weren't that sure about it." Later, after they sensed some resistance from their distributor about using a photo of the couple lost in a kiss, they'd heard enough. "That's when we decided we were gonna do it, because both of us were rebellious. John said, 'From now on, we'll only take photos of you and me looking at each other.'" That night, the Lennons celebrated the photo shoot by taking Shinoyama to Mr Chow.[302]

On Friday, September 19, Ono and Geffen met for the first time. When she asked the label head why they should go with him, he replied, "Because I will be very sensitive to who you are and deal with you straight and do a good job." With that, "Yoko told me that she wanted a million dollars," Geffen later recalled, "and that she wanted the contract all on one page. I agreed to all of that." The next day, they sealed the deal. "Don't you want to hear the record first?" Yoko asked with a twinkle in her eye. "No," Geffen answered. "I'll wait until whenever you want to play it for me." Yoko replied, "Well, if you wanted to hear the music before you made the deal, we wouldn't have gone with you."[303]

And with that, John joined them in Studio One. "They played me three tracks," said Geffen, "and I thought they were all hits." Geffen couldn't help noticing how much better John looked than the last time he'd seen him in the early 1970s; with Cher in tow, Geffen had visited Phil Spector when he was producing John's *Rock 'n' Roll* sessions. "That was a weird night, wasn't it?" said John. As he was leaving the Dakota, John pulled Geffen aside, telling him, "You know, we have to take care of Yoko. You and I have what we set out to have, but Yoko never got what she deserves. And that has to be our goal with this record." Later that night, John asked Fred to buy a copy of Donna Summer's recent single 'The Wanderer' so that he could get a look at the label. "I want to make sure we're dealing with a real record company." After studying the Geffen logo, John suggested that he and Yoko devise their own insignia for Lenono Music by superimposing the British and Japanese flags.[304]

In the meantime, overdubbing sessions continued unabated at the Hit Factory. Earlier, on September 15, John had completed work on 'Woman'. During that session, Lennon and McCracken had performed a layer of Beatlesque guitars for the song. John also remade his lead vocal, which he subsequently double-tracked in the isolation booth. "I love double-tracking," said John. "When we first discovered it, I'd double-track *everything*. On the second album [*With The Beatles* (1963)], he [George Martin] suddenly told us we can do this thing. I wouldn't let him have anything single-tracked from then on."

For John's lead vocals, Jack deployed a "pop filter" on his microphone in order to mitigate the popping sound associated with vocalising p's and s's. For 'Woman', Jack also supervised the overdubbing of a harmony arrangement that featured the voice of Eric Troyer, which was layered several times in post-production and included Beatle-like harmonies when he sang "yeah, yeah" during the song's fadeout. As he put the finishing touches on 'Woman', John appended a spoken-word introduction in which he dedicated the song "for the other half of the sky", paraphrasing a Chinese proverb attributed to Mao Zedong. Working with his fellow backup singers Cassandra Wooten, Michelle Simpson, and Cheryl Mason Jacks, Troyer also overdubbed a doo-wop-style chorus to '(Just Like) Starting Over', affording the song with the throwback feel that John had originally envisioned.

Continuing in a similar vein on September 17, John superimposed a spoken-word outro for 'Beautiful Boy (Darling Boy)', whispering, "Good night, Sean. See you in the morning." As with 'Woman', John re-recorded his lead vocals for 'Cleanup Time'. Engineer Lee DeCarlo created a nifty, artificial backing vocal for the song using a vocoder. As he later recalled, "In that song you hear the background vocal, 'Got to clean up, clean up'. I used the horns to trigger a vocoder. I think I sang 'Got to clean up' so it made the horns sound like vocals. They did the same thing on 'Bohemian Rhapsody' by Queen; the sound of all those background vocals is being done by a vocoder. You play a synthesizer, you sing into a microphone, and it picks up the characteristics of the chords and turns it into vocals. The background vocals in there are actually the horn players being turned into voices."[305]

On September 24, Jack and John continued post-production work on 'Watching The Wheels'. A few days earlier, John had remade his lead vocal. Since they had begun working on the song together, John had entreated Jack to make 'Watching The Wheels' more "circular". At this point, Jack hit upon the idea of overdubbing a hammer dulcimer on the track. After being unable to locate a studio musician through the musicians' union, Jack was on the verge of giving up on the idea when he saw a street musician at the corner of West 72nd Street and Columbus Avenue. "This guy's sitting on the street playing dulcimer," said Jack, "and people were throwing money in his box." Jack invited him to the Hit Factory to overdub the hammer dulcimer part.

A hippie with long scraggly hair, Matthew Cunningham was an accomplished player who hailed from Greenwich Village and plied his meagre trade on the streets of the city. As Davilio recalled, Cunningham seemed "pretty spaced out. When you play the dulcimer you sit in that Indian position on the floor. Jack told me, 'Tony, go out there and make sure he's in tune.' So I went over to the piano and plucked out some notes, and he kept shaking his head and said, 'That sounds sour, that's not in tune', but it was." And that's when John attempted to relay instructions to the musician over the studio's talkback. As Davilio looked on, "Matt squinted his eyes, looking at him, and said, 'What's your name?' And John gets back on the talkback and says, 'My name's John.' This guy's just staring at him and goes, 'Hi, John.' And then John says, 'Hi, Matt,' and then I see them all laughing in there because this guy didn't know who he was. Apparently, he was the only person in the country who wouldn't know John Lennon."[306]

With Cunningham's hammer-dulcimer overdub, Jack had finally achieved the circularity that John had wanted for 'Watching The Wheels'. That same day, John remade his lead vocal for 'I'm Losing You', singing "long, long, lost John" during the outro in reference to Lonnie Donegan's 1956 recording of 'Lost John', which Lennon had recorded with Ringo Starr and Klaus Voormann in 1970 during the *Plastic Ono Band* sessions. To keyboard player George Small's ears, the outro also made reference to George Harrison's Beatles classic 'Something' when John sings, "Don't want to lose you now". The September 24 session would end on a strange note, when Douglas announced that the *Double Fantasy* project would be relocated – lock, stock, and barrel – to the Record Plant. For his part, Jack preferred working at the venerable recording studio, and besides, he had long been concerned about the quality of the "bass definition" at the Hit Factory. As if on cue, Fred Seaman, Rich DePalma, and Mike Tree began packing up the Lennons' instruments and other belongings for the relatively short trip over to 44th Street.[307]

That Friday, September 26, John and Jack briefly set *Double Fantasy* aside to mix the album's first single, '(Just Like) Starting Over' b/w 'Kiss Kiss Kiss', for an October 24 release date. Working in the ground-floor mixing suite at the Record Plant, the production team was on a strict deadline, with Yoko having cautioned that a "significant moon change" was in the offing. For the folks mixing the two tracks for release, the 7 p.m. target she had set gave them a much-needed adrenalin rush. During the editing process, DeCarlo accidentally doubled Newmark's drum fill before the coda in '(Just Like) Starting Over', creating an anomaly that wasn't in the original take. As the engineer later recalled, "Everybody went, 'Oh, no!' and I yelled, 'I like it better!'" Fortunately for DeCarlo, John agreed with the edit, and the repeated fill became part of the final mix.[308]

During the post-production phase, John had experimented with a number of sound effects in order to enhance *Double Fantasy*'s tracks. For '(Just Like) Starting Over', he wanted to append the sound of a supersonic jet – à la the intro for the Beatles' *White Album* track 'Back In The USSR' – during the '(Just Like) Starting Over' coda. To John's mind, the sound of a jet would perfectly symbolise the song's theme of flying away and starting anew. When Jon Smith came up empty trying to find the supersonic sound that John was imagining, they turned instead to a sound-effects record featuring the voice of a female flight attendant.

While John, Jack, and the production team were hurrying to meet Yoko's deadline that evening, there was one final touch that Lennon wanted to superimpose as an intro to '(Just Like) Starting Over'. John had decided to add the sound of a wishing bell to the beginning of the song – indeed, the album – and dispatched Fred to locate a Tibetan bell that the Lennons had stored in apartment 71. Fred managed to arrive at the Record Plant in the nick of time. As Smith recalled, "We ran and got a mic and hooked it up. Time was running out so we really had to move. We recorded the bell and put it into the mix and finished with just a minute to spare. We laughed with joy at making it in time. I'm not sure, but I seem to remember John calling Yoko to tell her we made it and then the session was over." For the recording, John struck the tiny bell three times. In his mind, the tiny bell stood in stark contrast to the funereal bells tolling at the beginning of 'Mother' on *Plastic Ono Band* a decade earlier. He would later overdub the sound of the wishing bell onto the intro for 'Beautiful

Boy (Darling Boy)', affording the first side of *Double Fantasy* with a sense of symmetry. During the session, John cautioned the production team not to strike the bell too often. "You never know what's going to show up when you ring that bell."[309]

With the '(Just Like) Starting Over' b/w 'Kiss Kiss Kiss' single mixed and prepped for release, John had one last idea that he wanted to try. With the idea of creating a segue of sound effects from 'Watching The Wheels' to 'Yes, I'm Your Angel' at the beginning of *Double Fantasy*'s second side, John sent Seaman and Smith over to the Plaza Hotel on Monday, September 29. Armed with a Nagra tape recorder, their job was to capture a selection of period sound effects to usher in Yoko's throwback tune, for which bassist Tony Levin had whistled a whimsical introduction. After recording random street noise and the sounds of horse-drawn carriages clomping through Central Park, they strolled over to the Palm Court and captured the sounds of a violinist and a pair of pianists performing for the Plaza Hotel's smattering of tourists and other high-end clientele. "It was a real adventure," Smith recalled. "At first, the staff didn't want to let us in, having spotted the tape recorder, so we ordered drinks at the bar, sat down at a table, and activated the equipment."[310]

That evening, Jack and John supervised the superimposition of Fred and Jon's handiwork into the mix. As John later explained to *Rolling Stone*'s Jonathan Cott, he wanted to establish an ambience that transitioned from Small's piano finale for 'Watching The Wheels' into the windswept nostalgic past of 'Yes, I'm Your Angel'. According to John,

> One of the voices is me going, "God bless you, man, thank you, man, cross my palm with silver, you've got a lucky face", which is what the English guys who beg or want a tip say, and that's what you hear me mumbling. And then we re-created the sounds of what Yoko and I call the "Strawberries and Violin Room" – the Palm Court at the Plaza Hotel. We like to sit there occasionally and listen to the old violin and have a cup of tea and some strawberries. It's romantic. And so the picture is, there's this kind of street prophet, Hyde Park-corner-type guy who just watches the wheels going around. And people are throwing money in the hat. We faked that in the studio. We had friends of ours walking up and down, dropping coins in a hat. And he's saying "thank you, thank you", and then you get in the horse carriage and you go

around New York and go into the hotel and the violins are playing and then this woman comes on and sings about being an angel.[311]

As they completed work on *Double Fantasy*, the band members couldn't conceal their excitement about the potential of launching a tour with John and Yoko in 1981. During the final weeks of production, they had spoken glowingly about potential setlists and the nature of the stage production. After a while, even the Lennons got into the act, in spite of John's earlier misgivings during his conversation with Stan Vincent. "Sure, I'd like to get up on stage with Yoko and a good band and play these songs and really *do* 'em, because the band's hot as shit," said John. "They just come off the album and they were all good – we've got the good feeling among ourselves. So it would be great. I'm just a little nervous about all that goes on around it. But I think we can probably handle it a bit better this time."[312]

A number of ideas were in the air as work wrapped up on *Double Fantasy*, including the idea of pay-per-view events, as well as a full-scale domestic tour tentatively set to begin in March 1981. Slick recalled that by the end of the recording sessions for *Double Fantasy*, "it was all in place. We were going to come back in January and finish the tracks for the next album and get that ready to go. And then we were going to do a tour. I don't remember discussing going overseas, but I know we discussed the States. The band would have been the guys from the sessions: two guitar players, bass, drums, percussion, and John and Yoko." At one point, John suggested to photographer and close friend Bob Gruen that they might follow the March US dates with events in Tokyo, Paris, and a long-overdue return engagement back in England. In a conversation with sax player Howard Johnson, who had just completed a stint as a member of Paul Simon's touring band, John was surprised to learn that the nature of rock 'n' roll tours had changed considerably since the 1960s. As Johnson recalled, "John wanted to get some inside information about how Paul's tour was being set up. I said, 'It's a one-hour set, a 15-minute break, and then another one-hour set.' And he said, 'Simon's doing two hours?' I said, 'Yeah, that's kind of standard.' He said, 'Really? We'd just do a single 40 minute set!' And I said, '40 minutes? That shit went out with the Beatles!'"[313]

As for the concerts themselves, John had already begun considering several concepts, included an elaborate stage production, chock-full of special effects and other devices designed explicitly to enhance the audience's experience. They had even begun referring to the concert dates as the "One World, One People" tour. When it came to presenting the show, Jack recalled, John's "idea was the stage should look like either a space ship or a crab, depending on what your view was. It had two crab-like arms that came out and on the arms were cameras and the cameras moved around. There was gonna be a giant screen projecting all of this." Lee DeCarlo added that John "had really futuristic ideas. One was using holograms of the band onstage like *Star Trek*." In addition to playing the songs from the *Double Fantasy* sessions, John planned to perform contemporary arrangements of such Beatles megahits as 'She Loves You' and 'I Want To Hold Your Hand'. "I wanna do 'I Want To Hold Your Hand'," John explained to the band, "because that was mine, we did it in the Beatles, but it was *mine*. You're gonna do all of your wailing all that. You're gonna show them it's not old hat," adding that he hoped to hear the musicians' strut their "freak stuff" during the live shows. At that point, John unveiled an innovative bit of stage play involving his wife for 'I Want To Hold Your Hand'. "While he sang it," Yoko remembered, "he was going to kneel down and hold my hand. I said, 'I don't think that's going to go down too well.' But there was a sense of 'Let's take it to them.' He was feeling very rebellious."[314]

As September 1980 came to a close, John had clearly reached new levels of contentment. And outside of Yoko, nobody had been more privy to John's change of heart than Jack. During their many and long conversations – whether it be during their breakfasts together at Café La Fortuna or their late nights working in the studio – the two men had come to an understanding about the significance of what they had accomplished in just a few short months. "The 'well' album was our code name for *Double Fantasy*," Jack later recalled. "When you listen to the album, the word 'well' comes up a lot. After a lifetime of anger and uncertainty, he finally seemed to have *found* his centre. He was totally balanced and confident, and it came through in his music."[315]

By this juncture, John, Yoko, and Jack had settled on the final running order for *Double Fantasy*. Slated by Geffen Records for a November 17 release, the album still required additional post-production work – some balancing here, the refinement of a few vocals and sound effects there. As the much-vaunted Heart Play in the Lennons' romantic imagination, *Double Fantasy* now ranged across the spectrum of enduring love into middle-age – from the heart-warming affirmation of '(Just Like) Starting

Over' and the unfettered eroticism of 'Kiss Kiss Kiss' to the winsome childhood lullaby in 'Beautiful Boy (Darling Boy)', the self-actualising philosophy inherent in 'Watching The Wheels', and the hopeful rejoinder of 'Hard Times Are Over'. *Double Fantasy* had it all:

Side A:	*Side B:*
(Just Like) Starting Over	Watching The Wheels
Kiss Kiss Kiss	Yes, I'm Your Angel
Cleanup Time	Woman
Give Me Something	Beautiful Boys
I'm Losing You	Dear Yoko
I'm Moving On	Every Man Has A Woman Who Loves Him
Beautiful Boy (Darling Boy)	Hard Times Are Over

For the Lennons, there was never any question about incorporating a lyric sheet as part of the album's design. After all, John had pioneered the concept with the Beatles on *Sgt. Pepper* back in 1967. *Double Fantasy* was the "well" album all right: among the entire album's lyrics, the word "well" appears no fewer than 28 times – and exclusively within John's seven contributions to the record. But it was also destined to be an album founded on brute human faith. Take 'Watching The Wheels', with arguably John's most heartening phrase, "there's no problem, only solutions." And when it came to closing out the album, Yoko was right there alongside her husband. With the Benny Cummings Singers and the Kings Temple singing in all their glory, Yoko offered a pronouncement, elegant in its simplicity and reassurance: the hard times, she asserts, "are over, over for a while".

CHAPTER 13

Life Begins at 40

In the months after his Bermuda renaissance, John had rarely been short on inspiration. If anything, the Hit Factory sessions had elevated his creative sensibilities even more. With his birthday on the horizon – and a milestone at that – John composed 'Life Begins At 40'. Ringo Starr had turned 40 on July 7, and John intended to give the song, along with 'Nobody Told Me', to the drummer for his upcoming album *Can't Fight Lightning*. John wasn't alone in sharing material for Ringo's cause. McCartney had already authored two songs expressly for Ringo – 'Private Property' and 'Attention' – which they had recorded during the summer of 1980. In addition to performing a cover version of the Carl Perkins standard 'Sure To Fall (In Love With You)', McCartney and Starr had also recorded 'You Can't Fight Lightning', which Ringo had composed after he and his fiancée Barbara Bach had narrowly escaped a lightning strike. As for George Harrison, the Quiet Beatle had worked extensively with Ringo on a cover version of the romantic ballad 'You Belong To Me', as popularised by Gene Vincent, and they planned to record 'All Those Years Ago', a Harrison original that he had held over for Starr, later that fall at Harrison's Friar Park home studio.

For 'Life Begins at 40', John drew upon a long cultural lineage associated with milestones and aging. The phrase had been popularised in the 1930s in Will Rogers' *Life Begins At 40* (1935), the story of a newspaper columnist in small-town America. In the film, Rogers famously recited an original poem in which he explores the pitfalls of growing up and growing older:

> At 20, we don't care what the world thinks of us.
> At 30, we worry about what it thinks of us.
> At 40, we're sure it doesn't think of us.

By the 1970s, the phrase "life begins at 40" was rife among the popular culture of the day – joining such sayings as "Dirty 30" and "Nifty 50" on birthday paraphernalia, home décor, and gift-bag swag.[316]

For 'Life Begins At 40', John composed a sweet country lilt for his demo, which he performed on his acoustic guitar along with his drum machine. In many ways, the song featured the same kind of wit, albeit more self-effacing, as 'I'm The Greatest', John's concoction for Starr's bestselling 1973 LP *Ringo*. The home recording begins with John's comic preamble, which he delivers in a Southern drawl: "We'd like to welcome you here to the Dakota Country and Western Club. And in return for Mrs Yoko Ono's wonderful gift of a very strange head, I'd like this morning to sing you a little ditty that occurred to me in the throes of my sleep. It's called 'Life Begins at 40'." With his pseudo-country voice in full throttle, John sings about age being "just a state of mind". For John, his upcoming milestone birthday held a bittersweet significance. Earlier in the year, he had written to a cousin back in England, saying, "I'm 40 next. I hope life begins – i.e., I'd like a little less 'trouble' and more – what? I don't know." But for John, the act of aging brought along its own pitfalls – namely, the inevitable loss of loved ones along life's journey. "I'm almost scared to go to England," he wrote, "'cause I know it would be the last time I saw Mimi and I'm a coward about goodbyes."[317]

During the August sessions at the Hit Factory, John had briefly debuted a new composition entitled 'Gone From This Place'. That fall, he recorded a demo for the song, reeling off several takes in an effort to further refine the tune. With a tender acoustic guitar accompaniment, 'Gone From This Place' found John embroidering a carefree song about the simple joys of living juxtaposed with an abiding fear of untimely death. John made at least four passes at the song, briefly reviving 'She Runs Them Round In Circles', a song-fragment from his original composing session for 'Beautiful Boy (Darling Boy)'.

During this same period, John had also developed a song out of thin air in the company of Jack Douglas. As John had observed so many times before, it was his preferred means of composition – the sudden moment of inspiration, the bolt out of the blue. Tentatively entitled 'Street Of Dreams', the tune came into being in the wee hours of the morning after a late-night session. "After we left the studio," Jack recalled, "we used to go to Rousseau of London, which was the only place in New York where you could get a full English breakfast at two in the morning – grilled bread, greasy eggs, the whole bit. After we ate, we'd jump in the limo. We'd pass Carnegie Hall and I said to John, 'You know what they call this?' And he said, 'What?' And I said, 'the Street of Dreams'. At the turn of the century, all of the great musicians, opera singers, and the maestros were all on the street. People from all over the world came here to break into the industry. He said, 'I like that.'"[318]

The next day, John asked Jack to join him at the studio. He simply couldn't get the concept of the 'Street Of Dreams' out of his head. Jack's description of the artistic fusion in Old New York City had touched him deeply. Jon Smith was there, too, in the studio that day, and he recalled Lennon's evolving vision of a creative place where "the lights would shine on these things and it would sparkle in a very magical way." Sitting together at the piano, John and Jack took a crack at building a chorus. Fortunately, John produced a song-fragment that dated back as far as his mid-period days with the Fab Four. "That's a verse I've had since the Beatle days," he explained to Jack. "It was one he could never find a chorus for since the mid-Sixties," Jack later remembered. "It was very cool. All I remember is the chorus went, 'here on the street of dreams'. That was the opening line. The verse had a real Beatle-y feel. We made a little recording of it on the spot. Somewhere, there's a cassette of it. I've never heard it again." Smith couldn't help eavesdropping on the writing session. "He played it for us, and it was beautiful," said Smith. "I remember it being lovely. Sometimes, years later, when I'd be falling asleep, I could almost remember what it sounded like."[319]

As John's 40th birthday rapidly approached, the Lennons continued their media blitz. With a record deal in hand, they were slightly more than a month away from the much-anticipated release of what many in the industry were perceiving as their comeback album. The public response had been growing in direct relation to John and Yoko's increasing media presence. In late September, bodyguard Doug MacDougall had registered his concern that the number of fans loitering along the streetscape in front of the Dakota – and later, the studios themselves – had visibly swelled in recent weeks. His reservations about the Lennons' safety had been amplified after an interview appeared in the *Daily News* in which John and Yoko's daily routine seemed to be communicated in unnecessarily precise detail. For John, it all came back to his longstanding belief, driven by his overt pacifism, that beefing up security would be tantamount to placing his bodyguard in imminent danger, as much as himself, should violence, improbable as it may have seemed during that very different time, ensue.

On October 9, John's birthday passed with some fanfare. First up, the Lennons tasked Fred with distributing a press release, stating that "next Spring, John and Yoko will be touring Japan, USA, and Europe." In an instant, the media buzz understandably eclipsed the fervour that occurred four years earlier when McCartney toured the United States for the first time since the Beatles' final, scandal-ridden American tour in 1966. When that tour had concluded on August 29 of that year at San Francisco's Candlestick Park, the Beatles were at the apex of the "Beatles Are Bigger than Jesus Christ" scandal wrought by John's controversial remarks about religion that had been republished in an American teen magazine. At one point during the band's last American swing, a firecracker had been tossed onto the stage during an appearance at the Mid-South Coliseum in Memphis, Tennessee, where the Ku Klux Klan had staged a protest. For a split second, the bandmates thought that they were under attack, fearing that one of them had been assassinated. As John recalled, "There had been threats to shoot us, the Klan were burning Beatle records outside, and a lot of the crew-cut kids were joining in with them. Somebody let off a firecracker and every one of us – I think it's on film – look at each other, because each thought it was the other that had been shot. It was that bad."[320]

In the United States circa 1980, things could not have been more different than the country the Beatles had experienced back in the mid-Sixties. The notion that the Lennons would shortly be embarking upon a bona fide world tour was met with genuine excitement. For one thing, the onset of celebrity culture had done its work. American entertainment magazines like *People* and *Us Weekly* were always hungry for new content, and anything involving the ex-Beatles tended to increase newsstand sales. In contrast with the UK's hard-hitting scandal sheets, glossy US fan mags veered towards a gentler approach – after all, the celebrities themselves were the living embodiment of their publications' success or failure. As for the Lennons' concert tour plans, associating the story along with John's birthday ensured that it would enjoy widespread release.

As for John's birthday, the couple had originally intended to join Douglas and his production team in the studio that day. Not surprisingly, they begged off, preferring to spend the day at home with Sean, who was celebrating a fifth birthday himself. The night before, Jon Smith had thoughtfully, he believed at the time, placed a rolled-up joint with the words "Happy Birthday" written on it into John's jacket pocket. When he found the joint in his pocket, John had immediately flushed it in the toilet, still smarting over his immigration fight and fearing that the FBI had planted it on his person. When he found out that Smith was behind the furtive gift, John was both grateful and relieved. As for Smith, "I felt terrible, but it was a really good joint. He would have enjoyed it."[321]

In terms of the festivities, Yoko had marked her husband and son's birthdays by hiring a skywriter to display the message "Happy Birthday, John and Sean, Love Yoko" in the skies over Central Park. That afternoon, the family enjoyed birthday cake and gifts in the superkitchen. John wore a party hat fashioned from a brown-paper grocery bag. As for his presents, John would later be seen in photographs proudly wearing the new tie that his wife had knitted for him, along with a diamond- and ruby-studded US flag pin valued at $75,000 and a rare, priceless Patek Philippe watch. The US flag pin was an obvious reference to John's affinity for his adopted homeland – indeed, in 1981, he would be eligible to petition for American citizenship.

With John and Sean's annual twin birthday celebration set for the following week at Tavern on the Green, the Lennons returned to the studio to continue holding mixing sessions with Jack and his production team. At this point, John and Yoko had shifted their operation *back* to the Hit Factory after a meeting with Ed Germano, who was understandably eager to continue his association with the musicians. On October 10, *Los Angeles Times* reporter Robert Hilburn met with John during an extended mixing session for Yoko's 'Beautiful Boys', into which Douglas and his team were attempting to splice sound effects from a laser fight in *Star Wars* (1977). By this point, the *Double Fantasy* LP was chock-full of special effects, including the outro for 'I'm Losing You', which ostensibly included a Morse-code message that said, "I love you, Yoko", although Jon Smith later reported that "I don't remember if we actually did it or if it's just random Morse code that we found on a sound-effects record."[322]

As he sat with John in the Hit Factory control booth, Hilburn peppered Lennon with the usual questions about the genesis of *Double Fantasy*, which he warmly attributed to McCartney's recent hit single 'Coming Up', describing Paul as "my dear one". He also revealed a sense of fatherly pride over Sean's adoration for the Beatles' *Yellow Submarine* (1968) cartoon movie. "Sean loves it now," John told Hilburn. "All the little children do." The interview later took a more strident turn when the reporter questioned Yoko about the forthcoming LP's significance. As with her vigilance throughout the production of *Double Fantasy*, John's artistic welfare seemed to be her overarching goal. "I have two concerns in this album," she told Hilburn. "First, I hope that it reminds people of John's talent. Second, I hope the fact that I am working with him enhances the man-woman dialogue. At the same time, I don't want the situation to become negative because my songs are too far-out or anything. That's hurting the chances of the album reaching as many people as possible. That wouldn't be fair to John. So in selecting my songs, I was conscious about the ones that are not too – shall we say – offbeat. This album is like our first hello. When you say hello, you don't want to complicate things. Maybe in the second or third album, we can experiment more."[323]

For John, this was music to his ears. He had shared his concerns, especially with Jack, that his contributions to the album were largely "adult contemporary" in terms of genre, save for the edgier 'I'm Losing You'. Picking up on Yoko's thread about future recording efforts, John said, "Yes, this is just starting over. We're going to move forward in the next album. It's going to be even better, so people better get ready." By this juncture, John and Yoko had begun considering titles for their planned follow-up to *Double Fantasy*. After all, they currently held basic tracks for eight unused recordings in the Hit Factory vaults, with new compositions already in the works. Yoko was especially fond of the title *Milk And Honey*, given that she liked to think of the Lennons' journeys to the United States as an effort to partake in "the land of milk and honey" portended in Exodus 33:3, borrowing from the common historical notion that America was a land of fertility, promise, and possibility. Yoko also recognised that "in the Scripture, the land of milk and honey is where you go after you die, as a promised land". While evoking Exodus suggests that the *Milk And Honey* title enjoyed similarly innocent origins as *Double Fantasy*'s roots in the Bermuda Botanical Gardens, it may not have been entirely true. *Milk And*

Honey also happened to be the name of a mid-1970s collection of Asian erotic etchings.[324]

On Monday, October 14, the Lennons watched the Columbus Day parade in the company of their Dakota neighbours on the street side along Central Park West. President Jimmy Carter was ferried along the parade route, along with New York City Mayor Ed Koch and Mario Cuomo, the New York State Lieutenant Governor. Italian tenor Luciano Pavarotti served as Grand Marshal, leading the parade for nearly 30 blocks astride an ebony steed. Later that day, Yoko hosted John and Sean's annual birthday event at Tavern on the Green. Sean's kindergarten classmates ruled the roost, with entertainment provided by street magician Jeff Sheridan, a master of the sleight-of-hand who cut his teeth performing card manipulations in Central Park. Joining the Lennons were Peter Boyle and Loraine Alterman, along with a number of their fellow Dakotans, including Marnie Hair and Kay LeRoy. Boyle had recently been cast opposite Tommy Lee Jones in an Off-Broadway production of Sam Shepard's *True West* at the Public, Joseph Papp's theatre on Lafayette Street. The play was set to open in late December. Meanwhile, the birthday party featured plenty of hijinks. A camera-clad Boyle was giddily taking pictures, at one point telling Marnie that he would pay her 10 bucks if she would plant a kiss on John. Not missing a beat, Lennon exclaimed "Here's a picture that's worth a lot more!" and kissed Fred square on the lips.[325]

For the next few weeks, Fred was dispatched to Bermuda to prep Villa Undercliff for an upcoming Fairylands vacation for the Lennons, who were exhausted from having worked virtually nonstop since early August. By this juncture, they were only a handful of sessions away from completing post-production and mixing work on *Double Fantasy*. At one point, Jack supervised a 36-hour stint in the control booth with DeCarlo and Smith, where the production team refined the final mixes and made a host of last-minute corrections. John often sat beside Douglas at the mixing desk, with Yoko resting nearby on the control-room sofa. "You know, John, we're very lucky people," she said. "We'll be lucky if we finish this mix," John deadpanned. By Monday, October 20, *Double Fantasy* was completed after Yoko requested one final tweak for 'Cleanup Time'. With post-production and the mixing sessions having been completed, the LP's contents were scheduled for mastering by industry heavyweight George Marino at Sterling Sound. That same week, Geffen's bravura return to the music industry was the subject of a feature article in *The Wall Street*

Journal. With the release of the Lennons' new single fewer than 48 hours away, he plugged *Double Fantasy*. "The music is sensational," he told the *Journal*. "It's the most commercial record John Lennon has ever made. He sounds like his old Beatle self."[326]

That Friday, '(Just Like) Starting Over' b/w 'Kiss Kiss Kiss' was released to great fanfare and anticipation. As a message to their fans the world over, John and Yoko insisted that the record was mastered with the words ONE WORLD, ONE PEOPLE etched in the playout grooves. Robert Palmer's *New York Times* review of the single greeted the Lennons that morning. Palmer wrote movingly about the single's A-side: "Although its lyric is sentimental and somewhat obvious, only a curmudgeon could resist its melody, rich vocal harmonies, 50s-style triplet piano and heavy backbeat, and a vocal performance that combines vulnerability with some attractively Presley-like phrasing." But to John's delight, Palmer reserved his finest praise for 'Kiss Kiss Kiss', which he described as the "fresher" of the two songs. "This is real pop, 1980s style," Palmer wrote, noting that Yoko's song "wouldn't sound out of place on a new-wave radio show programmed next to, say, Lene Lovich." A few weeks later, Palmer visited the Dakota to conduct an interview with the couple. When John greeted the journalist at the door of apartment 72, he couldn't resist poking fun at *The New York Times* review of '(Just Like) Starting Over'. As Palmer later recalled, John stood there in the entryway, "smiling broadly, one hand on his heart, the other outstretched" as he proclaimed, "Pardon me, if I'm sentimental."[327]

John and Yoko celebrated the release of the '(Just Like) Starting Over' b/w 'Kiss Kiss Kiss' single by listening to the song's radio debut in the company of their close friend, photographer Bob Gruen. Rock radio was in its heyday back then, and the mark of success for any artist – including someone as esteemed as Lennon – was hearing their song over the airwaves for the very first time. "It's still a thrill to hear your record on the radio," said John. "It makes the music real to me even though I've heard the songs a million times in the studio." As he had earlier explained to Hilburn, John couldn't wait to get back behind the console. "Yoko and I are so excited," he added at the time, "that we're going right back into the studio to begin working on the next album. I feel just like a kid again." For Gruen, observing the Lennons as they heard '(Just Like) Starting Over' was a genuine pleasure. "John and Yoko danced around the room while the song played," he recalled. "Then the DJ came on and said he liked it so much he was gonna play it again."[328]

But when it came to the reviews for the new single, not everyone would prove to be as kind as Palmer had been in the venerable pages of *The New York Times*. In the UK's vaunted *NME* (*New Musical Express*), Julie Burchill derided '(Just Like) Starting Over', comparing John unfavourably to Paul in the process. "So much for McCartney writing slop and Lennon writing the shocking rockers!" Burchill opined, adding that John "either needs to be put away (if this record is meant to be good) or wants to be written off (if the direness of this dirge is intentional)." Meanwhile, *Billboard* magazine proved to be far more complimentary: "Lennon is back and sounding better than ever in this up-tempo, fresh-sounding rocker. The irresistible melody and lyric line is enhanced by an exceptional rhythm unit, while Lennon's vocal is strong and upfront."[329]

When he wasn't composing new music or pondering the upcoming release of *Double Fantasy*, John was fascinated with the vicissitudes of American politics. With the general election only a few weeks away, John observed the political scene as incumbent President Jimmy Carter sparred with Republican challenger Ronald Reagan. He particularly enjoyed engaging in spirited arguments with Fred's Uncle Norman, an old-school communist sympathiser, about the uncertain future of American politics. Not surprisingly, John particularly enjoyed getting the older man's goat as the election year heated up to a near-boiling point. In spite of his own well-known background as a 1960s peacenik of the highest order, John would feign allegiance to Reagan, a no-holds-barred, right-wing candidate, and watch Norman's blood pressure soar with disdain. Later, of course, he would let the older man down gently and remind him of his well-honed liberal positions. It had been no accident, after all, that John had landed on Nixon's notorious Enemies List back in the early 1970s.[330]

With the Iranian hostage crisis nearing its one-year anniversary with no hope in sight, John had been glued to the television. As October came to a close, Reagan trailed the president in national polls by eight points among registered voters. All that changed on October 28 during the presidential debate in Cleveland, Ohio. That evening, Reagan famously asked a massive American television audience, "Are you better off now than you were four years ago? Is it easier for you to go and buy things in the stores than it was four years ago? Is there more or less unemployment in the country than there was four years ago? Is America as respected throughout the world as it was? Do you feel that our security is as safe, that we're as strong as we were four years ago?" Within a matter of days, the answer to the challenger's questions would become clear. As the campaign moved into its final days, Reagan leapt ahead of the incumbent by three points, an incredible 11-point swing.

For John, Reagan's apotheosis was hardly a surprise, given the economic and political issues that had been plaguing the nation over the past few years – not to mention, the looming crises in the Middle East. Yet he also saw the political spectrum as a world where voters often made choices that had little to do with their personal needs or any lingering patriotic desires. Instead, he perceived the identification with ideologies and candidates as an artificial visit to the "dog pound of daddies", where we yearn to reconnect with our fathers, missing or otherwise. To John's mind:

> A lot of us are looking for fathers. Mine was physically not there. Most people are not there mentally and physically, like always at the office or busy with other things. So all these leaders, parking meters, are all substitute fathers, whether they be religious or political. All this bit about electing a president! We pick our own daddy out of a dog pound of daddies. This is the daddy that looks like the daddy in the commercials. He's got the nice grey hair and the right teeth and the parting's on the right side. Okay? This is the daddy we choose. The dog pound of daddies, which is the political arena, gives us a president. Then we put him on a platform and start punishing him and screaming at him because Daddy can't do miracles: Daddy doesn't heal us; we don't feel better. So then we move the daddy out in four years, and we get a new daddy.[331]

And sure enough on election day, Tuesday, November 4, the American electorate selected a "new daddy" and voted for Reagan in droves. Meanwhile, Fred had returned from Bermuda at the end of October, with the Lennons having decided against a vacation for the moment. Besides, John was enjoying his respite from the recording studio, having instructed his assistant to round up several books so that he could step up his reading schedule. For one thing, he wanted his copy of Heyerdahl's *The Tigris Expedition* back from Sam Green so that he could reread the book after his summer sailing adventures. He also hoped to take a crack at Susanne Steinem Patch's *Blue Mystery: The Story of the Hope Diamond*, presumably because he had learned about Brownie McLean's association with the legendary gem. Given McLean's status as the previous owner of the Lennons' Palm Beach Island estate, John wanted to learn more about the eccentric woman who had once called El Solano her home.[332]

By early November, John had been the subject of numerous articles – most often because of the upcoming release of *Double Fantasy*. And he was even the subject of an upcoming book publication. His former personal assistant Anthony Fawcett was set to publish a new edition of his 1976 biography *John Lennon: One Day at a Time*, on December 1. But in one of the year's most bizarre media incursions, John was the subject of a cover story in the November 1 issue of *Esquire*, written by Laurence Shames and entitled "John Lennon, Where Are You?" A slickly authored piece of quasi-detective journalism, Shames' subtitle announced that the writer was "In Search of the Beatle Who Spent Two Decades Seeking True Love and Cranial Bliss Only to Discover Cows, Daytime Television, and Palm Beach Real Estate".[333]

Of course, if John had been hiding over the past few months, he had clearly been doing it in plain sight. Since Cohen's August press release – and apparently unbeknown to Shames – the Lennons had been veritable media darlings. In terms of the magazine's reach, *Esquire* enjoyed an international profile, while also drawing a domestic readership that extended throughout the nation – from Alaska to Hawaii and all across the Lower 48. Shames framed his narrative as a kind of pop-culture mystery wherein the writer roamed the countryside in search of John, whom he described as "a 40-year-old businessman, who's got $150 million" and "stopped making music". When he couldn't seem to ferret out John's whereabouts, he sought out the prized Holsteins instead, finally locating them in the Catskill Mountains: "Lennon's cows lowed and mooed," Shames wrote, "and I wondered if they had any inkling that their owner had done amazing things a long time ago."[334]

Seemingly unable to find the ex-Beatle, Shames turned to the news bank to learn more about his subject. "There was a clear pattern in the newspaper clippings," Shames observed. "Lennon got written up when he bought something. He remained a celebrity because of his purchasing power." Having struck out in his quest to locate John in the northeast corridor, the writer turned to Florida, where he discovered that "the Palm Beachers *like* Lennon, which made me feel queasy. They think he's a swell neighbour. He's got tons of money and he doesn't litter." And that's when Shames happened upon the breaking news that the Lennons were planning to release an album. One of the author's contacts had spoken to him about John off the record, reporting that the project is "top secret right now, but it'll hit the papers any day. A Boston publicity firm is gonna let the news leak out in carefully measured doses. He's cutting it over at the Hit Factory. With Yoko. It might even turn out to be a double album." By this point, Shames had revealed himself not only to be journalism's hardscrabble equivalent to Sam Spade, but also, alas, a fan:

> The first reluctant stirrings of hope were starting up in me again, and I felt like a jerk for getting sucked back in. But that's the thing with Lennon's eerie stature: he could get the whole world jazzed about an album that might very well never see the light of day. And even if it did, with Yoko in on it, it could turn out to be the turkey of the season. Still, you hope. You know there's a hit-or-miss genius behind the microphone and maybe, just maybe, something startling will happen.[335]

With Shames' *Esquire* piece alighting newsstands the world over, John and Yoko settled into the home stretch of their autumn media blitz. On November 2, they sat for a session with Jack Mitchell, arguably New York City's most venerated photographer when it came to the arts. *The New York Times* had commissioned Mitchell to photograph the couple for the purposes of illustrating Palmer's upcoming *Double Fantasy* article. The session took place at the photographer's East 74th Street studio. Wearing sweaters, John and Yoko made themselves comfortable, while Mitchell prepped for the photo shoot. As Mitchell later recalled, "In an effort to gauge how much time I was going to have, I asked John if this was a stop en route to dinner. He replied, laughing: 'Dinner? I've not had breakfast yet!'" During breaks in the photo session, John admired Mitchell's recent portrait of Meryl Streep, explaining that he was a "Meryl Streep groupie", while pausing to pet Mitchell's ginger studio cat named Red. In Mitchell's memory, "John was especially spontaneous and loose. He seemed to be having fun and laughed a lot."[336]

After shooting eight rolls of black-and-white film and a half roll of colour film, Mitchell called it quits for the night. A week later, on November 9, one of Mitchell's photographs of the couple was published in *The New York Times*. Thrilled with the results, Yoko telephoned the photographer to see if she and John could use the photo for their Christmas card. Later, it occurred to Mitchell that he hadn't taken any solo photos of John and Yoko. He reminded himself that his assignment had been to photograph John and Yoko together, and besides, "they were just so together that it simply never occurred to me."[337]

Meanwhile, as the excitement over the Lennons' new recordings continued to build, even Fred got in on the act. Having recently reconnected with the folks back in Bermuda, he sent a copy of '(Just Like) Starting Over' b/w 'Kiss Kiss Kiss' to his island friends. "As promised," he wrote, "the new single. My spies in Disco 40 will check whether it gets played so you better not fuck around and play it only in the lounge (only kidding, of course). Anyway, thanks for making my stay in Bermuda more fun (though not necessarily more relaxing)." For Fred, working with John and Yoko during the production of *Double Fantasy* had been the most exciting and rewarding period of his Dakota employment. Since he had joined their staff the previous year, he had been hoping for the opportunity to witness the artists working in their element. And now it was really happening.[338]

Meanwhile, on the eve of *Double Fantasy*'s release date, John had begun working on several new compositions. Earlier that month, he'd started 'Dear John', a composition that took its name from the letters wartime GIs received from their unfaithful sweethearts back home. In the song-fragment, John works his Ovation acoustic, occasionally losing his place and laughing quietly to himself. "Dear John", he sings, "give yourself a break." Gently tapping out a beat for his accompaniment, he arrives at a moment of vital self-consolation: the race is done, "you've won". As the demo concludes, John whistles a sweet, lilting coda.

Arguably the strangest home recording of his solo career, 'Pop Is The Name Of The Game' found John improvising a furtive, funky little number with little in the way of lyrics beyond the title. During the same writing session, he took yet another pass at 'Serve Yourself', which remained unfinished and relatively unevolved since he last visited the song-fragment after returning from Bermuda. Recorded on November 14, 'You Saved My Soul (With Your True Love)' made for a different story, however. Singing against a driving electric rhythm guitar part, John composed a love paean for Yoko. Referencing the self-destructive tendencies he briefly displayed in his September 1979 audio diary, he thanked his wife for acting as his salvation. With a trace of rockabilly in his voice, he sings that "only you saved me" from jumping out of his New York apartment window.

The next day, John and Yoko travelled across the park to the Plaza Hotel, where they met Ringo and Barbara Bach. The couple was enjoying a stopover in New York City on their way to Los Angeles, where Ringo planned to continue work on *Can't Fight Lightning* with Harry Nilsson, who had composed 'Drumming Is My Madness' for the ex-Beatle. "I hadn't seen him for a while," Ringo recalled. "We see each other wherever we are, and he came over with Yoko." The Lennons had planned to spend an hour with them, but "we had such a great time", said Ringo, that "they stayed five hours". Before he returned to the Dakota with Yoko, John handed Ringo the demos for 'Nobody Told Me' and 'Life Begins At 40'. As the two old friends and bandmates parted ways, they locked in a recording date for January 14 in New York City to lay down the tracks.[339]

Later that evening, John would be the subject of a skit on NBC's *Saturday Night Live*. With the Lennons' comeback only a few days away, the city was abuzz about *Double Fantasy*. Comedian Charles Rocket – a new cast member of the variety show's Not Ready for Prime-Time Players – stood in front of the Dakota and made a nuisance of himself harassing passersby for any information about John and Yoko's new album. At one point, Rocket questioned an elderly Upper West Sider about John. "I know Lennon is in that building because all the youngsters gather there for an autograph," she told him. "Why do they allow them to gather up there?" After hassling the building's doorman about an overflowing pile of refuse outside of the archway, Rocket turned his attentions to the garbage collectors working behind the Dakota. "I don't know anything about that," one of the men replied, when the comedian asked him about the impending album release. "That's music," he curtly answered, tossing a handful of trash into his truck. "This is garbage." Standing on the streetscape in front of the Dakota, Rocket ended the sketch by recognising the futility of his efforts, exclaiming that "we're all gonna have to share the disappointment of not finding out anything at all."[340]

When the morning of the much-anticipated release of *Double Fantasy* finally arrived, John began the day by telephoning the folks back home. Up first was his half-sister Julia Baird back in Liverpool. During the call, John hatched a plan for making his triumphant return to the UK for the first time since 1971. Expecting his relations to come out in droves, John suggested that they stage the reunion at the large family home at Rock Ferry in Ardmore. "There are so many of you," he told her, that "we will have to get together at Ardmore." Over the past few months, he had begun to imagine returning to his homeland in fine style – sailing on the *Queen Elizabeth 2* up the Thames into London and making his grand comeback in the guise of a victorious conqueror. John's next call was to his Aunt Mimi, disapproving as ever of her nephew's penchant for extravagance. In celebration of the LP's release, he had gifted her with a matching pearl necklace and brooch from Cartier. "You're daft," she told him in reference to his indulgence.[341]

But for John, there was simply no way that his aunt's surly attitude could spoil his carefree outlook that day. "Go on, Mimi," he replied, laughing in the face of her frugality. "Spoil yourself – just for a change."[342]

CHAPTER 14

Record Plant

When John stepped out onto West 72nd Street later that day, he was in a buoyant, happy-go-lucky mood. He was carrying several pristine copies of *Double Fantasy* under his arm. As was true more often than not that fall, Paul Goresh was standing nearby. "You know the album came out today," John said excitedly to the amateur photographer. "Do you want one?" Goresh was delighted to take a copy of the LP off his hands. As if on cue, another bystander loped up and asked if he could have a copy, too. "Yeah," John replied. "Sam Goody's on 48th Street has them." Moments later, a beaming John posed with Goresh in front of the *porte-cochère*, with the doorman grinning from ear-to-ear in the background from his place near the copper-plated sentry box.[343]

For John and Yoko, *Double Fantasy* marked a new beginning. They were ecstatic about having brought the album from ideation to release in fewer than five months, to be sure. But they were possibly even more elated about having found the courage and resolve to imagine an artistic rebirth for themselves. "We feel like this is just the start and this is our first album," said John. "I know we've worked together before, and we've even made albums before, but we feel like this is the first album. I feel like nothing has happened before today."[344]

Given the hotly anticipated nature of its release, *Double Fantasy* was the subject of a bevy of early reviews. Stateside, the daily newspapers led the way. In *The Philadelphia Inquirer*, Jack Lloyd opined that "Lennon offers us no new vision concerning the future of pop music. But as a transitional album – one in which he felt compelled to get a few things off his chest – he has handled it with a fair amount of style," adding that "it's nice to have Lennon back again." Writing in the *Los Angeles Times*, Steve Pond panned the album, warning that "those expecting the return of the mythical Lennon – a man with an insightful, brilliant mind and a biting wit – will be sorely disillusioned by *Double Fantasy*." Pond concluded that "the worst thing about *Double Fantasy* is that it simply makes John and Yoko look like a pair of aged, lost hippies."[345]

The Washington Post's Richard Harrington mined a similar vein, writing that "$8.98 for a flaccid look at a family scrapbook is too much to ask," describing '(Just Like) Starting Over' as "an embarrassing pastiche of 50s and 60s influences." Harrington dismissed John's work as suffering from "a general lack of substance, lyrical directness, and undistinguished melodies." As for Yoko, her "warbling is more controlled than it was a decade ago, but her voice is still uninteresting." In a more charitable bent, Terry Lawson critiqued the album for Dayton, Ohio's *Journal Herald*, writing that "vocally, Lennon has never sounded better and Ono's odd singing style is used here to best advantage." Recognising that for many, "the criticism of *Double Fantasy* will undoubtedly centre on its simple tone, its failure to take real chances, its overriding sense of caution," Lawson swept any naysayers aside, concluding that "I'm happy enough to wallow in the fantasy." Meanwhile, other reviews were still in preparation from the likes of *Rolling Stone*'s Tom Carson, *The New York Times*' Stephen Holden, and *The Village Voice*'s Geoffrey Stokes.[346]

By contrast, the UK press was merciless. In the intervening years since John's last solo album, the county had become swept up in the scrappy, often violent punk movement and its growing clash with the industry's privileged, seemingly less-relevant mainstays. Clearly working from this perspective, an unsigned reviewer in *Melody Maker* commented that "the whole thing positively reeks of an indulgent sterility. It's a godawful yawn!" Writing in the November 22 issue of *NME*, Charles Shaar Murray continued the excoriation: "Lennon and Ono appear on the cover clamped in a passionate embrace," Murray writes. "The album celebrates their mutual devotion to each other and their son Sean to the almost complete exclusion of all other concerns. Everything's peachy for the Lennons and nothing else matters, so everything's peachy *QED*. How wonderful, man. One is thrilled to hear of so much happiness." Murray was complimentary of Yoko's tracks, observing that her "music sounds vastly more modern and considerably more interesting than Lennon's." In his summary, Murray admits that "I look forward to Yoko Ono's solo album," while wishing "that Lennon had kept his big happy trap shut until he has something to say that was even vaguely relevant to those of us not married to Yoko Ono."[347]

From their vantage point in the Dakota, John and Yoko were tuned into the album's performance, and, thanks to their clipping service, received all of the reviews almost as soon as they were published. Having devoted so much of her energy to helping John make music again, Yoko was understandably distraught – especially when '(Just Like) Starting Over' seemed to be stalling in the charts in spite of considerable airplay. As she later recalled,

> I went to John, who was sitting in a comfortable chair reading the papers.
> "John, I'm sorry. The single only went to number eight."
> "It won't move?"
> "No."
> He was thinking for a second, looking at me.
> Then he said, "It's all right. We have the family."[348]

As the reviews poured in, John was undoubtedly buoyed by his wife's positive notices. And with the press launch that they had orchestrated across print and radio media, the couple had rarely enjoyed so much attention in the media. That weekend, they made a return engagement, of sorts, to *Saturday Night Live*, when guest host Malcolm McDowell played Lennon against Denny Dillon's turn as Ono. In the skit, *SNL* cast member Charles Rocket interviews the pair about their new album. With McDowell and Dillon sitting in a mock-up of the superkitchen, the John character talks about his life as a househusband. "Yoko is just loco about my cocoa," he explains. As for *Double Fantasy*, "It's mainly love songs and a few oven-cooking tips," he remarks as a cake inside the oven behind them catches fire.[349]

For the Lennons, who enjoyed the humorous take on their lifestyle, the moment must have seemed surreal as they watched the live television programme across town in apartment 72. As the month wore on, John and Yoko geared up for yet more media forays, with several radio spots scheduled for early December. Up first was a November 26 video shoot in Central Park for a '(Just Like) Starting Over' promo film with photographer Ethan Russell, who had covered the Beatles' final photo session at Tittenhurst Park in August 1969, and cinematographer Don Lenzer. By this point, John had apparently abandoned the concept of a promo video of himself flying, monster-like above the park. As the Lennons strolled along the wooded pathways, John made conversation, pointing in the direction of the city and saying, "Hey, Yoko, why don't you buy that building? You could have one room to keep your fur coats in, the rest we could keep cats in." Russell later recalled John's good humour on that crisp autumn day. During a break, John laughed and said, "This reminds me of *Rubber Soul*, only my face has fallen."[350]

That evening, the scene shifted to SoHo's Sperone Gallery on Greene Street. With Allan Tannenbaum on hand to capture still photographs, John and Yoko entered a film set arrayed entirely in white. The sparse setup included a faux staircase, stepladder, and a bed. For the first phase of the session John and Yoko donned kimonos, their customary daywear, as Lenzer, Russell, and Tannenbaum shot their footage. During the second phase, the Lennons disrobed, feigning intercourse while the amatory sounds of 'Kiss Kiss Kiss' blared from a nearby boombox. As the clock struck 11 p.m., the session wrapped up for the night, with John and Yoko posing for photographs and signing autographs for the crew.

For the Lennons, Thanksgiving Day festivities included observing the annual parade with their neighbours along Central Park West. They marked the day by donating a selection of cakes, cookies, and other assorted foodstuffs to the folks at the Spofford Juvenile Detention Center in the Bronx. As was their custom, they also disseminated their annual holiday message to the world: "On this day of Thanksgiving, we are thinking of you. We wish you a happy life." The next day, November 28, John was placed under oath in relation to Apple Corps' ongoing lawsuit against the creators of *Beatlemania*, who were planning to produce a movie based on the hit Broadway show. As with McCartney's 1979 Columbia contract, Lennon made special mention of potential future Fab Four output – in this instance, a documentary. As John stated, "I and the other three former Beatles have plans to stage a reunion concert." Over the past several years, Apple Corps director Neil Aspinall had been compiling a documentary to be entitled *The Long And Winding Road*, which would have included a live performance by the Beatles as the movie's climactic scene.[351]

As November came to a close, John and Yoko's well-known yen for social activism had been reignited by recent events on the West Coast. Since November 13, Japanese teamsters had been on strike against a powerful consortium of Japanese food importers and distributors. They planned to travel to San Francisco on December 14 to participate in a protest march. In the meantime, they composed a statement of support for the striking workers in California. "We are with you in spirit," the Lennons wrote. "Both of us are subjected to prejudice and abuse as an Oriental family in the Western world. In this beautiful country, where democracy is the very foundation of its Constitution, it is sad that we have to still fight for equal rights and equal pay for the citizens. Boycott it must be, if it is the only way to bring justice and restore the dignity of the Constitution for the sake of all citizens of the United States and their children."[352]

For the Lennons, early December began with a flourish of excitement. First up was the forthcoming release of the 'Woman' b/w 'Beautiful Boys' single, which was slated for a January 1981 release. For the picture sleeve, the Lennons selected one of the photos from their session with Jack Mitchell a month earlier. And then there was the upcoming cover story by Peter Occhiogrosso entitled "Yoko Only" for the *SoHo Weekly News*. Adorned with a photograph by Allan Tannenbaum, the article's publication was a great source of pride for John, who sent Fred out to area newsstands to purchase 100 copies of the issue. Any evidence that Yoko was beginning to be seen as an artist in her own right was welcome news to him.

That afternoon, John and Yoko were joined by photographer and fellow Dakotan Annie Leibovitz, who visited apartment 72 for an upcoming cover feature in *Rolling Stone*. She had photographed the couple in the early Seventies for a *Rolling Stone* cover story associated with Jann Wenner's *Lennon Remembers* interviews. The December 3 photo shoot began in the superkitchen, where John and Yoko reclined in the director's chairs around the butcher-block table. Later, in the master bedroom, Leibovitz took pictures of John lying in bed, strumming his candy apple red Fender Stratocaster. When the photographer left that afternoon, they made plans for a second photo shoot on Monday.

As far as the Lennons were concerned, the most pressing story that day would be unfolding a few dozen blocks to the south at the Record Plant. Earlier that week, John had telephoned Jack Douglas, announcing the couple's intentions to get back to work. "We're going back. *Again*. I feel like I just don't want to leave the studio," John told the producer. "Just you and me and Yoko. That's all I want. Get an assistant, get an engineer, and produce." With John and Yoko's profile continuing to soar even higher in the wake of *Double Fantasy*'s release, the Record Plant hired a bodyguard, six-foot-six Robert "Big Bob" Manuel, to accompany them when they were on the premises.[353]

Studio assistant Danny Caccavo recalled the moment when the Lennons arrived at the Record Plant that day. Apparently self-conscious about the couple's shifting allegiances between the Hit Factory and its arch-rival studio four blocks away, Yoko told the studio's receptionist, Rabiah Seminole that "we really do love it at Record Plant. We're here to stay." Jack met the Lennons in a small 10th-floor studio, where they began hatching plans to return to 'Walking On Thin Ice', one of the unused tracks from the *Double Fantasy* sessions. "We only had a germ of that record, so we made a loop of I think eight bars," Jack later recalled. "It's just loop-based. And a loop then was just a tape machine, I had it on a two-track spinning back to a multitrack, cutting bars together." The tape loop formed a basic rhythm track for 'Walking On Thin Ice', including Newmark's original drum work, along with Tony Levin's driving bass. To round out his production team, Jack invited 23-year-old Steve Marcantonio to serve as engineer for the track. Marcantonio had worked at the Record Plant since 1978 and had recently engineered *The Blues Brothers* soundtrack.[354]

As for the session's outcome, Jack and the Lennons weren't entirely sure at this point. They had begun with the idea of creating a "Yoko Only" record of dance remixes for 'Kiss Kiss Kiss', 'Every Man Has A Woman Who Loves Him', 'Walking On Thin Ice', and 'Open Your Box', the suggestive B-side to John's 1971 hit 'Power To The People'. But as they quickly discovered that night, 'Walking On Thin Ice' was brimming with possibilities all on its own. With the tape loop in place, Jack and John were able to begin overdubbing voices and instruments to the song. For his part, Marcantonio was impressed with John's facility at the console. "He was very much a part of the record-making process," Marcantonio recalled. "He knew the signal flow, and he knew what he wanted and how he liked things to sound." On that first night back in the studio, Yoko remade her lead vocal, while also recording a spoken-word middle section: "I knew a girl who tried to walk across the lake," she said in an intentionally nonchalant, even disconnected voice. "Course it was winter, when all this was ice." As Jack remembered, "Yoko was great," and her poetic interlude was the turning point for the song. "John knew that Yoko was onto something with that one – especially with that spoken-word."[355]

During the session that night at the Record Plant, Bob Gruen photographed the couple in the studio. Several photos depict the Lennons posing with *Baby Grand Guitar*, a sculpture from John and Yoko's 1971 *This Is Not Here* exhibition that they had donated to the Record Plant. For the occasion, John had worn a brand-new black leather jacket that he had purchased at the Gap over on Broadway and 69th Street, a few blocks away from the Dakota. Energised by the first session associated with 'Walking On Thin Ice', John and Yoko were back at the Record Plant with Jack by Thursday afternoon. Yoko remade aspects of her lead vocals, while Jack fashioned a percussion track and John played keyboards. For Jack, the vibe in the studio was even more electric than back at the Hit Factory. It "was very wild", he recalled. "We were having a blast. We just felt like we had complete freedom to do whatever we wanted."[356]

One of the finest moments of John's storied career emerged during the evening part of the session, when he overdubbed a sizzling guitar part onto 'Walking On Thin Ice'. As usual, Fred had carted a selection of John's guitars over from the Dakota. Caccavo remembered that John picked up the candy apple red Strat that day – or perhaps it might have been the red "Rick N Hamer" that Nielsen had presented to him back in August. But when it came to the guitar that John used to perform the solo on 'Walking On Thin Ice', Jack didn't have any doubt about the instrument's identity. "It was the Capri," he recalled, referring to John's fabled 1958 Rickenbacker 325. While many of John's older guitars had fallen into disrepair, the Capri was in playing shape. After May Pang brought the guitar back from England in 1971, John had turned it over to luthier Ron DeMarino, who stripped away the jet-black finish and sanded the instrument down to its original wood-grain appearance. In the last few months, with the concept of a spring tour gathering steam, John planned to restore the guitar to the jet-black colouring that had wowed fans on *The Ed Sullivan Show* back in February 1964.[357]

For the guitar solo, John simply wailed on the guitar, executing a series of power chords as Douglas, sitting nearby, reached over and worked the instrument's Bigsby tailpiece. As with a whammy bar, the Bigsby tremolo arm allowed the producer to manipulate the vibrato sound and heighten the eerie ambience they had been creating for 'Walking On Thin Ice'. Shortly afterwards, John explained that he modelled his solo on Sanford Clark's 1956 rockabilly hit 'The Fool'. Almost as soon as they had completed the take, John, Yoko, and Jack found themselves mesmerised by Lennon's guitar work. As Marcantonio later recalled, "John laid down this really cool guitar solo that was so John Lennon, and every time the solo came up he would turn to me and we'd play air guitar to each other."[358]

In the wee hours of the morning, John took a break from the session in the company of Peter Occhiogrosso, to whom he was grateful for authoring such an inspiring profile on Yoko for the *SoHo Weekly News*. As they stepped outside, they were joined by Big Bob, who reminded John that the Record Plant was in a dicey neighbourhood. "Well, I don't have my handgun with me," John quipped, "so it's every man for himself." As it turned out, John had an ulterior motive, hoping to learn from Occhiogrosso about whether an EP comprised of 'Yoko Only' dance mixes made sense or a conventional 45 RPM single. "I've got a great single for the flip side," said John, "but I think we're gonna go with her songs."[359]

As it happened, John and Yoko were still working some six hours later, finally calling it quits around 8.30 on the morning of Friday, December 5. They were joined by Bob Gruen, who photographed them on the streetscape in front of the building. John was wearing yet another new jacket, which he had purchased just around the corner from the Dakota at the trendy boutique Charivari 72. This time, John's jacket was eminently more exotic than his leather outfit from the Gap. Designed by Kansai Yamamoto, who had fashioned David Bowie's Ziggy Stardust costumery, the jacket was embroidered with a dragon's head, along with *The Heart Sutra*, the Buddhist saying that is translated as "form is empty / Emptiness is form".[360]

As they waited for the limo to ferry them back to the Dakota, John assured Gruen that the mixed nature of *Double Fantasy*'s record reviews had left him unscathed. As Gruen later recalled, "He wasn't sorry that reviewers said Yoko's songs were more avant-garde, modern, and interesting than John's songs, which they described as being more MOR, middle-of-the-road. And he said, 'That's fine because we're going right down the middle-of-the-road to the bank.'"[361]

Back at the Dakota, John began making plans in earnest for the family's 1981 trip to the UK. By this point, Aunt Mimi was on high alert, certain that she would be seeing her nephew before too long. She had recently received her annual holiday card from the Lennons, inscribed "Happy Christmas and a brand-new year. We wish you health! Wealth!? Wisdom???! And the time to enjoy it! Love, John, Yoko, Sean".

That same day, John telephoned Mimi at her home on the English coast and began firming up his plans to introduce Sean to his British relations. As Mimi later recalled, "He rang and said he was looking out of a window in New York, looking at the docks and ships and wondering whether any of them were going to Liverpool. It made him homesick. He was coming home. He was coming here to Poole, Dorset, and going to Liverpool." When she hung up the telephone that day, the 74-year-old Mimi was convinced that John was serious this time, and she began preparing a bedroom for his visit. Yoko was fairly certain about John's plans, too, recalling that "he was so happy, laughing and joking and looking forward to coming over to England. It was like a new John." But she also knew that John had begun to yoke his plans for a UK reunion with the chart-topping success of '(Just Like) Starting Over'. If the single captured the number-one spot, they'd book passage on the *QE2*, "show Sean to Aunt Mimi and also say hello to Liverpool," said Yoko. If the record came up short, though, "we had to chuck that plan altogether."[362]

Later that day, John and Yoko had returned to the Record Plant yet again. John pulled Jack aside, saying, "Listen, this 'Walking On Thin Ice' idea, I really wanna finish it because it's the one that's gonna set her off." Since hearing of the B-52's blaring over the PA at Disco 40 back in July, John had been convinced that Yoko's time had arrived, that people would begin to take her seriously as a bona fide rock singer. For years, he had described his wife as the "world's most well-known, unknown artist", and with 'Walking On Thin Ice' he was determined to see her become *known* for the quality of her musical gifts and not merely because of her famous husband.[363]

As John and Yoko continued refining 'Walking On Thin Ice' that afternoon with Jack in the studio, *Rolling Stone*'s Jonathan Cott joined the couple for an interview. John had been eager to show off his wife's hot new track for the journalist, and Cott was decidedly impressed. Earlier that day, Cott had spent time with the couple at the Dakota. For Cott, interviewing the Lennons made for a homecoming of sorts. He had first interviewed them back in September 1968, marking John's first full-length spread in the magazine. John's fate had also seemed to be intertwined with the pioneering rock magazine, which published a film still of Lennon from *How I Won the War* (1967) as the cover photograph of its inaugural issue.

During the interview, John brought up a recent fan letter that he received from a British girl named Tali Onon. A few months back, John had been very taken with her story – namely, her social struggles as a student of mixed parentage. At the time, John had a few spare postcards left from his visit to Bermuda, and he dropped one in the mail to ensure that she received a response. As he told Cott that day, "I get truly affected by letters from Brazil or Poland or Austria – places I'm not conscious of all the time – just to know somebody is there, listening. One kid living up in Yorkshire wrote this heartfelt letter about being both Oriental and English and identifying with John and Yoko. The odd kid in the class. There are a lot of those kids who identify with us. They don't need the history of rock 'n' roll. They identify with us as a couple, a biracial couple, who stand for love, peace, feminism and the positive things of the world." Things took a different turn when Cott asked John about the vexing nature of fame and success, which found John venting his disgust with Laurence Shames' *Esquire* article. "They only like people when they're on the way up," said John, "and when they're up there, they've got nothing else to do but shit on them. I cannot be on the way up again. What they want is dead heroes, like Sid Vicious and James Dean. I'm not interested in being a dead fucking hero."[364]

When Cott questioned John about his interest in inspiring people to find the best version of themselves, John replied that "it's still there", adding that he continues to believe in "give peace a chance, not shoot people for peace. All we need is love. I believe it. It's damn hard, but I absolutely believe it." As for the musicians of the present, John strikes a word of caution for the superstars of the moment, having swiftly returned to his earlier discourse on hero worship. "God help Bruce Springsteen when they decide he's no longer God," said John, who reserved high praise for 'Hungry Heart', the Boss' latest radio hit. "Right now, his fans are happy. He's told them about being drunk and chasing girls and cars and everything, and that's about the level they enjoy. But when he gets down to facing his own success and growing older and having to produce it again and again, they'll turn on him, and I hope he survives it." By the time the interview had concluded, it was nearly 3 a.m. As he prepared to leave John and Yoko in the studio, where Douglas was preparing to take another stab at mixing 'Walking On Thin Ice', Cott couldn't help telling John how exhilarated he was at seeing the Lennons in such fine fettle. "I love her, and we're together," said John, simply. "Goodbye, till next time."[365]

Back at the Dakota, John settled into a protracted session listening to Jack's latest mix of 'Walking On Thin Ice'. Giving her husband some space to concentrate on the song, Yoko strolled over to a newsstand, where she bought him some chocolates as a surprise. "He loved chocolates," said Yoko, "but it was not in our sugarless diet at that point. After the drug binges of the Sixties, John wanted both of us to clean up and be healthy 'for Sean's sake too'." When she got back to apartment 72, she was startled when he opened the door. "How did you know I was coming back just now?" she asked. "Oh, I know when you're back," he replied, delighted at the sight of the chocolates.[366]

That afternoon, John managed to pause his 'Walking On Thin Ice' playback sessions long enough to take a late brunch with the *SoHo Weekly News*' John Miller at Wylie's, an upscale East Side restaurant. John spoke animatedly about *Double Fantasy*, although both men ended up engaging in a lengthy conversation about death. "I used to worry about death when I was a kid," said John. "Now the fear of it means less and less to me." In the Beatle days, "when we were the rage, we used to use around-the-clock bodyguards because we genuinely feared for our lives. Now that we've been disbanded for so long, it's a great relief that the terror has disappeared from our lives."[367]

That evening, John and Yoko returned to the Hit Factory for the first time in weeks. The occasion was an interview with BBC Radio 1's Andy Peebles. Jon Smith was in attendance, having been tapped to engineer the recording. Before the interview started, John hustled Smith into the control booth. "You have to come hear this! Put it on!" John said to Smith as they cued up the latest mix of 'Walking On Thin Ice'. Smith couldn't believe his ears. The song had been absolutely transformed since the *Double Fantasy* sessions back in August. "It was just mind-blowing," Smith recalled.[368]

As for the Peebles interview, John had proven to be even more forthcoming than his earlier visit with Cott. To Yoko's mind, it came down to the simple fact that Peebles was British. "John greeted me like a long-lost friend," Peebles later recalled. "It was quite extraordinary. I think the reason he was so great with us was because of the BBC. Yoko said to me that he listened a lot to the BBC World Service and every time Liverpool was mentioned he would get very tearful and homesick, and start frantically reminiscing." Throughout the entire session, John was in remarkable spirits. After three hours, he suggested that Peebles continue his interview with the Lennons over an equally lengthy dinner at

Mr Chow. For his part, Peebles would never forget the moment of their arrival at the restaurant, which, to his mind, summed up John's sense of humour perfectly:

> As we stood at the top of the staircase and the maître d' almost started to run up the stairs, John looked down and saw everyone in the restaurant looking up because they'd realized who'd just arrived. In that wonderful Liverpool voice, he said, "Look at this, our Andrew, look at these people down there, they're all going, 'Who the fuck's that with Andy Peebles?'" That was an old Jimmy Tarbuck line, who was the big comedian to come out of Liverpool at the same time as the Beatles.[369]

When he woke up on Sunday, December 7, John resumed his marathon 'Walking On Thin Ice' listening session, at times playing the song at an increasing volume as if he were attempting to ferret out every last morsel of sound. By this point, Yoko recalled, "We were both haunted by the song. I remember I woke up in the morning and found John watching the sunrise and still listening to the song. He said I had to put it out right away as a single. He wanted to be on the B-side of it. I didn't think that was wise. 'Nobody's going to listen to the A-side then.'" At this point, John countered, saying, "Hey, I've got a good idea. How about sending just the A-side to the DJs and keep the B-side a total secret until it's sent to the shops?" Yoko knew enough about the record business – and its overwhelming fascination with her husband – to realise that his plan wouldn't be successful. "Nice try, John. You know it's not going to work," she told him. Finally, John came to agree with Yoko. "You're probably right," he said, concluding that "we have to put you out as a solo artist." In this way, the question was finally settled. The 'Walking On Thin Ice' single would indeed be released as 'Yoko Only'. Now all they needed was a B-side.[370]

That same day, John managed to eke out an hour on the telephone with Aunt Mimi, who had caught on to the increasing frequency of her nephew's calls. "It was the same old John, funny and happy, telling me he was coming and couldn't wait to see me," she recalled. As he'd done several times before, John suggested that she relocate Stateside and move into the Dakota with him. "I couldn't live in America," she said. "And, you see, with him phoning for so long, certainly once a week and sometimes twice a week, the phone is so clear I didn't feel that he'd been away at all. It was as good as seeing him."[371]

That night, they held yet another late-night 'Walking On Thin Ice' mixing session at the Record Plant. As Steve Marcantonio later recalled, Jack and the Lennons were "burning the candle at both ends" and determined to finish the record. In the wee hours of the morning, they finally decided to take a break, agreeing to come back on Monday evening to listen to the latest version and carry out any last-minute tweaks. Desperate for some fresh air, the young assistant engineer went outside, only to be trailed by John. "I could not believe he came with me," Marcantonio recalled. "He told me a story about when the Beatles first started out, they used to run away from thugs. Here I am walking down the street in New York City expecting, 'Hey, look at you, you're walking down the street with John Lennon!' I wanted to share it with the world, but there was no one on the street at all."[372]

Within a matter of hours, Yoko was back in action, telephoning veteran British journalist Ray Connolly. The old newspaperman had been trying to arrange an interview with the Lennons for the past several weeks, only to be "very pleasantly fobbed off". He was surprised to hear from Yoko that Monday, having given up on the prospect of catching up with his old friends. It was "December 8th, when I suddenly got a call in London from Yoko wanting to know why I hadn't gone to New York to do the interview. 'I'll come tomorrow morning', I told her, and booked my flight with British Airways."[373]

"We woke up to a shiny blue sky spreading over Central Park," Yoko later recalled. "The day had an air of bright eyes and bushy tails." And it was destined to be a busy day at that, given the Lennons' dawn-to-dusk schedule, which included a photo shoot, an interview, and another bout at the Record Plant that evening. After the couple took their breakfast at Café La Fortuna, John made his way over to Viz-à-Viz for a quick trim. When he stepped out of the hair salon that morning, he sported a retro style akin to his pre-fame Hamburg look.[374]

Back at apartment 72, Annie Leibovitz was preparing to complete the photo shoot. Geffen had been working diligently behind the scenes to ensure that John and Yoko would be the next *Rolling Stone* cover story. Meanwhile, back at the magazine, editor Jann Wenner was pressuring Leibovitz to engineer a "John only" cover shot, claiming that too many fans blamed Yoko, albeit erroneously, for breaking up the Beatles. Leibovitz felt this tension acutely as she arrived at the Lennons' apartment that morning. "John came to the door in a black leather jacket," she recalled, "and he had his hair slicked back. I was thrown a little bit by it. He had that early Beatle look." Almost immediately, John made it clear that he would be pleased if Yoko was in the cover shot along with him. Pointing at Yoko, he said, "I want to be with *her*." Not wanting to disappoint her subjects, while trying to balance Wenner's concern, the photographer reasoned that "we have to do something extraordinary."[375]

In Leibovitz's mind, a concept began to develop around the withering place of romantic love in contemporary culture. By way of contrast, she had been inspired by the black-and-white *Double Fantasy* cover depicting John and Yoko in a gentle kiss. And she had heard about the recent SoHo video shoot and the image of the couple making love. "In 1980," she recalled, "it felt like romance was dead. I remembered how simple and beautiful that kiss was, and I was inspired by it." To this end, she began to envision a vulnerable rendering of the famous couple. "It wasn't a stretch to imagine them with their clothes off, because they did it all the time," she thought. Only this time, Yoko wasn't having it. She offered to remove her top as a form of compromise, but then John and Leibovitz hit upon the idea of a naked John – save for his ever-present diamond pendant – embracing a fully clothed Yoko in a foetal pose. Leibovitz photographed them lying on the cream-coloured carpet in their living room.[376]

After Leibovitz took a Polaroid test shot, John could barely contain himself. "This is it!" he exclaimed. "This is our relationship!" That day, Leibovitz only shot a single roll of film, including the cover photo and various images of John posing around the apartment. In some instances, he pulled up the collar of his leather jacket from the Gap to assume the look of an early 1960s tough. In other shots, he can be seen reclining on the living room furniture or posing inside a window dormer with the image of Central Park unfolding in the background.[377]

By the time that Leibovitz completed her photo shoot, John was already due downstairs in Studio One, where a team from RKO Radio had already started interviewing his wife. The group was led by radio personality Dave Sholin, who had flown in from San Francisco the night before with scriptwriter Laurie Kaye, producer Ron Hummel, and Warner Bros. label rep Bert Keane. The interview had come about at the urging of David Geffen, who had approached Sholin back in September. During their meeting, Geffen played '(Just Like) Starting Over' for the radio host without identifying the artist. "I fell in love with it," Sholin recalled. "I'm a huge Elvis fan. And John sang the song with a lot of Elvis-like inflections."[378]

When Sholin and his crew began interviewing the Lennons that afternoon, they were understandably nervous. After making their way through a maze of back offices into Studio One, they removed their shoes, in keeping with the Asian custom, and everyone began to relax, taking in the cloud-painted ceiling high above their heads. And that's when John joined them in Studio One. "You get those butterflies, you get excited," Sholin recalled, "but John loosened everybody up immediately." Within a matter of moments, John was cracking wise about his daily routine – "I get up about six. Go to the kitchen. Get a cup of coffee. Cough a little. Have a cigarette" – and watching *Sesame Street* with Sean: "I make sure he watches PBS and not the cartoons with the commercials – I don't mind cartoons, but I won't let him watch the commercials." All the while, Sholin had become fascinated with John and Yoko. "The eye contact between them was amazing. No words had to be spoken," Sholin recalled. "They would look at each other with an intense connection."[379]

During the interview, John spoke perceptibly about the Lennons' audience, whom he had begun to see in a very different light via the production and release of *Double Fantasy*: "I'm 40," said John, "and I wanna talk to the people my age. I'm happy if the young people like it, and I'm happy if the old people like it," but with *Double Fantasy*, "I'm talking to guys and gals that have been through what we went through, together – the 60s group that has survived. Survived the war, the drugs, the politics, the violence on the street – the whole shebang – that we've survived it and we're here."[380]

As the interview pressed on, John began to fixate on balancing his desire for a lasting, peaceful humanity – the nascent globalism of "one world, one people" – and his personal conflict with encroaching middle-age, necessitated, no doubt, by his recent milestone birthday. "I hope I die before Yoko," he said, "because if Yoko died I wouldn't know how to survive. I couldn't carry on." Yet his thoughts were always buoyed, it seemed, by an inherent optimism. In this vein, he had begun to perceive his music as part of a larger continuum. "I always considered my work one piece, whether it be with Beatles, David Bowie, Elton John, Yoko Ono," he told Sholin, "and I consider that my work won't be finished until I'm dead and buried, and I hope that's a long, long time." And speaking of his collaborations, John made a point of noting that "there's only been two artists I've ever worked with for more than a one night stand, as it were. That's Paul McCartney and Yoko Ono. I think that's a pretty damn good choice. As a talent scout, I've done pretty damn well."[381]

As the interview wrapped up that afternoon, John and Yoko began posing for photos and signing autographs for the RKO crew. John made a special point of signing the picture sleeve of the '(Just Like) Starting Over' single for Sholin's fiancée Debbie, scrawling "see you in San Francisco!" across the photo of John kissing Yoko near Central Park's Bow Bridge back in September. Meanwhile, as John struggled to sign his name on copies of *Double Fantasy* – with the LP's slick, plasticine finish – Yoko took to the Studio One telephone to round up the couple's limo to the Record Plant that evening. For her part, Laurie Kaye thanked John profusely for his generosity that afternoon. "Oh, it's a pleasure," John replied, as he signed a copy of the album for her. "I'm a fan of people, too, you know. I like people to sign their books when they give 'em to me and all that."[382]

And with that, Sholin and his RKO team took their leave and began carting their equipment – tape recorders, microphones, and the like – out to their chauffeured Lincoln Town Car in front of the *porte-cochère*. Hurrying to make their flight across town at JFK, they were stowing their equipment in the trunk when John and Yoko strolled out of the archway. As they emerged from the building, Yoko could see that their limo had not arrived, and she began to get frustrated. "John liked being prompt," she recalled. "John was English, I was Japanese. The result was both of us possessed extreme austerity and hilarity back to back." And now, to top it off, their car wasn't there to ferry them to the Record Plant.[383]

Meanwhile, John was thinking about other things. When they stepped onto the sidewalk along West 72nd Street, the area around the entrance to the Dakota was unusually vacant. "Where are my fans?" John asked. At that point, Goresh walked up to show John the photo proofs from a recent visit. "John looked great that day," the photographer recalled. He had "that Teddy Boy look with the Elvis pompadour." As John scanned the proofs, another fan walked up, sheepishly extending a copy of *Double Fantasy* and a pen in his direction. "Do you want me to sign that?" John asked. As he scrawled "John Lennon 1980" across the cover, Goresh snapped a photo of John and the fan, a bespectacled fellow in a rumpled overcoat. "Is that okay?" John asked, with his eyebrows raised. As the man edged away, John turned back to Goresh and shot him a quizzical look.[384]

And that's when John asked Sholin if the RKO team could give the couple a lift to the Record Plant in their Town Car. As Yoko later recalled, she had seen "John still signing an autograph for a guy in front of the Dakota. 'John, we'll be late!' I remember being a bit irritable. 'Why one more autograph?' I thought." With Sholin's good-natured urging, John and Yoko climbed into the backseat. As the car pulled away, Goresh saw John wave goodbye to him. Seizing the moment as their driver piloted the Town Car through the snarling Midtown traffic, Sholin resumed their conversation, asking John about his current relationship with Paul. For his part, John didn't miss a beat, telling Sholin that their rift had been "overblown" and that Paul was "like a brother. I love him. Families – we certainly have our ups and downs and our quarrels. But at the end of the day, when it's all said and done, I would do anything for him, and I think he would do anything for me."[385]

By this point, Sholin sorely wished that he had been recording their chitchat in the Town Car, especially after John began showing off his "Elvis Orbison" voice and singing impromptu rock 'n' roll tunes by the likes of Little Richard and Jerry Lee Lewis. "It was great," Sholin recalled. "He was singing all this Fifties stuff, and it was so enjoyable." After they said their goodbyes to the RKO crew, John and Yoko joined Jack upstairs at the Record Plant. As it happened, Charly Roth, the piano tech from Manny's Music who had serviced John's Yamaha back in January 1979, was working just down the hall that night with his fledgling band Regina and the Red Hots.

By this point, 'Walking On Thin Ice' had evolved into a discothèque-friendly six-minute opus, complete with Yoko's eerie vocal sound effects, spoken-word poem, and Lennon's wailing guitar solo, with a much-needed assist from Douglas. John was ecstatic as he listened to the mix in all of its glory. "From now on," he told Yoko, "we're just gonna do this. It's great!" – adding that "*this* is the direction!" In need of a B-side for the proposed 'Walking On Thin Ice' single, John had telephoned Fred back at the Dakota, asking him to rummage through apartment 71 and find an old box of cassette outtakes. John was particularly interested in finding a Yoko tune called 'It Happened', which she had recorded with guitarist David Spinozza back in 1974. Around the same time that Fred was searching for the cassette, Ray Connolly telephoned Studio One to confirm his plans for a Tuesday interview with the Lennons. As the journalist recalled, an assistant informed him that "Yoko says to come straight over to the apartment when you get in. John will be waiting for you. He's looking forward to seeing you again."[386]

Not long afterwards, Fred ferried the cassette over to the Record Plant, where he was joined on his elevator ride to the 10th floor by David Geffen, who was accompanied by Felix Cavaliere of the Young Rascals, one of the music exec's clients. Upstairs, Felix and John wasted little time in discussing promoter Sid Bernstein, who had formerly managed the Young Rascals – and badly, in Felix's opinion, by distributing unauthorised tracks. For his part, John vented about Bernstein's seemingly nonstop efforts to reunite the Beatles. Realising that the conversation about Bernstein needed to remain private, John turned to Yoko, saying, "Remind me to erase everything in the track. What would happen if I died?"[387]

After listening to the latest mix of 'Walking On Thin Ice' with Geffen and Douglas, John proclaimed that "it's better than anything we did on *Double Fantasy*", adding "let's put it out before Christmas!" Recognising that the holiday season was scarcely two weeks away, Geffen countered, "Let's put it out after Christmas and really do the thing right. Take out an ad." Now he had John's undivided attention. "An ad!" said John. "Listen to this, Mother, you're gonna get an ad!" Geffen shifted the conversation back to *Double Fantasy*, informing the Lennons that the album was climbing the UK charts, having already earned a gold disc in John's homeland. As he made his pronouncement, Yoko caught the music mogul's eye. "Yoko gave me this real funny look," Geffen recalled, "like it better be number one in England. That was the thing she was interested in, not for herself but because John wanted it so badly."[388]

Over the next few hours, Jack and the Lennons made a few last-minute refinements on 'Walking On Thin Ice'. Finally, they called it quits for the evening, having decided to meet bright and early the next morning at Sterling Sound to begin the mastering process. Besides, John and Yoko were exhausted, having worked almost nonstop over the past week on their new creation. They planned to grab a bite to eat – perhaps at the Stage Deli over on 7th Avenue and a few blocks away from Carnegie Hall.

Making their way to the elevator, John paused at the reception desk, where he presented Rabiah Seminole with a surprise. She had previously mentioned to a member of the Record Plant staff that she was hoping to get John and Yoko's autographs, and Lennon was happy to oblige. As she later recalled, "John gave me a little piece of yellow notepaper with their signatures, which also had his and Yoko's caricatures and the date

'1980' written on it. I was thrilled. Then I laughingly told him that he had misspelled my name, and he said, 'It's the way it sounds to me, luv.'"[389]

As they stepped into the elevator, John and Yoko were joined by Big Bob. "John was so happy," the bodyguard later remembered, "because Yoko was finally getting respect from the press. That meant the world to him." On a whim, John asked Big Bob to join them for a late meal. "I'm sick to my stomach," Big Bob replied, begging off. "I don't feel good." John placed his arm around the bodyguard's shoulders. "Don't worry," he said. "You go home, feel better, we'll do it another night."[390]

By the time John and Yoko had made their way downstairs from the Record Plant, they had decided that they wanted to go straight home and say goodnight to Sean, who was back in apartment 72 with Helen Seaman. They could get a bite to eat later. After all, this was New York, "the city that never sleeps". As they stepped outside the building, the streetscape was fairly quiet for a late Monday evening. Only this time, the limousine was parked right out front, ready and waiting to ferry the couple back to the Dakota.

Pulling away from the Record Plant, the limo made the short drive northward through the upper recesses of Midtown, rolling through Columbus Circle and up Central Park West before making the sharp left turn onto West 72nd Street, where a taxi cab was discharging a customer in front of the Dakota. Forced to double-park, the limo coasted to a stop in front of the *porte-cochère*, where the building's gaslights illuminated the night-time air. Yoko climbed out of the vehicle first and began walking towards the archway. John followed suit, strolling a few paces behind his wife and clutching a stack of cassettes, including the latest mix of 'Walking On Thin Ice', in his hand.

It was just after 10.45 p.m.

EPILOGUE

Season of Glass

The evening of Monday, December 8, 1980, had been unseasonably warm on the Upper West Side. At dusk, the thermometer had registered a whopping 64 degrees Fahrenheit (18 degrees Celsius) – a full 18 degrees above average. It had been a fairly quiet night on the streetscape in front of the Dakota – until it suddenly wasn't.

Actress Ruth Ford was startled to hear the report of the bullets from her open kitchen window above the archway. She had been writing out Christmas cards and enjoying the night air when the sound of five shots and a smattering of broken glass echoed across the courtyard below her apartment. Artist Robert Morgan heard the bullets detonate from his apartment in the Majestic building just across West 72nd Street from the Dakota. He was astonished by the sheer noise of the shots, the sound of which reverberated loudly in the *porte-cochère* before dissipating into the Dakota's cavernous courtyard. Within a few moments, Morgan heard the sound of police sirens. Ruth Ford had dialled 9-1-1 within a matter of seconds, while Jay Hastings, the Dakota's night manager, had pressed the alarm button at his desk, summoning the police from the 20th Precinct on West 82nd Street.[391]

Morgan observed the ensuing drama from his 12th-storey window. He could clearly make out the sight of police officers climbing out of their squad car, doors flung open wide, with guns drawn. Instinctively, he reached for his handy Nikkormat, which had been outfitted with a

226

105-millimetre telephoto lens. "The night was clear and the scene was lit up," Morgan remembered, and his camera was loaded with high-speed black-and-white film. As the police lumbered out of the archway with the dying man in their arms, Morgan placed his finger on the shutter release. But he simply couldn't do it. "This isn't my work," the artist told himself, taking up his paintbrush instead. "Whoever is there deserves a final moment of privacy."[392]

As he watched from his perch high above West 72nd Street, Morgan observed the police as they hurriedly placed the victim in back of the squad car. In their haste, they hadn't noticed that one of the backdoors had bounced open after coming into contact with the victim's feet. Seeing this, one of the officers came around and gently arranged the man's legs in the backseat. Within moments, the police car was hurtling towards Columbus Avenue to make the short southerly trip, sirens blaring, to Roosevelt Hospital. As the tragedy unfolded a dozen blocks away, Morgan began working his brush along the canvas, desperate to capture the scene before it faded from memory. By this juncture, he was beyond certain that the victim was his famous neighbour across the way on the Dakota's seventh floor, the one with whom he had shared a "nodding acquaintance". Morgan understood that the personal trauma he experienced with his fellow Upper West Siders would shortly take on global proportions:

> When I tell people, "I was there when John Lennon was shot," they invariably ask: "Did you have a camera?"
> "Yes, I did," I respond.
> "So, where is the photo?"
> "I didn't take one. I painted a picture."[393]

Millions of American television viewers would learn the awful truth only a few minutes later, when ABC sportscaster Howard Cosell interrupted the *Monday Night Football* matchup between the New England Patriots and the Miami Dolphins to deliver the news:

> We have to say it. Remember, this is just a football game. No matter who wins or loses. An unspeakable tragedy confirmed to us by ABC News in New York City. John Lennon, outside of his apartment building on the West Side of New York City, the most famous, perhaps, of all of the Beatles, shot twice in the back,

rushed to Roosevelt Hospital, dead on arrival. Hard to go back to the game after that newsflash, which in duty bound, we had to take.

Before the night was out, Yoko made the awful trip back to the Dakota without her husband. Accompanied by David Geffen, she entered the building through a side entrance. When they arrived at the entryway to apartment 72, Geffen spotted a copy of the latest *Billboard* charts that someone had affixed to the door. "Back then," said Geffen, "they used to have the four-fold *Billboard* chart that was four times the size of the magazine. That week on the charts, I think the record [*Double Fantasy*] was at number nine with a bullet. On the chart, they had circled the record with an arrow to number one. And, of course, on the next *Billboard* chart, it was number one.[394]

Some 3,500 miles away in London, Ray Connolly prepared to make his way to Heathrow for his early morning flight to New York City. He had spoken to Yoko just 12 hours earlier about his impending interview with the Lennons, but now he found himself with just 45 minutes in which to compose John's obituary for the *Evening Standard*. "It was a pretty tearful morning," Connolly recalled. In an instant, he had to switch gears from going to meet his old friend across the Atlantic to writing up John's death notice for the morning papers. For Ray, the agony of losing his friend was suddenly compounded by the harrowing physical act of filing his story:

> In those pre-computer days, articles written out of the newspaper office would be "phoned over" to people called copytakers who would sit in a row, each with a typewriter and headphones, and type out the article being dictated. The death of John was the most difficult piece I ever had to write or dictate, having to stop talking several times as emotion overtook me. The copytaker, a nice Irishman who had typed so many of my stories, was kindness itself. "Just take your time, Ray. We'll get there," he said quietly as he waited.[395]

That same morning, the staff at EMI's Abbey Road Studios began making their way into work. A crowd of mourners was already beginning to congregate at the famous recording studio – the very place where John and the Beatles had recorded their most lasting masterworks. Studio head

Ken Townsend, broken-hearted after suffering such a deeply personal loss, opened the windows of the old Edwardian estate and played a recording of John's 'Imagine' for the gathering throng. As the regular coterie of tourists strolled past the nearby zebra crossing made famous by the Beatles' *Abbey Road* cover art, Townsend threw open the gates of the car park and urged the fans to share their unspeakable grief together.[396]

On Tuesday morning, Dave Sholin's red-eye flight landed at San Francisco International Airport in the wee hours. As it turned out, the RKO crew had barely made their plane back at JFK after dropping John and Yoko off at the Record Plant. When they landed on the West Coast, Sholin and his team were still ecstatic over their interview with the Lennons. After sharing a high-five with engineer Ron Hummel, Sholin jumped in his car to drive home. And that's when he tuned the radio to his home station and realised that something wasn't quite right:

> Our station, WCBS FM, which was Top 40, was playing a *Beatles* song, a ballad. I thought, "this is strange, because it's not their format to do oldies." Then there was another Beatles song, another slow one. It could have been 'Imagine' or something, too, I don't remember. And then I thought, "okay this is really strange." Because I just was with him. So then the DJ, Broadway Bill Lee, announced what had happened. I was just in shock. It was the most surreal moment of my life. The day was now both the best and the worst day of my life. It went from wonderful on a real high to totally devastating in a heartbeat.[397]

Later that Tuesday, Yoko issued her first statement to a bewildered world. She was now widowed and ensconced in the Dakota, which had been besieged by grieving fans almost as soon as word of the murder had hit the media. She announced that "there is no funeral for John. John loved and prayed for the human race. Please do the same for him. Love, Yoko and Sean." Shell-shocked in his grief, Jack Douglas appeared as Tom Snyder's guest on the *Tomorrow* show that same day. Jack looked beyond his own, unimaginable loss to share John's hopeful vision for the future. John "saw the beginning of the Seventies, as we all did, as a time for 'me', a time for us all to say, 'now I'm going to do something for *me*. I've spent the Sixties fighting for the cause' – whatever cause it was," said Jack. "And he was looking at the Eighties as a time to say, 'I'm going to do something for me, but I'm not going to step on anyone else to do it. I'm not going to exclude anyone else.' And that's what he was looking for in the Eighties."

That night, Bruce Springsteen and the E Street Band took to the stage at Philadelphia's Spectrum arena. Just two months into his bravura tour for *The River*, the evening had begun for the rock icon with a backstage argument about whether they should be performing at all in light of what had happened the night before in New York City. Reluctantly pressing on with the show, Springsteen addressed the audience before playing a single note. "The first record that I ever learned was a record called 'Twist And Shout'," he said, his voice audibly shaken, "and if it wasn't for John Lennon, we'd all be in some place very different tonight. It's an unreasonable world and you have to live with a lot of things that are just unlivable, and it's a hard thing to come out and play. But there's just nothing else you can do." And with that, the band launched into an impassioned version of the anthemic 'Born To Run'.[398]

At Yoko's request, a 10-minute silent vigil was held on Sunday, December 14, at 2 p.m. Eastern Standard Time. Across the globe, radio stations honoured the occasion by going silent. For the grieving masses, the vigil would serve as John's de facto funeral, with his body having been cremated within hours of his death. It would be a means for anyone who hoped to celebrate John's life to "participate from where you are", in Yoko's words. In his hometown of Liverpool, some 30,000 mourners gathered, while more than 50,000 fans assembled in Central Park for a sombre remembrance of the man who had so proudly called New York City his home.

At nearly the same time down in Palm Beach, more than 200 people congregated outside the gates of El Solano. They had arrived to hold a prayer vigil in concert with the thousands of other such events being held around the world. John Hochella, one of the estate's caretakers, remembered that the visitors had begun "climbing over the walls". Cars had been parked illegally up and down South Ocean Boulevard and had even begun spilling over into the side streets. Eventually, a police officer arrived with a bullhorn in an effort to quell the unfolding mayhem. As Hochella later recalled, "Yoko gave the command to open the gates", asking the caretaker to "please let the kids in on the front lawn".[399]

At 2 p.m., the mourners filed into the front courtyard, depositing wreaths and flowers along the edge of the saltwater swimming pool. As a lay minister, Hochella delivered an impromptu eulogy for the visitors.

"That was tough for me," he said, "because I didn't know where John stood religiously, what his beliefs were. I tried to keep it as subtle as I could." With the mourners amassed on the lawn in front of El Solano, Hochella shared his words of comfort. "We unite in prayer and meditation at this moment with others all over the world to pray for the soul of John Lennon," he said. "John believed in the unity of mankind. He believed in peace and in the brotherhood of all. His music is evidence of this. And his music tells us that John Lennon will always be with us in spirit."[400]

For the surviving Beatles, John's murder made for a devastating loss, with each of the bandmates experiencing it in different ways – and perhaps even in different wavelengths as the finality of his absence reverberated through their lives. On the morning after the tragedy, Paul McCartney and producer George Martin reasoned that they could somehow dull their pain by keeping their date at AIR Studios. In truth, McCartney and Martin could barely keep it together. The Beatles' engineer Geoff Emerick was there, too, whiling away that awful day in the control booth. Finally, all three old friends stood together, struggling to come to terms with their despair. "For a few moments," Geoff later wrote, "the three of us stood there numbly, reminiscing about the impact John Winston Ono Lennon had had on our lives, focusing on the positive, the light-hearted, the absurd. We smiled as we conjured up pleasant memories, but there were tears behind our laughter. Somehow none of us could seem to come up with the right words to say. There probably *were* no right words to say."[401]

For Paul, this last aspect would become horribly true as he walked away from the studio that evening. Confronted by reporters, he could barely muster a response when asked about John having been suddenly wrenched from the world, remarking that "it's a drag, innit?" McCartney was subsequently pilloried in the British press, but for his part, Martin understood implicitly the sense of shocked detachment that Paul was feeling in that moment. During an interview with the BBC's Gavin Hewitt, the producer described the rage that was boiling up inside of him. "I feel frightfully sorry for Yoko and Sean," he said, "and all the people who loved him so much. But I also feel very angry that it's such a senseless thing to happen. That one of the great people that happened this century was just wiped out by madness. I'm very angry about it."[402]

As for Ringo, he had left New York City just 10 days earlier. "We rented a plane as early as we could and we flew up to New York, not that you can do anything, but you just have to go and say hello," he remembered. "I said to Yoko, 'You know I know how you feel.' And the woman, straight as a die, in all honesty, said, 'No, you don't.' Because no matter how close I was to him, I was not half as close as she was to him. And that blew me away, more than anything." At this point, Ringo simply didn't have the stomach, understandably, for taking 'Nobody Told Me' and 'Life Begins At 40' into the studio. And he never would.[403]

For George Harrison, John's untimely death meant that the two former Beatles' rift would remain unsettled. In a public statement, Harrison commented that "after all we went through together, I had and still have great love and respect for him. I am shocked and stunned. To rob life is the ultimate robbery in life. This perpetual encroachment on other people's space is taken to the limit with the use of a gun. It is an outrage that people can take other people's lives when they obviously haven't got their own lives in order."[404]

In the months before his old friend's murder, George had penned a song called 'All Those Years Ago' for Ringo to perform on *Can't Fight Lightning*, which was later retitled as *Stop And Smell The Roses*. While Ringo had recorded the track in November 1980 at George's home studio at Friar Park, he found the song difficult to sing, given its high register. Searching for a means to express his unimaginable grief, Harrison transformed 'All Those Years Ago' into a celebration of John's life, with key references to such tunes as 'All You Need Is Love' and 'Imagine'. 'All Those Years Ago' emerged as a mini-Beatles reunion of sorts, with Paul and Linda McCartney joining Harrison and Starr on the track, along with Wings sideman Denny Laine. To round out the experience, George Martin and Geoff Emerick joined the others at Harrison's estate to honour their fallen comrade. That summer, 'All Those Years Ago' would land a Top 5 hit for John's grieving ex-mates.

In the new year, *Double Fantasy*'s sales figures would continue to balloon. The album topped the charts in 11 countries, eventually earning triple-platinum status from the Recording Industry Association of America for eclipsing sales of more than three million units. As Geffen had predicted during his last moments with John at the Record Plant, '(Just Like) Starting Over' b/w 'Kiss Kiss Kiss' had topped the US charts. Released posthumously in January 1981, 'Woman' b/w 'Beautiful Boys' followed suit. *Double Fantasy*'s final single 'Watching The Wheels' b/w 'Yes, I'm Your Angel' was released in March 1981 and registered a Top 10 showing; the single's picture sleeve was adorned with Paul Goresh's August 7, 1980, photograph of John and Yoko exiting the Dakota's archway.

On January 20, 1981, Ronald Reagan was inaugurated as the 40th President of the United States. In the same moment that the new chief executive recited his speech on the steps of the US Capitol, the 52 American hostages were released after 444 days in captivity in Iran. Former President Jimmy Carter flew to West Germany, where he received them at the Rhein-Main Air Base, bringing the nation's long dispiriting drama to an end. That May, John's reggae idol Bob Marley collapsed onstage and died at age 36 in Miami, where he had been seeking cancer treatment.

As John had predicted, 'Walking On Thin Ice' eventually topped the charts. Yoko released the single b/w 'It Happened' on January 24, 1981. "Getting this together after what happened was hard," Yoko wrote in the liner notes. "But I knew John would not rest his mind if I hadn't. I hope you like it, John. I did my best." In its initial pass at the *Billboard* charts, 'Walking On Thin Ice' landed a number-58 showing. But even more impressively, it fell into heavy rotation in the underground dance clubs. In the new century, 'Walking On Thin Ice' enjoyed new life through a series of dance club remixes and cover versions by the likes of the Pet Shop Boys. And in 2003, John's prophecy came true when the track notched the number-one spot on the US Hot Dance Club charts.

When it came to *Double Fantasy*, Yoko didn't have to wait quite so long to see her final LP with John honoured on pop music's grandest stage. On February 24, 1982, she and Sean accepted the Album of the Year statuette at the 24th Annual Grammy Awards at LA's Shrine Auditorium. When the capacity crowd learned that the Lennons' comeback album had taken the top award that night, they rose to their feet, cheering and crying in nearly the same instant. In 1984, John and Yoko would enjoy an encore of sorts with the belated release of *Milk And Honey*. 'Nobody Told Me' emerged as a Top 5 US hit, and, for a moment at least, a new John Lennon song lorded over the airwaves.

As for Julian, John's eldest son hit pay dirt during his 21st year with the release of his debut album *Valotte*. Produced by longtime Billy Joel producer Phil Ramone, the LP generated a pair of Top 10 hits in the title track and 'Too Late For Goodbyes'. In 1985, he would earn his own Grammy Award for Best New Artist. In later years, he established a charity known as the White Feather Foundation, which he named in honour of his lost father. As Julian explained, his dad once told him that "if anything happens to me, and you see a white feather floating evenly across the room, you'll know that's me." As with Yoko, Julian had to wait a long time to see his father's prophecy come to fruition, but in 2007 – 27 years after John's death – it finally happened. Working on the film set for *Whaledreamers* in Australia, he accompanied an aboriginal elder to a tribal ritual where Julian was presented, to his incredible shock and surprise, with a white feather. He's worn the feather attached to a pendant around his neck ever since.

As the years rolled by, John would be honoured with an assortment of memorials, including Strawberry Fields, the Central Park acreage that was dedicated to John's memory in 1985. On December 13, 1980, during the week after John's death, the Central Park Task Force and the Central Park Community Fund joined forces to establish the not-for-profit Central Park Conservancy, which had been expressly formed to stem the park's ongoing blight and secure private resources to reclaim the city's most vital greenspace. Strawberry Fields marked one of the earliest projects for the newly formed Conservancy. With the Imagine mosaic as its centrepiece, the parklet included the teardrop-shaped portion of Central Park across the street from the Dakota. The City of Liverpool would honour their favourite son with a statue on Mathew Street near the Cavern Club, later rechristening their airport as Liverpool John Lennon Airport, complete with the evocative motto "above us only sky".

A Lennon statue would later be unveiled on a Havana park bench. Immortalised in bronze relief by President Fidel Castro, the statue has received countless visitors over the years, including Sir George Martin, who famously sat in quiet repose across from the statue, gazing admiringly at the spitting image of his lost friend. Bermuda would eventually get into the act, erecting a sculpture named 'Double Fantasy' at the Masterworks Museum of Bermuda Art. Situated at the northeast corner of the Bermuda Botanical Gardens, the memorial marks the occasion when John found his inspiration for the *Double Fantasy* LP. Easily the most elaborate of the attendant tributes, Iceland's Imagine Peace Tower was dedicated by Yoko on October 9, 2007 – the date that would have marked John's 67th birthday. In addition to featuring the words "Imagine Peace" in 24 languages, the tower is constructed of 15 searchlights that reflect a vertical column of light into the sky – sometimes as high as 4,000 feet. In Yoko's vision, the Imagine Peace Tower acts as a global wishing well, a place where the world may yet, as John sings so poignantly in 'Imagine', live as one.

McCartney would create a lasting memorial of his own with his song 'Here Today', which he featured on the Martin-produced *Tug Of War*

(1982) LP. A regular staple in his concerts, 'Here Today' acts, in the tradition of literature's finest poetic odes, as an attempt to immortalise the subject's life through the power of language. Paul does exactly that, honouring the memory of his fallen mate by celebrating their enduring friendship through the creative act of songwriting. That same year, McCartney was a guest on BBC Radio 4's ever-popular *Desert Island Discs*, where he proclaimed 'Beautiful Boy (Darling Boy)' to be the record he would long for most if he happened to be shipwrecked on some remote tropical isle.

As for Yoko, the very same heroism and resourcefulness that found her buttressing John's spirit to embark upon his comeback had seen her through John's unspeakable murder and four decades of widowhood. As the years rolled by, she would never drift very far away from that terrible night back on December 8, 1980. For her, it was truly the worst of nights, but in its own way, it had proven to be something entirely different before they left the Record Plant for that final, fateful drive back to the Dakota. As Yoko recalled:

> The studio work went until late at night. In a room next to the control room, just before we left the studio, John looked at me. I looked at him. His eyes had an intensity of a guy about to tell me something important. "Yes?" I asked. And I will never forget how with a deep, soft voice, as if to carve his words in my mind, he said the most beautiful things to me. "Oh," I said after a while, and looked away, feeling a bit embarrassed. In my mind, hearing something like that from your man when you were way over 40... well... I was a very lucky woman, I thought. Even now, I see his piercing eyes in my mind. I don't know why he decided, at that very moment, to say all that as if he wanted me to remember it forever.[405]

Even later still, Sean would find his own way to memorialise the father that he lost when most kids his age were just starting to go to kindergarten. Not surprisingly, his adult memories of his dad take root through the images from a child's eyes. He would especially remember bedtime, when his father would slip into his room to check on him before settling down for the night. As he recalled, John would say, "'Goodnight, Sean', and he'd flick the light switch in the rhythm of his words, so that they'd wink in time. There was always something very comforting about that. I had a bunkbed even though I was the only child in the house, and a mobile of silver airplanes above my head." As he lay there in his bed, on the verge of drifting off to sleep, he would watch "the shadows that were cast on the wall by the cars going along Central Park West, seven flights down. I remember watching those shadows move by, from left to right, and I remember thinking of the words 'watching shadows on the wall' from 'Watching The Wheels'." Could it be, Sean wondered, that when his father composed that very song "he'd been watching the same shadows I had"?[406]

Acknowledgements

A project of this magnitude could not possibly come to fruition without the efforts of a host of friends and colleagues. I am particularly grateful to Mario Casciano, Ray Connolly, Jack Douglas, Roger Farrington, Troy Germano, Mike "Tree" Medeiros, Nancy Gosnell Molineux, Robert Morgan, Willie Nile, May Pang, Charly Roth, Fred Seaman, Dave Sholin, Earl Slick, Jon Smith, Brenda Spencer, Ken Townsend, and Stu Zolotorow for sharing their memories of John Lennon's life and times. This book would not have been possible without the generosity and professional expertise of Isabel Atherton, Stephen Bard, Ken Campbell, Scott Cardinal, Al Cattabiani, Mike Cavallo, Jeff Copeland, Jeroen Dekker, Peter Doggett, Howie Edelson, Matthew Elblonk, Scott Erickson, Tom Frangione, Scott Freiman, Joe Goodden, Rob Guertsen, Jude Southerland Kessler, Clive Kirkwood, Mark Lapidos, Mark Lewisohn, Cha-Chi Loprete, Chip Madinger, George A. Martin, Wenty Morris, Garson O'Toole, Kit O'Toole, John Peden, Shaun Phillips, Scott Raile, Scott Reda, Robert Rodriguez, Jim Ryan and Susan Ratisher Ryan, Ken Sharp, Jeff Slate, Guy Story, Iqbal Surve, Al Sussman, Kurt Wagner, and Eddie Zareh. I am also thankful for the encouragement and support of Steven Bachrach, Eileen Chapman, John Christopher, Lynne Clay, Chris DeRosa, Mike Farragher, Will Jones, Jacob Michael, Carmen Nitsche, Mike Plodwick, Ed Rakowski, Vernon and Patti Ralph, Joe Rapolla, Mark Rodriguez, George and Kathy Severini, Joe Studlick, Michael Thomas, Bill Timoney,

Rich Veit, Fred Womack, and Eddie Zareh. I owe a debt of gratitude to the folks at Omnibus and the Music Sales Group for their patience and unfailing goodwill, especially David Barraclough, Lucy Beevor, Imogen Gordon Clark, and Robert Thompson. My indefatigable publicist Nicole Michael deserves special thanks, as does my family – particularly my wife Jeanine, who makes all things possible.

Bibliography

"April 24, 1976: John and Paul Almost Go on *SNL*." *Best Classic Bands* April 24, 2017, bestclassicbands.com/lennon-mccartney-snl-4-24-17/.

Badman, Keith. *The Beatles Diary, Volume 2: After the Break-Up, 1970-2001*. London: Omnibus, 2009.

Beatles, The. *The Beatles Anthology*. San Francisco: Chronicle, 2000.

"Ben Stiller Says NYC Is an Exciting Place for Kids." *People* August 11, 2008, people.com/parents/ben-stiller-sta/.

Birmingham, Stephen. *Life at the Dakota: New York's Most Unusual Address*. 1979. New York: Open Road, 2015.

Bocaro, Madeline. "Gone Utterly Beyond". *Madelinex* December 7, 2018, madelinex.com/2018/12/07/gone-gone-gone-beyond-gone-utterly-beyond/.

———. "Just a Story: 'Walking on Thin Ice'". *Madelinex* December 8, 2016, madelinex.com/2016/12/08/yoko-songs-walking-on-thin-ice/.

Boyle, Peter. Interview by Allan Neuwirth. Archives of American Television, 2005.

Caccavo, Danny. "Reference Library: Catharsis 101". *The Beatles Again* October 1998, www.beatlesagain.com/breflib/john.html.

Capozzi, Joe. "John Lennon's Last Years in Palm Beach". *The Palm Beach Post* November 1, 2018. www.palmbeachpost.com/news/20181101/john-lennons-last-years-in-palm-beach/1.

Carter, Jimmy. *Why Not the Best?: The First 50 Years.* Fayetteville: University of Arkansas Press, 1996.

Cohen, Alina. "How Annie Leibovitz Perfectly Captured Yoko and John's Relationship". *Artsy* December 6, 2019, www.artsy.net/article/artsy-editorial-annie-leibovitz-perfectly-captured-yoko-johns-relationship.

Connolly, Ray. *Being John Lennon: A Restless Life.* New York: Pegasus, 2018.

———. "The Dream Weaver… Surrealist of Rock". *Evening Standard* December 9, 1980: 1.

———. "I Remember the Real John Lennon, Not the One Airbrushed by History", *The Daily Telegraph* December 4, 2010, www.telegraph. co.uk/culture/music/the-beatles/8179356/I-remember-the-real-John-Lennon-not-the-one-airbrushed-by-history.html.

———. *The Ray Connolly Beatles Archive.* London: Plumray Books, 2018.

Cott, Jonathan. *Days That I'll Remember: Spending Time with John Lennon and Yoko Ono.* London: Omnibus, 2013.

———. "John Lennon: The Last Interview". *Rolling Stone* December 23, 2010, www.rollingstone.com/music/music-news/john-lennon-the-last-interview-179443/.

———. "Yoko Ono and Her 16-Track Voice". *Rolling Stone* March 18, 1971, www.rollingstone.com/music/music-news/yoko-ono-and-her-sixteen-track-voice-237782/.

Cott, Jonathan, and Christine Doudna, eds. *The Ballad of John and Yoko.* New York: Rolling Stone, 1982.

Cushman, Jim. "A Beatle Slept with This: Pieces of the Mania". *Collectors Weekly* March 11, 2011, www.collectorsweekly.com/articles/a-beatle-slept-with-this-pieces-of-the-mania/.

Davilio, Tony, with Mary Vicario. *The Lennon Sessions: An Introspective Chronicle from the Arranger on Double Fantasy.* Victoria, BC: Trafford, 2004.

Dekker, Jeroen. "One World, One People: John Lennon's Spring 1981 Tour". *Lennon Chords* 2005, lennonchords.info/1981/index.htm.

Di Perna, Alan. "Rick Nielsen, Earl Slick, and Jack Douglas Discuss the Recording of John Lennon's Final Album *Double Fantasy*". *Guitar World* December 8, 2015, www.guitarworld.com/magazine/interview-earl-slick-rick-nielsen-and-jack-douglas-tell-story-behind-john-lennons-double-fantasy.

Doggett, Peter. *The Art and Music of John Lennon*. London: Omnibus, 2009.

Dowlding, William J. *Beatlesongs*. New York: Simon and Schuster, 1989.

Emerick, Geoff, and Howard Massey. *Here, There, and Everywhere: My Life Recording the Music of the Beatles*. New York: Gotham, 2006.

Fraley, Jason. "Willie Nile Shares New Details on the Night John Lennon Was Killed". *WTOP* March 30, 2017, wtop.com/entertainment/2017/03/exclusive-new-details-night-john-lennon-killed/.

Gaddis, William. *J R*. New York: Knopf, 1975.

Gambaccini, Paul. "The Jailhouse Blues, a New LP, and McCartney". *San Francisco Examiner* June 27, 1980: 63.

Gilmore, Mikal. *Stories Done: Writings on the 1960s and Its Discontents*. New York: Free Press, 2008.

Goddard, Peter. "A Crowd of People Stood and Stared: Remembering John Lennon". *The Star* December 9, 2010, www.thestar.com/entertainment/music/2010/12/09/a_crowd_of_people_stood_and_stared_remembering_john_lennon.html.

Goresh, Paul. Television interview. 1990. www.youtube.com/watch?v=vgzEDoFTvUY.

Green, John. *Dakota Days: The True Story of John Lennon's Final Years*. New York: St. Martin's, 1983.

Gubler, Fritz. *Great, Grand, and Famous Hotels*. Sydney: Great, Grand, and Famous Hotels, 2008.

Haughney, Christine. "Sharing the Dakota with John Lennon". *The New York Times* December 6, 2010, www.nytimes.com/2010/12/07/nyregion/07appraisal.html.

Hayes, Milton. 'The Green Eye Of The Little Yellow God'. Sheet music. London: Reynolds, 1911.

Heyerdahl, Thor. *Kon-Tiki: Across the Pacific by Raft*. Trans. F.H. Lyon. Chicago: Rand McNally, 1950.

Hickox, Katie. "John Lennon's Country Girl Gets Beatles-Styled Wedding in Vegas". *Beatle News* April 16, 2009, www.beatlesnews.com/news/the-beatles/200904160703/john-lennons-country-girl-gets-beatles-styled-wedding-in-vegas.html.

Hilburn, Robert. *Corn Flakes with John Lennon and Other Tales from a Rock 'n' Roll Life*. New York: Rodale, 2009.

Holden, Stephen. "*McCartney II*". *Rolling Stone* July 24, 1980, www.rollingstone.com/music/music-album-reviews/mccartney-ii-188055/.

Hopkins, Jerry. *Yoko Ono*. New York: Macmillan, 1986.

Iscove, Charles. *The Lost Lennon Tapes Project: An Unauthorized Guide to the Complete Radio Series, 1988–1992*. Milton Keynes: Lightning Source, 2010.

Jackson, Andrew Grant. *Still the Greatest: The Essential Solo Beatles Songs*. Lanham, MD: Scarecrow, 2012.

Jones, Jeannine. "A Writer Shares 1980s UWS Memories and Asks for Yours". *West Side Rag* November 24, 2013, www.westsiderag.com/2013/11/24/a-writer-shares-1980s-uws-memories-and-asks-for-yours.

Kane, Larry. *Lennon Revealed*. Philadelphia: Running Press, 2005.

Kehew, Brian. "Flight of the Sardonyx". *Vintage Guitar* May 2012: 46–47.

Lawson, Terry. "*Double Fantasy* Isn't Bold or Adventurous". *Journal Herald* November 22, 1980: 24.

Lennon, John. *The John Lennon Letters*. Ed. Hunter Davies. New York: Little, Brown, 2012.

———. *Lennon Remembers*. Interview by Jann Wenner. 1970. New York: Verso, 2000.

———. *Skywriting by Word of Mouth and Other Writings, including "The Ballad of John and Yoko"*. New York: Harper and Row, 1986.

Lennon, John, and Yoko Ono. *All We Are Saying: The Last Major Interview with John Lennon and Yoko Ono*. Interview by David Sheff. Ed. G. Barry Golson. New York: Griffin, 2000.

———. *Double Fantasy: A Heart Play*. Geffen, 1980.

———. *John Lennon: The Man, the Memory – Last Interview Special*. Interview by Dave Sholin and Laurie Kaye. RKO Radio, 1980.

———. *The Lennon Tapes*. Interview by Andy Peebles. London: BBC, 1981.

———. *Milk and Honey: A Heart Play*. Geffen, 1984.

Lennon, Sean. "Sean Lennon's Holidays with His Father". *The Times* January 16, 2010, www.thetimes.co.uk/article/sean-lennons-holidays-with-his-father-lpwkwcwvzvg.

Lescaze, Lee, and Tom Zito. "The Beatles May Reunite in Benefit for Boat People". *The Washington Post* September 21, 1979, www.washingtonpost.com/archive/lifestyle/1979/09/21/the-beatles-may-reunite-in-benefit-for-boat-people/efb6848f-3235-4896-a9de-b6d6a24cf6fb/.

Lewisohn, Mark. *Tune In: The Beatles – All These Years*. New York: Crown, 2013.

Lipton, Dave. "That Time Paul McCartney Spent Nine Days in Jail". *Ultimate Classic Rock* January 26, 2015, ultimateclassicrock.com/paul-mccartney-tokyo-bust/.

Lloyd, Jack. "Lennon's Expected Splash Is Instead a Strong Ripple". *The Philadelphia Inquirer* November 30, 1980: 142.

———. "Yoko Ono Puts John Lennon's Pen-and-Ink Art on Display". *Philadelphia Inquirer* October 15, 1993: 36.

Lorenzo, Rosaura Lopéz. *En Casa de John Lennon*. Coruña: Hércules Ediciones, 2005.

Madinger, Chip, and Mark Easter. *Eight Arms to Hold You: The Solo Beatles Compendium*. Springfield, MO: Open Your Books, 2018.

Madinger, Chip, and Scott Raile. *Lennonology: Strange Days Indeed – A Scrapbook of Madness*. Springfield, MO: Open Your Books, 2015.

Marcantonio, Steve. "Eight Days in the Studio with John Lennon and Yoko Ono". Interview by Joe Pagetta. Nashville Public Television, November 10, 2018, blogs.wnpt.org/mediaupdate/2010/11/18/eight-days-in-the-studio-with-john-lennon-and-yoko-ono/.

Marsh, Dave. "Ghoulish Beatlemania: Thoughts on the Death of John Lennon". *Rolling Stone* January 22, 1981: www.rollingstone.com/music/music-news/ghoulish-beatlemania-thoughts-on-the-death-of-john-lennon-74513/.

Martin, George. "'They Were My Boys, the Greatest in the World': An Interview with George Martin (1993)". Interview by Bill DeYoung. January 3, 2016. www.billdeyoung.com/tag/george-martin-beatles/.

Martin, George, with Jeremy Hornsby. *All You Need Is Ears*. New York: St. Martin's, 1979.

Martin, George, with William Pearson. *With a Little Help from My Friends: The Making of Sgt. Pepper*. Boston: Little, Brown, 1994.

McCarthy, John. "How John Lennon Rediscovered His Music in Bermuda". *The Daily Beast* November 3, 2013, www.thedailybeast.com/how-john-lennon-rediscovered-his-music-in-bermuda.

Miles, Barry. *Paul McCartney: Many Years from Now*. New York: Holt, 1997.

Miller, Sara Cedar. *Strawberry Fields: Central Park's Memorial to John Lennon*. New York: Abrams, 2011.

Mitchell, Jack. "A Final Record". *The New York Times* December 8, 2005, www.nytimes.com/2005/12/08/opinion/a-final-record.html.

Moniz, Jessie. "Was John Lennon's Double Fantasy a Freesia or a Hibiscus?" *The Royal Gazette* November 23, 2011, www.royalgazette.com/article/20111123/NEWS/711239919.

Morgan, Robert. "The Photograph Not Taken: The Night John Lennon Died". *Princeton Alumni Weekly* December 2, 2015, paw.princeton.edu/article/photograph-not-taken-night-john-lennon-died.

Neil, Scott. *Lennon Bermuda*. Bermuda: Freisenbruch Brannon Media, 2012.

Norman, Philip. *John Lennon: The Life*. London: Ecco, 2008.

Ono, Yoko. *John Lennon: Summer of 1980*. New York: Perigee, 1983.

———. "John Lennon's Last Days: A Remembrance by Yoko Ono". *Rolling Stone* December 23, 2010, www.rollingstone.com/music/music-news/john-lennons-last-days-a-remembrance-by-yoko-ono-62533/.

———. *Season of Glass*. Geffen, 1981.

———. "The Tea Maker". *The New York Times* December 7, 2010, www.nytimes.com/2010/12/08/opinion/08ono.html.

———. "'Walking On Thin Ice' b/w "It Happened". Geffen, 1981.

O'Toole, Garson. "Life Is What Happens to You While You're Busy Making Other Plans". May 6, 2012, quoteinvestigator.com/2012/05/06/other-plans/.

———. "When You're 60, You Realize No One Was Ever Thinking of You". June 1, 2019, quoteinvestigator.com/2019/06/01/worry/.

Pang, May, and Henry Edwards. *Loving John: The Untold Story*. New York: Warner, 1983.

Petty, Moira. "Decline of a Rock Genius". *The Times* September 29, 2000: 2, 8.

Pond, Steve. "Lennon, Ono in Yesteryear". *Los Angeles Times* November 30, 1980: 79.

Recchia, Philip. "Paul: We Can Work It Out; '79 Deal Ok'd Beatles Reunion any Time at All". *New York Post* December 5, 2005, nypost.com/2005/12/05/paul-we-can-work-it-out-79-deal-okd-beatles-reunion-any-time-at-all/.

Richmond, Len, with Gary Noguera, eds. *The New Gay Liberation Book: Writings and Photographs about Gay (Men's) Liberation*. 1973. Palo Alto: Ramparts, 1979.

Riley, Tim. *Lennon: The Man, the Myth, the Music*. New York: Hyperion, 2011.

Rodriguez, Robert. *Fab Four FAQ 2.0: The Beatles' Solo Years, 1970–1980*. Milwaukee: Backbeat, 2010.

Rogan, Johnny. *Lennon: The Albums*. London: Omnibus, 1982.

Roth, C.P. "My Visit with John Lennon at the Dakota". *The Huffington Post* December 8, 2011, www.huffpost.com/entry/my-visit-with-john-lennon_b_1136589.

Starr, Michael Seth. *Ringo: With a Little Help*. Milwaukee: Backbeat, 2016.

Saunders, Allen. "Quotable Quotes". *Reader's Digest* January 1957: 32.

Schaffner, Nicholas. *The Beatles Forever*. New York: McGraw-Hill, 1977.

Seaman, Frederic. *The Last Days of John Lennon: A Personal Memoir*. New York: Birch Lane, 1991.

Shames, Laurence. "John Lennon, Where Are You?: In Search of the Beatle Who Spent Two Decades Seeking True Love and Cranial Bliss Only to Discover Cows, Daytime Television, and Palm Beach Real Estate". *Esquire* November 1, 1980, classic.esquire.com/article/1980/11/1/john-lennon-where-are-you.

Sharp, Ken. *Starting Over: The Making of John Lennon and Yoko Ono's Double Fantasy*. New York: Gallery, 2010.

Slate, Jeff. "Earl Slick: My 12 Greatest Recordings of All Time". *Music Radar* February 26, 2013, www.musicradar.com/news/guitars/earl-slick-my-12-greatest-recordings-of-all-time-571523.

Smith, Liz. "Insults, Intrigues, and Indignities". *Daily News* March 23, 1980: 6.

Solt, Andrew, dir. *Imagine: John Lennon*. Warner Brothers, 1988.

Swanson, Dave. "That Time the Beatles Received a $230 Million Offer". *Ultimate Classic Rock* September 19, 2015, ultimateclassicrock.com/beatles-turn-down-230-million-reunion-offer-september-19-1976/.

Tannenhauser, Carol. "An Optometrist Recalls Late Night Chats with John Lennon and that Awful Night". *West Side Rag* December 8, 2017, www.westsiderag.com/2017/12/08/an-optometrist-recalls-late-night-chats-with-john-lennon-and-that-awful-night.

"Throwback Thursday: Fantastic Video Surfaces of the UWS in 1977", *West Side Rag* December 3, 2015, www.westsiderag.com/2015/12/03/throwback-thursday-fantastic-video-surfaces-of-the-uws-in-1977.

A Toot and a Snore in '74. Mistral Music, 1992.

Twarowski, Christopher. "Imagine: John Lennon on Long Island". *Long Island Press* October 5, 2013, www.longislandpress.com/2013/10/05/imagine-john-lennon-on-long-island/.

Wiener, Jon. *Come Together: John Lennon in His Time*. Urbana: University of Illinois Press, 1984.

Wildes, Leon. *John Lennon vs. the USA: The Inside Story of the Most Bitterly Contested and Influential Deportation Case in United States History*. New York: American Bar Association, 2016.

Williams, Alex. "Rex Reed Bangs a Gong on the Mediocrity of Modern Life". *The New York Times* January 10, 2010, www.nytimes.com/2018/01/10/style/who-is-rex-reed.html.

Wright, Minnie. "John Lennon: What Yoko Ono *Really* Thought about His Affair with May Pang – in Her Words". *Daily Express* November 29, 2019, www.express.co.uk/entertainment/music/1211066/John-Lennon-Yoko-Ono-May-Pang-The-Beatles-affair.

Yakas, Ben. "Record Producer Jack Douglas Opens Up about Working with John Lennon". *Gothamist* July 18, 2016, gothamist.com/arts-entertainment/record-producer-jack-douglas-opens-up-about-working-with-john-lennon.

Notes

Chapter 1 Kitchen Diplomacy

1   Keith Badman, *The Beatles Diary, Volume 2: After the Break-Up, 1970–2001* (London: Omnibus, 2009), pp. 643–44.

2   Dave Marsh, "Ghoulish Beatlemania: Thoughts on the Death of John Lennon", *Rolling Stone* (January 22, 1981), www.rollingstone.com/music/music-news/ghoulish-beatlemania-thoughts-on-the-death-of-john-lennon-74513/.

3   Stephen Birmingham, *Life at the Dakota: New York's Most Unusual Address* (New York: Open Road, 2015), p. 20.

4   Birmingham, *Life at the Dakota*, p. 40.

5   Birmingham, *Life at the Dakota*, p. 74.

6   Birmingham, *Life at the Dakota*, p. 79.

7   Birmingham, *Life at the Dakota*, p. 192.

8   Christine Haughney, "Sharing the Dakota with John Lennon", *The New York Times* December 6, 2010, www.nytimes.com/2010/12/07/nyregion/07appraisal.html.

9   Rosaura Lopéz Lorenzo, *En Casa de John Lennon* (Coruña: Hércules Ediciones, 2005), p. 35.

10 Interview with Jim Ryan and Susan Ratisher Ryan, November 2, 2019.

11 Peter Goddard, "A Crowd of People Stood and Stared: Remembering John Lennon", *The Star* December 9, 2010, www.thestar.com/

entertainment/music/2010/12/09/a_crowd_of_people_stood_and_stared_
re-membering_john_lennon.html; Carol Tannenhauser, "An Optometrist
Recalls Late Night Chats with John Lennon and that Awful Night".
West Side Rag December 8, 2017, www.westsiderag.com/2017/12/08/
an-optometrist-recalls-late-night-chats-with-john-lennon-and-that-awful-
night.

12 Lorenzo, *En Casa de John Lennon*, p. 10; Chet Flippo, "The Private Years",
The Ballad of John and Yoko, ed. Jonathan Cott and Christine Doudna (New
York: Rolling Stone, 1982), p. 178; Alex Williams, "Rex Reed Bangs a
Gong on the Mediocrity of Modern Life", *The New York Times* January 10,
2010, www.nytimes.com/2018/01/10/style/who-is-rex-reed.html.

13 Frederic Seaman, *The Last Days of John Lennon: A Personal Memoir* (New
York: Birch Lane, 1991), p. 83.

14 Seaman, *The Last Days of John Lennon*, p. 83.

15 Interview with Jim Ryan and Susan Ratisher Ryan, November 2, 2019.

16 John Lennon and Yoko Ono, *All We Are Saying: The Last Major Interview
with John Lennon and Yoko Ono*, interview by David Sheff, ed. G. Barry
Golson (New York: Griffin, 2000), p. 82.

17 George Martin, "'They Were My Boys, the Greatest in the World': An
Interview with George Martin (1993)", interview by Bill DeYoung, January
3, 2016, www.billdeyoung.com/tag/george-martin-beatles/.

18 George Martin with William Pearson, *With a Little Help from My Friends:
The Making of Sgt. Pepper* (Boston: Little, Brown, 1994), p. 24; Philip
Norman, *John Lennon: The Life* (London: Ecco, 2008), p. 783.

Chapter 2 The Dakoterie

19 Birmingham, *Life at the Dakota*, pp. 147–48.

20 Sara Cedar Miller, *Strawberry Fields: Central Park's Memorial to John Lennon*
(New York: Abrams, 2011), p. 39.

21 Jeannine Jones, "A Writer Shares 1980s UWS Memories and Asks
for Yours", *West Side Rag* November 24, 2013, www.westsiderag.
com/2013/11/24/a-writer-shares-1980s-uws-memories-and-asks-for-yours;
"Throwback Thursday: Fantastic Video Surfaces of the UWS in 1977",
West Side Rag December 3, 2015, www.westsiderag.com/2015/12/03/
throwback-thursday-fantastic-video-surfaces-of-the-uws-in-1977.

22 Tannenhauser, "An Optometrist Recalls Late Night Chats with John
Lennon and that Awful Night"; "Ben Stiller Says NYC Is an Exciting Place
for Kids", *People* August 11, 2008, people.com/parents/ben-stiller-sta/.

23 Interview with Jim Ryan and Susan Ratisher Ryan, November 2, 2019.

24   Interview with Jim Ryan and Susan Ratisher Ryan, November 2, 2019; interview with Robert Morgan, January 2, 2020.

25   Seaman, *The Last Days of John Lennon*, p. 27.

26   Seaman, *The Last Days of John Lennon*, pp. 9, 14.

27   Lennon and Ono, *John Lennon: The Man, the Memory – Last Interview Special*, interview by Dave Sholin and Laurie Kaye, RKO Radio, December 8, 1980.

28   Lorenzo, *En Casa de John Lennon*, p. 64.

29   Birmingham, *Life at the Dakota*, p. 171.

30   Katie Hickox, "John Lennon's Country Girl Gets Beatles-Styled Wedding in Vegas", *Beatles News* April 16, 2009, www.beatlesnews.com/news/the-beatles/200904160703/john-lennons-country-girl-gets-beatles-styled-wedding-in-vegas.html; Seaman, *The Last Days of John Lennon*, p. 109.

31   Birmingham, *Life at the Dakota*, p. 217.

32   Birmingham, *Life at the Dakota*, p. 216.

33   Birmingham, *Life at the Dakota*, p. 230.

34   William J. Dowlding, *Beatlesongs* (New York: Simon and Schuster, 1989), p. 184.

35   Haughney, "Sharing the Dakota with John Lennon".

36   Lorenzo, *En Casa de John Lennon*, p. 30.

37   *Imagine: John Lennon*, dir. Andrew Solt, Warner Bros., 1988.

38   Liz Smith, "Insults, Intrigues, and Indignities", *Daily News* March 23, 1980, p. 6.

39   Moira Petty, "Decline of a Rock Genius", *The Times* September 29, 2000, pp. 2, 8.

40   See Jim Cushman, "A Beatle Slept with This: Pieces of the Mania", *Collectors Weekly* March 11, 2011, www.collectorsweekly.com/articles/a-beatle-slept-with-this-pieces-of-the-mania/.

41   The Beatles, *The Beatles Anthology* (San Francisco: Chronicle, 2000), p. 354; *The Lennon Tapes*, interview by Andy Peebles (London: BBC, 1981), p. 95.

Chapter 3 A Phantom

42   Interview with Robert Thompson, January 3, 2020.

43   *All We Are Saying*, p. 56; Norman, *John Lennon*, p. 768.

44   Lorenzo, *En Casa de John Lennon*, pp. 31–32.

45   Paul Goresh, television interview, 1990, www.youtube.com/watch?v=vgzEDoFTvUY; Yoko Ono, *John Lennon: Summer of 1980* (New York: Perigee, 1983), p. 88.

46 Ibid.

47 Ibid.

48 Ibid.

49 Seaman, *The Last Days of John Lennon*, p. 38; interview with Mark Lapidos, January 6, 2020.

50 Seaman, *The Last Days of John Lennon*, p. 41.

51 John Lennon, *The John Lennon Letters*, ed. Hunter Davies (New York: Little, Brown, 2012), p. 363.

52 Larry Kane, *Lennon Revealed* (Philadelphia: Running Press, 2005), p. 211.

53 *All We Are Saying*, pp. 22–23.

54 *All We Are Saying*, p. 21.

55 Tim Riley, *Lennon: The Man, the Myth, the Music* (New York: Hyperion, 2011), p. 557.

56 Riley, p. 567.

57 May Pang and Henry Edwards, *Loving John: The Untold Story* (New York: Warner, 1983), p. 61; Minnie Wright, "John Lennon: What Yoko Ono *Really* Thought about His Affair with May Pang – in Her Words", *Daily Express* November 29, 2019, www.express.co.uk/entertainment/music/1211066/John-Lennon-Yoko-Ono-May-Pang-The-Beatles-affair.

58 Norman, *John Lennon*, p. 712; Robert Hilburn, *Corn Flakes with John Lennon and Other Tales from a Rock 'n' roll Life* (New York: Rodale, 2009), p. 119.

59 Riley, *Lennon*, p. 577; see *A Toot and a Snore in '74* (Mistral Music, 1992).

60 Joe Capozzi, "John Lennon's Last Years in Palm Beach", *The Palm Beach Post* November 1, 2018, www.palmbeachpost.com/news/20181101/john-lennons-last-years-in-palm-beach/1.

61 Pete Hamill, "Long Night's Journey into Day", *The Ballad of John and Yoko*, ed. Jonathan Cott and Christine Doudna (New York: Rolling Stone, 1982), p. 150; interview with May Pang, June 23, 2018.

62 Kane, *Lennon Revealed*, p. 237; Wright, "John Lennon".

63 Norman, *John Lennon*, p. 675.

64 C.P. Roth, "My Visit with John Lennon at the Dakota", *The Huffington Post* December 8, 2011, www.huffpost.com/entry/my-visit-with-john-lennon_b_1136589.

65 Ibid.

66 Ibid.

67 Ibid.

68 Seaman, *The Last Days of John Lennon*, pp. 27–28.

69 Chip Madinger and Scott Raile, *Lennonology: Strange Days Indeed – A Scrapbook of Madness* (Springfield, MO: Open Your Books, 2015), p. 448.

70   Jonathan Cott, *Days That I'll Remember: Spending Time with John Lennon and Yoko Ono* (London: Omnibus, 2013), p. 187–88.

71   Ray Connolly, "I Remember the Real John Lennon, Not the One Airbrushed by History", *The Daily Telegraph* December 4, 2010, www. telegraph.co.uk/culture/music/the-beatles/8179356/I-remember-the-real-John-Lennon-not-the-one-airbrushed-by-history.html.

72   Chip Madinger and Mark Easter, *Eight Arms to Hold You: The Solo Beatles Compendium* (Springfield, MO: Open Your Books, 2018), p. 111; Pang and Edwards, *Loving John*, pp. 325–27; Ray Connolly, *Being John Lennon: A Restless Life* (New York: Pegasus, 2018), p. 390.

Chapter 4 Emotional Wreck

73   Norman, *John Lennon*, p. 770.

74   John Lennon, *Skywriting by Word of Mouth and Other Writings, including "The Ballad of John and Yoko"* (New York: Harper and Row, 1986), p. 11.

75   Len Richmond with Gary Noguera, eds., *The New Gay Liberation Book: Writings and Photographs about Gay (Men's) Liberation* (Palo Alto: Ramparts, 1979), p. 95; Lennon, *Skywriting by Word of Mouth*, p. 28.

76   Lennon, *Skywriting by Word of Mouth*, p. 12.

77   Seaman, *The Last Days of John Lennon*, pp. 185–86.

78   Madinger and Raile, *Lennonology*, p. 442.

79   *All We Are Saying*, p. 61; Mikal Gilmore, *Stories Done: Writings on the 1960s and Its Discontents* (New York: Free Press, 2008), p. 173.

80   Interview with Seaman, September 19, 2019; Cott, *Days That I'll Remember*, p. 153; Lorenzo, *En Casa de John Lennon*, p. 17.

81   *All We Are Saying*, pp. 5, 61.

82   Jon Wiener, *Come Together: John Lennon in His Time* (Urbana: University of Illinois Press, 1984), pp. 258–59.

83   Leon Wildes, *John Lennon vs. the USA: The Inside Story of the Most Bitterly Contested and Influential Deportation Case in United States History* (New York: American Bar Association, 2016), p. 71.

84   Wildes, *John Lennon vs. the USA*, pp. 6–7, 71; see Peter Doggett, *The Art and Music of John Lennon* (London: Omnibus, 1998), ch. 14.

85   *All We Are Saying*, p. 225.

Chapter 5 Mind Movies

86   Robert Rodriguez, *Fab Four FAQ 2.0: The Beatles' Solo Years, 1970–1980* (Milwaukee: Backbeat, 2010), p. 341.

87   Jack Lloyd, "Yoko Ono Puts John Lennon's Pen-and-Ink Art on Display",
      Philadelphia Inquirer October 15, 1993, p. 36.
88   *Skywriting by Word of Mouth*, p. 85; *The John Lennon Letters*, p. 342.
89   *Skywriting by Word of Mouth*, pp. 93, 98, 127, 160.
90   *Skywriting by Word of Mouth*, p. 132.
91   Lorenzo, *En Casa de John Lennon*, pp. 68–69.
92   Barry Miles, *Paul McCartney: Many Years from Now* (New York: Holt,
      1997), p. 587.
93   Jimmy Carter, *Why Not the Best?: The First 50 Years* (Fayetteville:
      University of Arkansas Press, 1996), p. 165.
94   Seaman, *The Last Days of John Lennon*, p. 183.
95   Interview with Pang, February 28, 2019.
96   Dave Swanson, "That Time the Beatles Received a $230 Million Offer",
      Ultimate Classic Rock September 19, 2015, ultimateclassicrock.com/beatles-
      turn-down-230-million-reunion-offer-september-19-1976/; "April 24,
      1976: John and Paul Almost Go on *SNL*", *Best Classic Bands* April 24, 2017,
      bestclassicbands.com/lennon-mccartney-snl-4-24-17/.
97   Lee Lescaze and Tom Zito, "The Beatles May Reunite in Benefit for Boat
      People", *The Washington Post* September 21, 1979, www.washingtonpost.
      com/archive/lifestyle/1979/09/21/the-beatles-may-reunite-in-benefit-for-
      boat-people/efb6848f-3235-4896-a9de-b6d6a24cf6fb/.
98   Nicholas Schaffner, *The Beatles Forever* (New York: McGraw-Hill, 1977),
      p. 186; Philip Recchia, "Paul: We Can Work It Out; '79 Deal Ok'd Beatles
      Reunion any Time at All", *New York Post* December 5, 2005, nypost.
      com/2005/12/05/paul-we-can-work-it-out-79-deal-okd-beatles-reunion-
      any-time-at-all/.
99   Lorenzo, *En Casa de John Lennon*, p. 70.
100   Connolly, *Being John Lennon*, pp. 285–86; Miles, *Paul McCartney*, p. 567.
101   Ken Sharp, *Starting Over: The Making of John Lennon and Yoko Ono's Double
      Fantasy* (New York: Gallery, 2010), p. 13.
102   Ben Yakas, "Record Producer Jack Douglas Opens Up about Working
      with John Lennon", *Gothamist* July 18, 2016, gothamist.com/arts-
      entertainment/record-producer-jack-douglas-opens-up-about-working-
      with-john-lennon.
103   *The Last Lennon Tapes* was presented in serial form and hosted by Elliot
      Mintz for the Westwood One Radio Network from January 24, 1988, to
      March 29, 1992. For a detailed catalogue of the recordings, see Charles
      Iscove's *The Lost Lennon Tapes Project: An Unauthorized Guide to the Complete
      Radio Series, 1988–1992* (Milton Keynes: Lightning Source, 2010).
104   Madinger and Raile, *Lennonology*, p. 508.
105   Madinger and Raile, *Lennonology*, p. 509.

106 Mark Lewisohn, *Tune In: The Beatles – All These Years* (New York: Crown, 2013), p. 825.

107 Madinger and Raile, *Lennonology*, p. 514.

108 *John Lennon: The Man, the Memory.*

Chapter 6 El Solano

109 Seaman, *The Last Days of John Lennon*, p. 81.

110 Jerry Hopkins, *Yoko Ono* (New York: Macmillan, 1986), p. 218; Seaman, *The Last Days of John Lennon*, p. 24.

111 Yoko Ono, "The Tea Maker", *The New York Times*, December 7, 2010, www.nytimes.com/2010/12/08/opinion/08ono.html.

112 *The John Lennon Letters*, p. 363.

113 *All We Are Saying*, pp. 4–5; Lorenzo, *En Casa de John Lennon*, p. 44.

114 *All We Are Saying*, pp. 4–5.

115 Birmingham, *Life at the Dakota*, pp. 185–86.

116 *John Lennon: The Man, the Memory.*

117 *All We Are Saying*, p. 211.

118 Seaman, *The Last Days of John Lennon*, p. 84.

119 Interview with Pang, February 28, 2019.

120 Lewisohn, *Tune In*, p. 81.

121 Madinger and Raile, *Lennonology*, p. 509; Seaman, *The Last Days of John Lennon*, p. 90.

122 Madinger and Raile, *Lennonology*, p. 511.

123 *All We Are Saying*, p. 83.

124 Seaman, *The Last Days of John Lennon*, p. 92; Lorenzo, *En Casa de John Lennon*, p. 30.

125 Dave Lipton, "That Time Paul McCartney Spent Nine Days in Jail", *Ultimate Classic Rock* January 26, 2015, ultimateclassicrock.com/paul-mccartney-tokyo-bust/; John Green, *Dakota Days: The True Story of John Lennon's Final Years* (New York: St. Martin's, 1983), p. 238.

126 Madinger and Raile, *Lennonology*, p. 511.

127 Seaman, *The Last Days of John Lennon*, p. 94; Peter Boyle, interview by Allan Neuwirth, Archives of American Television, 2016.

128 Seaman, *The Last Days of John Lennon*, p. 95.

129 Seaman, *The Last Days of John Lennon*, p. 97.

130 Seaman, *The Last Days of John Lennon*, p. 98.

131 *The John Lennon Letters*, pp. 216–17.

132 Madinger and Raile, *Lennonology*, p. 511; Seaman, *The Last Days of John Lennon*, p. 99.

133 Seaman, *The Last Days of John Lennon*, p. 103.
134 Seaman, *The Last Days of John Lennon*, p. 105; Riley, *Lennon*, p. 628.
135 Seaman, *The Last Days of John Lennon*, p. 108.
136 Sean Lennon, "Sean Lennon's Holidays with His Father", *The Times* January 16, 2010, www.thetimes.co.uk/article/sean-lennons-holidays-with-his-father-lpwkwcwvzvg.
137 Seaman, *The Last Days of John Lennon*, p. 94.
138 Seaman, *The Last Days of John Lennon*, p. 100; Capozzi, "John Lennon's Last Years in Palm Beach".
139 Seaman, *The Last Days of John Lennon*, p. 101.
140 Dowlding, *Beatlesongs*, p. 275.
141 *The John Lennon Letters*, p. 373.
142 Seaman, *The Last Days of John Lennon*, p. 122.
143 Stephen Holden, "*McCartney II*", *Rolling Stone* July 24, 1980, www.rollingstone.com/music/music-album-reviews/mccartney-ii-188055/.
144 Paul Gambaccini, "The Jailhouse Blues, a New LP, and McCartney", *San Francisco Examiner* June 27, 1980, p. 63; Dowlding, *Beatlesongs*, p. 78; Geoff Emerick and Howard Massey, *Here, There, and Everywhere: My Life Recording the Music of the Beatles* (New York: Gotham, 2006), p. 8.
145 Lennon, interview with Robert Hilburn, October 10, 1980.
146 Ibid.
147 Seaman, *The Last Days of John Lennon*, p. 124.
148 Riley, *John Lennon*, p. 615; interview with Pang, June 23, 2018.
149 Sean Lennon, "Sean Lennon's Holidays with His Father".
150 Madinger and Raile, *Lennonology*, p. 513.
151 Seaman, *The Last Days of John Lennon*, p. 129.
152 Madinger and Raile, *Lennonology*, p. 513.
153 Seaman, *The Last Days of John Lennon*, p. 132.
154 Sean Lennon, "Sean Lennon's Holidays with His Father"; Norman, *John Lennon*, p. 811.
155 Seaman, *The Last Days of John Lennon*, p. 131.
156 Hilburn, *Corn Flakes with John Lennon*, p. 118.
157 Madeline Bocaro, "Just a Story: 'Walking On Thin Ice'", *Madelinex* December 8, 2016, madelinex.com/2016/12/08/yoko-songs-walking-on-thin-ice/.
158 Jonathan Cott, "Yoko Ono and Her 16-Track Voice", *Rolling Stone* March 18, 1971, www.rollingstone.com/music/music-news/yoko-ono-and-her-sixteen-track-voice-237782/.

Chapter 8 Megan Jaye

159 Madinger and Raile, *Lennonology*, p. 513.

160 The Beatles, *The Beatles Anthology*, p. 14.

161 Thor Heyerdahl, *Kon-Tiki: Across the Pacific by Raft*, trans. F.H. Lyon (Chicago: Rand McNally, 1950), p. xi.

162 Madinger and Raile, *Lennonology*, p. 513.

163 Badman, *The Beatles Diary*, p. 592.

164 Interview with Iqbal Surve, January 20, 2020.

165 Norman, *John Lennon*, p. 781.

166 Fritz Gubler, *Great, Grand, and Famous Hotels*, (2008), p. 238.

167 Pang and Edwards, *Loving John*, pp. 327–31; interview with Pang, June 23, 2018, and October 21, 2018.

168 Madinger and Raile, *Lennonology*, p. 514.

169 Scott Neil, *Lennon Bermuda* (Bermuda: Freisenbruch Brannon Media, 2012), p. 15.

170 Neil, *Lennon Bermuda*, p. 16.

171 Madinger and Raile, *Lennonology*, p. 515; Neil, *Lennon Bermuda*, p. 16.

172 Neil, *Lennon Bermuda*, p. 19.

173 Madinger and Raile, *Lennonology*, p. 515.

174 Neil, *Lennon Bermuda*, p. 17.

175 Neil, *Lennon Bermuda*, pp. 17–18.

176 Neil, *Lennon Bermuda*, pp. 17, 19.

177 Neil, *Lennon Bermuda*, p. 18.

178 Neil, *Lennon Bermuda*, pp. 19–20.

179 Neil, *Lennon Bermuda*, p. 20.

180 Madinger and Raile, *Lennonology*, p. 515; Neil, *Lennon Bermuda*, p. 20.

181 Connolly, *Being John Lennon*, p. 392.

182 Neil, *Lennon Bermuda*, pp. 20, 24.

183 Neil, *Lennon Bermuda*, p. 24.

184 Neil, *Lennon Bermuda*, p. 26.

185 Madinger and Raile, *Lennonology*, p. 515.

186 Neil, *Lennon Bermuda*, pp. 28, 29.

187 Neil, *Lennon Bermuda*, pp. 32, 33.

188 Seaman, *The Last Days of John Lennon*, p. 147.

189 Seaman, *The Last Days of John Lennon*, p. 152.

190 Neil, *Lennon Bermuda*, p. 35.

191 Seaman, *The Last Days of John Lennon*, p. 151.

192 Seaman, *The Last Days of John Lennon*, p. 154.

193 Ibid.

Chapter 9 Fairylands

194 Seaman, *The Last Days of John Lennon*, pp. 158–59.

195 Seaman, *The Last Days of John Lennon*, p. 164.

196 *John Lennon: The Man, the Memory*.

197 *John Lennon: The Man, the Memory*; Jessie Moniz, "Was John Lennon's Double Fantasy a Freesia or a Hibiscus?" *The Royal Gazette* November 23, 2011, www.royalgazette.com/article/20111123/NEWS/711239919.

198 Seaman, *The Last Days of John Lennon*, p. 170.

199 Allen Saunders, "Quotable Quotes", *Reader's Digest* January 1957, p. 32; William Gaddis, *J R* (New York: Knopf, 1975), p. 394; see Garson O'Toole, "Life Is What Happens to You While You're Busy Making Other Plans", May 6, 2012, quoteinvestigator.com/2012/05/06/other-plans/.

200 Sean Lennon, "Sean Lennon's Holidays with His Father".

201 Madinger and Raile, *Lennonology*, p. 517.

202 Seaman, *The Last Days of John Lennon*, p. 172.

203 Seaman, *The Last Days of John Lennon*, pp. 173–74.

204 *All We Are Saying*, p. 223.

205 Sharp, *Starting Over*, p. 154.

206 Sharp, *Starting Over*, p. 15.

207 Sharp, *Starting Over*, p. 16; interview with Jack Douglas, August 11, 2018.

208 Sharp, *Starting Over*, p. 17.

209 Seaman, *The Last Days of John Lennon*, p. 176; see the liner notes for Lennon and Ono's *Milk And Honey* (1984).

210 *Milk And Honey* liner notes.

211 Madinger and Raile, *Lennonology*, p. 517; Neil, *Lennon Bermuda*, p. 90.

212 Neil, *Lennon Bermuda*, p. 86.

213 Madinger and Raile, *Lennonology*, p. 518; John McCarthy, "How John Lennon Rediscovered His Music in Bermuda", *The Daily Beast* November 3, 2013, www.thedailybeast.com/how-john-lennon-rediscovered-his-music-in-bermuda.

214 Interview with Mike Medeiros, January 20, 2020; Madinger and Raile, *Lennonology*, p. 518.

215 *All We Are Saying*, p. 222.

216 *All We Are Saying*, p. 223.

217 *All We Are Saying*, p. 182.

218 Jonathan Cott, "The Last *Rolling Stone* Interview", *The Ballad of John and Yoko*, ed. Jonathan Cott and Christine Doudna (New York: Rolling Stone, 1982), p. 189.

Chapter 10 Hit Factory

219 Seaman, *The Last Days of John Lennon*, pp. 186–87.

220 Neil, *Lennon Bermuda*, pp. 90–91.

221 Seaman, *The Last Days of John Lennon*, p. 185.

222 Seaman, *The Last Days of John Lennon*, pp. 188–90.

223 Neil, *Lennon Bermuda*, p. 91; Seaman, *The Last Days of John Lennon*, p. 189.

224 Sharp, *Starting Over*, p. 17; interview with May Pang, January 21, 2020.

225 Sharp, *Starting Over*, pp. 31, 33.

226 Interview with Jon Smith, February 7, 2020.

227 Sharp, *Starting Over*, p. 26.

228 Sharp, *Starting Over*, pp. 22, 24.

229 Riley, *Lennon*, p. 536.

230 Seaman, *The Last Days of John Lennon*, pp. 192–93.

231 Sharp, *Starting Over*, p. 27.

232 Interview with Earl Slick, August 30, 2019.

233 Seaman, *The Last Days of John Lennon*, pp. 194–95.

234 Sharp, *Lennon*, p. 156.

235 Brian Kehew, "Flight of the Sardonyx", *Vintage Guitar* May 2012, pp. 46–47.

236 Sharp, *Lennon*, p. 29; interview with Douglas, August 11, 2018.

237 *All We Are Saying*, pp. 112–13.

238 Interview with Roger Farrington, January 6, 2020.

239 Ibid.

240 Ibid.

241 Ibid.

242 Interview with Farrington, January 6, 2020; interview with Slick, August 30, 2019.

243 Interview with Slick, August 30, 2019; Madinger and Raile, *Lennonology*, p. 520.

244 Interview with Farrington, March 24, 2020.

245 Tony Davilio with Mary Vicario, *The Lennon Sessions: An Introspective Chronicle from the Arranger on Double Fantasy* (Victoria, BC: Trafford, 2004), p. 43.

Chapter 11 A Heart Play

246 Alan di Perna, "Rick Nielsen, Earl Slick, and Jack Douglas Discuss the Recording of John Lennon's Final Album *Double Fantasy*", *Guitar World* December 8, 2015, www.guitarworld.com/magazine/interview-earl-slick-rick-nielsen-and-jack-douglas-tell-story-behind-john-lennons-double-fantasy; Sharp, *Starting Over*, p. 34.

247 Madinger and Raile, *Lennonology*, p. 520.

248 Sharp, *Starting Over*, p. 36.

249 Sharp, *Starting Over*, pp. 36–37; Davilio, *The Lennon Sessions*, p. 47.

250 Sharp, *Starting Over*, p. 49.

251 Sharp, *Starting Over*, p. 46.

252 *All We Are Saying*, p. 130.

253 Jeff Slate, "Earl Slick: My 12 Greatest Recordings of All Time", *Music Radar* February 26, 2013, www.musicradar.com/news/guitars/earl-slick-my-12-greatest-recordings-of-all-time-571523.

254 Sharp, *Starting Over*, pp. 150–51.

255 Norman, *John Lennon*, p. 781.

256 *All We Are Saying*, p. 221.

257 Ibid.

258 Sharp, *Starting Over*, p. 67; interview with Douglas, August 11, 2018.

259 Sharp, *Starting Over*, p. 165.

260 Cott, "The Last *Rolling Stone* Interview", p. 190.

261 Sharp, *Starting Over*, p. 113.

262 Sharp, *Starting Over*, p. 117.

263 Miles, *Paul McCartney*, p. 146.

264 *All We Are Saying*, p. 226.

265 Riley, *Lennon*, p. 630.

266 Di Perna, "Rick Nielsen, Earl Slick, and Jack Douglas Discuss the Recording of John Lennon's Final Album *Double Fantasy*".

267 Sharp, *Starting Over*, p. 98.

268 Sharp, *Starting Over*, pp. 98–99.

269 Riley, *Lennon*, pp. 632–33.

270 Sharp, *Starting Over*, p. 160.

271 *All We Are Saying*, p. 148.

272 Di Perna, "Rick Nielsen, Earl Slick, and Jack Douglas Discuss the Recording of John Lennon's Final Album *Double Fantasy*".

273 George Martin with Jeremy Hornsby, *All You Need Is Ears* (New York: St. Martin's, 1999), p. 130.

274 Seaman, *The Last Days of John Lennon*, p. 206.

275 Sharp, "Beatle Stories in the Studio".

276 Sharp, *Starting Over*, p. 169; *Lennonology*, p. 521.

277 Sharp, *Starting Over*, p. 169.

278 Sharp, *Starting Over*, p. 162.

279 Ibid.

280 Riley, *Lennon*, p. 632.

281 Di Perna, "Rick Nielsen, Earl Slick, and Jack Douglas Discuss the Recording of John Lennon's Final Album *Double Fantasy*".

282 Slate, "Earl Slick: My 12 Greatest Recordings of All Time"; Sharp, *Starting Over*, p. 156.

283 Madinger and Raile, *Lennonology*, p. 521.

Chapter 12 Stepping Out

284 Madinger and Raile, *Lennonology*, p. 522.

285 Madinger and Easter, *Eight Arms to Hold You*, p. 131.

286 Di Perna, "Rick Nielsen, Earl Slick, and Jack Douglas Discuss the Recording of John Lennon's Final Album *Double Fantasy*"; Seaman, *The Last Days of John Lennon*, p. 205.

287 Sharp, *Starting Over*, p. 85.

288 Sharp, *Starting Over*, p. 169.

289 Madinger and Raile, *Lennonology*, p. 522.

290 Madinger and Raile, *Lennonology*, p. 522.

291 Interview with Stuart Zolotorow, January 24, 2020.

292 Ibid.

293 Sharp, *Starting Over*, pp. 139–40.

294 Madinger and Raile, *Lennonology*, p. 523.

295 Madinger and Raile, *Lennonology*, p. 523.

296 Ibid.

297 *All We Are Saying*, pp. 3–4, 102; Cott, *Days That I'll Remember*, p. 162.

298 *All We Are Saying*, p. 18.

299 Madinger and Raile, *Lennonology*, p. 524.

300 Sharp, *Starting Over*, p. 175.

301 Sharp, *Starting Over*, p. 176.

302 Sharp, *Starting Over*, pp. 135–36.

303 Riley, *Lennon*, p. 633.

304 Madinger and Raile, *Lennonology*, p. 526; Seaman, *The Last Days of John Lennon*, p. 209.

305 Sharp, *Starting Over*, p. 153.

306 Sharp, *Starting Over*, pp. 160–61.

307 Interview with Douglas, August 11, 2018.

308 Sharp, *Starting Over*, pp. 147–48.

309 Sharp, *Starting Over*, p. 148; Madinger and Raile, *Lennonology*, p. 528.

310 Interview with Smith, February 7, 2020.

311 Cott, *Days That I'll Remember*, pp. 167–68.

312 *All We Are Saying*, p. 17.

313 Sharp, *Starting Over*, p. 201.

314 Jeroen Dekker, "One World, One People: John Lennon's Spring 1981

Tour", *Lennon Chords* 2005, lennonchords.info/1981/index.htm; Sharp, *Starting Over*, p. 200.

315 Sharp, *Starting Over*, p. 241; interview with Douglas, August 11, 2018.

Chapter 13 Life Begins at 40

316 Garson O'Toole, "When You're 60, You Realize No One Was Ever Thinking of You", June 1, 2019, quoteinvestigator.com/2019/06/01/worry/.
317 Badman, *The Beatles Diary*, p. 618.
318 Sharp, *Starting Over*, pp. 91–92.
319 Ibid.
320 The Beatles, *The Beatles Anthology*, p. 277.
321 Madinger and Raile, *Lennonology*, p. 529.
322 Sharp, *Starting Over*, p. 156.
323 Hilburn, *Corn Flakes with John Lennon*, p. 119.
324 *Milk And Honey* liner notes; Madinger and Easter, *Eight Arms to Hold You*, p. 131.
325 Seaman, *The Last Days of John Lennon*, p. 219.
326 Madinger and Raile, *Lennonology*, p. 531; interview with Smith, February 7, 2020.
327 Ibid.
328 Sharp, *Starting Over*, p. 180.
329 Madinger and Raile, *Lennonology*, p. 531.
330 Interview with Seaman, December 16, 2017.
331 *All We Are Saying*, pp. 125–26.
332 *The John Lennon Letters*, p. 382.
333 Laurence Shames, "John Lennon, Where Are You?: In Search of the Beatle Who Spent Two Decades Seeking True Love and Cranial Bliss Only to Discover Cows, Daytime Television, and Palm Beach Real Estate", *Esquire* November 1, 1980, classic.esquire.com/article/1980/11/1/john-lennon-where-are-you.
334 Ibid.
335 Ibid.
336 Jack Mitchell, "A Final Record", *The New York Times* December 8, 2005, www.nytimes.com/2005/12/08/opinion/a-final-record.html.
337 Ibid.
338 Madinger and Raile, *Lennonology*, p. 531; interview with Seaman, September 19, 2019.
339 Madinger and Raile, *Lennonology*, p. 532.

340 *Saturday Night Live*, NBC Television, Season Six, Episode 1, November 15, 1980.

341 Badman, *The Beatles Diary*, p. 684.

342 Ibid.

Chapter 14 Record Plant

343 Sharp, *Starting Over*, p. 180.

344 *John Lennon: The Man, the Memory*.

345 Jack Lloyd, "Lennon's Expected Splash Is Instead a Strong Ripple", *The Philadelphia Inquirer* November 30, 1980, p. 142; Steve Pond, "Lennon, Ono in Yesteryear", *Los Angeles Times* November 30, 1980, p. 79.

346 Madinger and Raile, *Lennonology*, p. 533; Terry Lawson, "*Double Fantasy* Isn't Bold or Adventurous", *Journal Herald* November 22, 1980, p. 24.

347 Badman, *The Beatles Diary*, p. 684; Johnny Rogan, *Lennon: The Albums* (London: Omnibus, 1982), ch. 12.

348 Yoko Ono, "John Lennon's Last Days: A Remembrance by Yoko Ono", *Rolling Stone* December 23, 2010, www.rollingstone.com/music/music-news/john-lennons-last-days-a-remembrance-by-yoko-ono-62533/.

349 *Saturday Night Live*, NBC Television, Season Six, Episode 2, November 22, 1980.

350 Cott and Doudna, *The Ballad of John and Yoko*, p. 227.

351 *The John Lennon Letters*, p. 384; Rodriguez, *Fab Four FAQ 2.0*, p. 398.

352 Madinger and Raile, *Lennonology*, p. 534.

353 Ben Yakas, "Record Producer Jack Douglas Opens Up about Working with John Lennon", *Gothamist* July 18, 2016, gothamist.com/arts-entertainment/record-producer-jack-douglas-opens-up-about-working-with-john-lennon.

354 Yakas, "Record Producer Jack Douglas Opens Up about Working with John Lennon".

355 Steve Marcantonio, "Eight Days in the Studio with John Lennon and Yoko Ono", interview by Joe Pagetta, Nashville Public Television, November 10, 2018, blogs.wnpt.org/mediaupdate/2010/11/18/eight-days-in-the-studio-with-john-lennon-and-yoko-ono/; Yakas, "Record Producer Jack Douglas Opens Up about Working with John Lennon".

356 Yakas, "Record Producer Jack Douglas Opens Up about Working with John Lennon".

357 Danny Caccavo, "Reference Library: Catharsis 101", *The Beatles Again* October 1998, www.beatlesagain.com/breflib/john.html; interview with Douglas, August 11, 2018.

358 Marcantonio, "Eight Days in the Studio with John Lennon and Yoko Ono".

359 Madinger and Raile, *Lennonology*, p. 534.

360 Madeline Bocaro, "Gone Utterly Beyond", *Madelinex* December 7, 2018, madelinex.com/2018/12/07/gone-gone-gone-beyond-gone-utterly-beyond/.

361 Sharp, *Starting Over*, p. 207.

362 Badman, *The Beatles Diary*, pp. 688, 692; Ono, "John Lennon's Last Days".

363 Sharp, *Starting Over*, p. 212; Jonathan Cott, "Yoko Ono and Her 16-Track Voice".

364 Cott, "The Last *Rolling Stone* Interview", p. 190.

365 Cott, "The Last *Rolling Stone* Interview", pp. 191, 192.

366 Ono, "John Lennon's Last Days".

367 Madinger and Raile, *Lennonology*, p. 536.

368 Interview with Smith, February 7, 2020.

369 Sharp, *Starting Over*, pp. 209, 211.

370 Ono, 'Walking On Thin Ice' liner notes, January 24, 1981.

371 Madinger and Raile, *Lennonology*, p. 537.

372 Sharp, *Starting Over*, p. 212.

373 Connolly, *The Ray Connolly Beatles Archive* (London: Plumray Books, 2018), p. 166.

374 Ono, "John Lennon's Last Days".

375 Sharp, *Starting Over*, p. 217; Alina Cohen, "How Annie Leibovitz Perfectly Captured Yoko and John's Relationship", *Artsy* December 6, 2019, www.artsy.net/article/artsy-editorial-annie-leibovitz-perfectly-captured-yoko-johns-relationship.

376 Cohen, "How Annie Leibovitz Perfectly Captured Yoko and John's Relationship".

377 Ibid.

378 Interview with Dave Sholin, February 8, 2020.

379 *John Lennon: The Man, the Memory*; interview with Sholin, February 8, 2020.

380 *John Lennon: The Man, the Memory*.

381 Ibid.

382 Ibid.

383 Ono, "John Lennon's Last Days".

384 Sharp, *Starting Over*, p. 228.

385 Ono, "John Lennon's Last Days"; interview with Sholin, February 8, 2020.

386 Interview with Sholin, February 8, 2020; Sharp, *Starting Over*, p. 229; Connolly, *The Ray Connolly Beatles Archive*, p. 171.

387   Sharp, *Starting Over*, p. 230.

388   Riley, *Lennon*, p. 640.

389   Sharp, *Starting Over*, p. 230.

390   Jason Fraley, "Willie Nile Shares New Details on the Night John Lennon Was Killed", *WTOP* March 30, 2017, wtop.com/entertainment/2017/03/exclusive-new-details-night-john-lennon-killed/.

Epilogue: Season of Glass

391   Rex Reed, *Good Morning America*, December 9, 1980; interview with Morgan, January 2, 2020.

392   Robert Morgan, "The Photograph Not Taken: The Night John Lennon Died", *Princeton Alumni Weekly* December 2, 2015, paw.princeton.edu/article/photograph-not-taken-night-john-lennon-died.

393   Interview with Morgan, January 2, 2020; Morgan, "The Photograph Not Taken: The Night John Lennon Died".

394   Sharp, *Starting Over*, p. 181.

395   Interview with Ray Connolly, January 20, 2020; Connolly, "The Dream Weaver... Surrealist of Rock", *Evening Standard* December 9, 1980, p. 1; Connolly, *The Ray Connolly Beatles Archive*, p. 168.

396   Interview with Ken Townsend, September 27, 2019.

397   Interview with Dave Sholin, February 8, 2020.

398   Riley, *Lennon*, p. 646.

399   Capozzi, "John Lennon's Last Years in Palm Beach".

400   Capozzi, "John Lennon's Last Years in Palm Beach".

401   Emerick, *Here, There, and Everywhere*, p. 359.

402   George Martin, interview with Gavin Hewitt, *BBC Evening News*, December 9, 1980.

403   Michael Seth Starr, *Ringo: With a Little Help* (Milwaukee: Backbeat, 2016), ch. 16.

404   Badman, *The Beatles Diary*, p. 703.

405   Ono, "John Lennon's Last Days".

406   Sean Lennon, "Sean Lennon's Holidays with His Father".